RED STAR
UNDER THE
BALTIC

RED STAR UNDER THE BALTIC

A Soviet Submariner's Personal Account 1941–1945

by

Victor Yemelianovich Korzh

Translated by
Dr Clare Burstall and
Dr Vladimir Kisselnikov

Pen & Sword
MARITIME

First published in Great Britain in 2004 by
Pen & Sword Maritime
an imprint of
Pen & Sword Books Ltd
47 Church Street
Barnsley
South Yorkshire
S70 2AS

ISBN 1 844151387

A CIP catalogue record for this book is
available from the British Library

Typeset in Sabon by Phoenix Typesetting, Auldgirth, Dumfriesshire
Printed and bound in England by CPI UK

Pen & Sword Books Ltd incorporates the imprints of Pen & Sword Aviation,
Pen & Sword Maritime, Pen & Sword Military, Wharncliffe Local History,
Pen and Sword Select, Pen and Sword Military Classics and Leo Cooper.

For a complete list of Pen & Sword titles please contact
PEN & SWORD BOOKS LIMITED
47 Church Street, Barnsley, South Yorkshire, S70 2AS, England
E-mail: enquiries@pen-and-sword.co.uk
Website: www.pen-and-sword.co.uk

CONTENTS

FOREWORD

by
Rear Admiral Valentin Stepanovich Kozlov

It was with some satisfaction that I accepted the invitation to write a foreword to Viktor Korzh's book *Red Star under the Baltic*. For me, a veteran of the war, a submariner, the events described in the book are very familiar, bringing to mind the names of those who never returned from patrol, who did not live to celebrate the approaching sixtieth anniversary of the victory over Nazi Germany and the end of the Second World War.

During the war the Baltic Sea theatre was one of the most treacherous and perilous for submarine operations; complicated from the navigational standpoint, shallow water for the most part. In the first months of the war the enemy succeeded in capturing our bases in the central sea area, with the result that the ships of the Baltic Fleet were obliged to take up positions in Kronstadt and Leningrad. Trying not to let them get out of there, and as a top priority, to keep the submarines locked up in the Gulf of Finland, the *Kriegsmarine* high command exerted a great deal of effort to create apparently impenetrable anti-submarine defences. The Gulf of Finland, especially the narrow part of it, was ringed around with both shore-based and seaborne anti-submarine devices, including special nets. The waters of the Gulf were thickly sown with various kinds of mines, numbered in their tens of thousands. Numerous anti-submarine vessels, motor torpedo boats and aircraft kept under constant surveillance the routes thought to be used for the deployment of the Soviet submarines.

I am emphasizing the specific features of the Baltic theatre and

vii

the countermeasures of the anti-submarine forces because there is nowadays too much uncritical praise in foreign and translated literature of the so-called 'aces' of the Third Reich. They are held to be the champions in terms of Allied shipping sunk which, on the whole, happened during the first years of the Second World War.

In those days the Nazi 'wolf pack' captains were hunting down defenceless merchant ships and tankers (including those of neutral countries) virtually without opposition and sending them to the bottom in considerable numbers. Everything changed from the beginning of 1943, when the Allies began the wide scale use of aircraft in anti-submarine attack, new types of radar and sonar were introduced, and shipping in transit began to be organized into defended convoys. The enemy began to lose dozens of their boats every month, and the success rate of their attacks decreased sharply.

In the Baltic the Nazis were transporting military cargoes by ship, as well as troops, fuel for their field units and the iron ore from Sweden that was crucial for the Third Reich. In this situation it was the submarines alone that could sever their lines of communication, sink enemy ships, disrupt traffic and, by so doing, provide vital assistance to the front.

Recognizing the extreme significance of the tasks set them by the high command, the submariners, in spite of all the hazards, made forced passages extending almost 200 miles through the Gulf of Finland at great risk.

The submarines would break through to the open sea at the cost of considerable sacrifice: of thirty-eight boats that were lost on patrol, more than twenty were to lie forever on the bottom of the Gulf, the majority destroyed by mines. In spite of this, the submarines of the Baltic Fleet carried out 196 sorties, the length of which frequently exceeded the limits laid down for independent operations at sea. With torpedoes, mines and artillery fire they sank 124 enemy vessels and also twenty warships and motor torpedo boats.

The author of the book, by profession a mechanical engineer, has described taking part in three war patrols, setting down with an excellent grasp of the subject matter all the vicissitudes that he had to cope with at sea, in which the submariners acquitted themselves with honour. It is remarkable how favourably fate treated Viktor Korzh. After his safe return to base from patrol on the submarine S-7 in the summer of 1942, 'Seven' – by then with a different engineer officer – came to a sad end during her next mission in the autumn. Viktor had been promoted and would later put to sea in other submarines.

I was closely acquainted with Sergei Lisin, the captain of S-7, and I found out a great deal from him in the post-war period. He had lived through the catastrophic loss of his own boat as well as through personal tragedy. S-7 was torpedoed by a Finnish submarine, with the loss of almost the entire crew, except for the captain and three seamen who happened to be on the bridge. They were thrown into the sea by the shock wave, were picked up by the Finns and were then taken into captivity. Captain Lisin, stood up to all the privations of imprisonment and resisted pressure from the enemy to change sides, even at the risk of his own life.

When Finland withdrew from the war in 1944, he was released from prison, was rehabilitated and was granted the Hero of the Soviet Union medal (the highest decoration), which had been awarded to him before his boat was sunk for the sinking of four enemy freighters.

On his second patrol the author put to sea in S-12, under the command of Vasili Turayev. Her crew outlasted double the amount of time prescribed for boats of this type to remain at sea, stood up to massive bombardment. Later on, experts at headquarters calculated that each of the Baltic Fleet submarines had, on average, been subjected to bombardment by forty depth charges. This was how the strength of the submariners and their boats was tested.

S-12 sank two freighters at one go with a two-torpedo salvo, returned safely to Kronstadt. But the following year this boat was lost as well, this time sailing without either Viktor Korzh or Captain Turayev. They had been posted to other boats.

The third patrol described by the author was undertaken on board a large minelaying submarine – L-21 – in March 1945. The Divisional Commander, Alexander Oryol, (as Admiral, the future commander of the Baltic Fleet) was on board the submarine, acting as mentor to her young captain. Victory was approaching, the enemy was urgently evacuating his troops from the Baltic region and the Soviet submarines in this closing stage were striking the final blows at the enemy. The three warships and a tanker sunk by *L-21* added to the contribution made by the Baltic submariners to the general victory over Nazi Germany.

The publication of this book in English will not only show the reader how complicated were the circumstances in which the Soviet submariners were fighting, but will also serve as a reminder, particularly to a younger generation that, in that bitter war, victory over the enemy was achieved by British naval forces working together with seamen of the United States and the Soviet Union.

The history of cooperation in battle between the submariners of our two countries goes back a long way. Already in the First World War, English submarines were entering the Baltic Sea and conducting joint operations with Russian boats. And from 1941 to 1942 submarines from Great Britain were temporarily based in our port of Polyarnyy and they too joined together with the submariners of the Northern Fleet in the fight against the common foe.

Today too, our nations are facing a common foe and we veterans of the last World War respond positively to the fact that, in the fight against international terrorism, we find ourselves once more on the same side of the front line. Nowadays veteran submariners from a number of countries gather together in submariners' International Congresses. In 2000 the thirty-seventh such congress took place in St Petersburg and last year the fortieth was held in Chatham, England.

Viktor Korzh's book, written about forty years ago, contributes to the memory of those for whom the front line extended beneath the water, whose courage and fortitude triumphed over the hardships of war. The author, a distinguished submariner, a war veteran, lived a richly creative life. In the years following the war he was engaged in research and teaching activities on behalf of the submarine service. He died in 1993.

Ever more distantly into the realms of history recede the events, the names and the fates of those who took part in the Second World War – for Russians, the Great Patriotic War. Ever fewer are the number of participants and witnesses who remain alive. For this reason it is absolutely essential to preserve the heroic and tragic truth about the war, without retouching or distortion, to protect it from attempts to reappraise its outcomes. The publication of *Red Star under the Baltic* will serve these purposes well.

St Petersburg, 30 January 2004

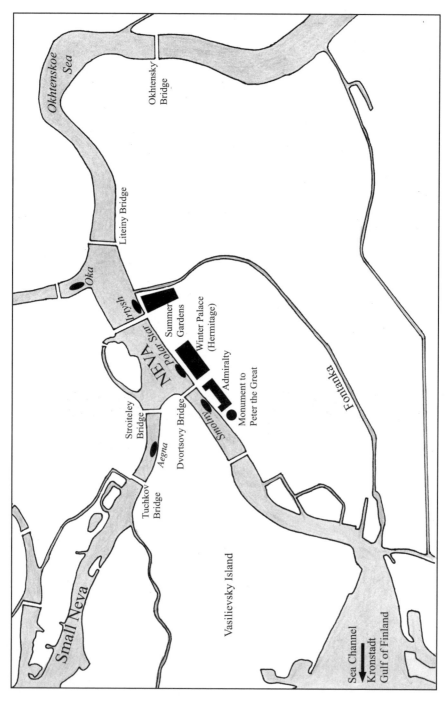

The positions of the submarines' floating bases on the Neva, Leningrad, 1941–1942

Chapter One

THE NEVA ICE

Operation NS

In the evening we were going to go to *La Traviata*; Lieutenant Captain Loshkariov had got hold of three tickets. 'Put warmer clothes on,' he had warned Ilyin and me, 'and I shall wear my felt boots as well, seeing that I'm on patrol duty immediately after the performance.'

The cloakroom was not operating. In the auditorium everyone was wearing greatcoats and sheepskin jackets; hats with earflaps on their heads. When we had taken our seats, I risked removing my hat, but replaced it at once: my ears were freezing.

A mist was swirling about in the auditorium from the hundreds of people breathing. Muffled up in overcoats and scarves, the members of the orchestra were blowing on their fingers. But the conductor rubbed his hands, waved his baton, and the very first strains of the overture made us forget everything: we no longer heard the booming rumble of the guns firing nor the fitful crackle of the shells bursting.

The brocade curtain rose smoothly. Loshkariov grabbed me by the arm, 'This is senseless!' Violetta had darted out onto the stage – gay, full of *joie de vivre*, the way she really should be. But my heart ached for her, in a flimsy dress, with bare shoulders, fragile and appealing; what must she have been going through at that moment! I know that I was not the only one who wanted to tear off his greatcoat and shield the singer from the cold. But Violetta was living in a different world. Her voice, melodious and poignant, filled the enchanted auditorium. And Alfredo, graceful and elegant, was passionately declaring his love for her,

1

a love which neither the years nor the vicissitudes of life could ever cool.

Deeply moved, we were walking along the street afterwards, not even noticing the cruel frost, nor the shifting snowdrifts, nor the trams stuck fast in the snow, riddled with shrapnel, nor the crimson reflections of the fires. Somewhere something was on fire again. Fires had become more frequent. They were set off not only by incendiary bombs, but by crude little heating-stoves too. A weakened person would throw the last fragments of a chopped-up chair into a red-hot stove, would become drowsy in the warmth and fall asleep – for all eternity. It no longer mattered to him that hot embers were dropping from the open stove door onto the floor and that the whole room was already ablaze. And it was becoming increasingly difficult to put the fires out: the water-supply had frozen up; they were lugging water from the ice-holes in the Neva and the Fontanka.

'Senseless!' Loshkariov kept repeating. He was still thinking about the half-naked singer in the unheated theatre.

'Selfless,' Ilyin corrected him. 'She warms the Leningraders with her singing.' The Divisional Navigator was, as ever, precise. They don't come more precise than him.

The next day I was sent for by the commander of the submarine brigade, Captain Second Rank A.V. Tripolsky: 'An urgent task for you. The city needs our help. Take two of the more robust engine-room mechanics and make your way to the Serafimovskoye Cemetery. Something has gone wrong with an excavator there.'

'We'll be off to the cemetery then!' I replied. I went to my boat, chose the sturdiest of the lads – malnutrition was telling on us – too, and we picked up some tools. We stepped out through the snowdrifts.

'What are we going to do there?' asked the sailors.

'Repair an excavator.'

'And have you had to do this before?'

'Never in my life.'

'Us neither,' sighed the sailors.

Never mind, it was no great problem. In Leningrad we were doing many things for the first time. The siege would teach us how to do everything. Something else was bothering me: whether I had understood the Brigade Commander correctly. Well, an excavator – fair enough. But how did the cemetery come into it?

We overtook a line of people. Bundled up to their very eyes, they were shuffling along bent over and dragging sleds behind them, both big ones and absolutely tiny ones; children's ones. Feet in woollen socks had poked out from under a short flannel blanket and were being dragged through the snow. And there was an arm drooping from a sled. Coiled waxen fingers raked the snow . . .

Lumbering heavily in the ruts, a truck rumbled by. After it another and yet another. We tried to thumb a lift; not one of them stopped. My sailors were beginning to lose their tempers. They showered the next truck with the choicest of swear words. The vehicle halted; the driver, wearing a grease-stained quilted jacket, swaying with fatigue, got down from the cab and glared at us angrily. 'Why are you kicking up such a fuss? Take a look!' He drew the tarpaulin aside. 'Where would you sit? On their heads or on their legs?'

We recoiled: in the truck bed were corpses. We didn't ask anyone else to give us a lift, although it was a fair distance – beyond Novaya Derevnya.

A lot of people were milling about at the cemetery – truck-drivers, paramedics, housing management and militia representatives, relatives of the dead. Eventually I tracked down the man in charge. He was glad to see me; he sent for the driver. We went over to the excavator, its bucket collapsed helplessly in a trench. We set to work. We replaced the worn cables and started up the engine which had gone cold. The pale-faced, skinny driver clambered up into his seat with a struggle and gripped the levers. The steel bucket scooped some frozen sand up and emptied it into a deep pit, on the bottom of which the bodies of men, women and children – with or without a covering sheet – were laid out in rows. And the trucks kept on coming. The paramedics would produce the lists, unload the vehicles. A new truck would roll up to take the place of the one that had left. They were bringing them in from the military and civilian hospitals, the mortuaries, the housing estates . . .

Side by side at the bottom of the communal grave were ranged the soldier who died of his wounds, the workman who stood at his lathe until his last breath, the old man who couldn't make it to the shop to collect his tiny ration of bread, and the little girl with plaits who was caught by an enemy shell in the doorway of her house . . . They were all being buried together, because in besieged Leningrad everyone was a fighter, regardless of profession, sex or age.

We stood by the huge grave for a long time. The frost scorched our cheeks as it did before. But we had removed our hats. May I burn in hell, if I ever forget this!

Oh, how impatient we were then to go to war! Each of us would have given his life without a second thought, simply to repay the enemy for these victims, for the grief and wounds of Leningrad! But the battle was still a long way off. The Gulf of Finland had frozen over. Our submarines were held fast in the Neva ice. For the time being it only remained for us to share with besieged Leningrad all its sorrows and to prepare ourselves for the fight to come.

The ships of the brigade had entered the Neva in late autumn. They had arrived after carrying out patrols, after the bitterness of retreat, after the loss of their bases – Libava, Riga, Tallinn.

The enemy was bombing and shelling the city. He directed his blows against our ships, too. The naval gunners were on watch around the clock, helping the ground forces' anti-aircraft batteries to repel air attacks.

A new menace had appeared as well. During a routine air-raid alert, Rim Yulievich Gintovt, the Chief Engineer Officer for one of the submarine divisions, had not gone down to the air-raid shelter but had stayed in the submarine shore base. Having thrown his greatcoat over his shoulders, Rim Yulievich had flung open the window of his fourth-floor office. Somewhere over to one side bombs were screaming down; everything around was shaking from the explosions. Suddenly the spotters of the anti-aircraft defence post which had been set up on the roof of the base building showed signs of alarm and trained their machine guns on a parachute dropped from a plane. Considerably higher up and further away over the Neva, a second canopy could be seen. Both were coming down at an unusually rapid rate. When the nearer parachute was about 100 metres from the ground, Gintovt realized what was going on. He shouted loudly to the spotters: 'Get down! It's a mine!'

4

The spotters dropped to the roof. Gintovt took shelter behind a wall as well. And almost at once there was an explosion of incredible force. The window frames blew out to the sound of breaking glass; the doors flew open with cracking noises. When Gintovt looked out of the window, the four-storey building on the corner opposite had been completely demolished. In the courtyard the sailors found the parachute and an 'alarm clock' – some kind of complicated mechanical device – squashed flat as a pancake.

The incident was reported without delay to the city's anti-aircraft defence headquarters. The order went out from there to surround the garden on Vasilievsky Island where the second mine had gone down. It had not detonated. Naval mine experts disarmed it and took it to a special site. It was an extremely timely find: similar 'windfalls' had begun to drop on the navigation channel from time to time, and there was an urgent need to find ways to combat them. Scientists helped the naval specialists to unravel the secret of the novelty, a German magnetic mine, and to devise a means of rendering it harmless.

Intelligence sources reported that the Nazis had concentrated a mass of floating mines in the upper reaches of the Neva. It was known to us that the enemy had already used floating mines in rivers to destroy bridges. By order of the Fleet Commander, artillery watches were instituted on all ships, with the aim of destroying any suspicious object found floating with the current. Old wooden barges were placed in front of the ships; a mine would bump into the obstacle and explode before it could float up to the ship. A few kilometres upstream, beyond the bridge named after Volodarsky, special lookout posts were set up. All these measures had their effect: the mines were destroyed long before they were able to get close to the ships.

The early coming of the cold froze the Neva solid; the Nazis were obliged to refrain from sending the floating 'surprises'. The artillery watches were stood down; the lookout posts on the other side of the Volodarsky Bridge were abolished. Until the spring, the mine threat came off the agenda.

So, we were stationed on the Neva. *Smolny*, the 1st Submarine Division's floating base, was made fast by the granite wall opposite the Admiralty, whose golden spire had been covered with a canvas sheath. Here, not far from the gigantic wooden crate covering the monument to Peter the Great in Alexandrovsky Garden, an army anti-aircraft machine-gun battery had snugly and securely dug itself in. Having such neighbours relieved the floating-base gunners of the necessity to open fire with their weaker guns in the event of an air raid. The division's boats were dispersed from the monument to Peter the Great to the Dvortsovy Bridge.

The 2nd Division and its floating base, *Irtysh*, had settled down by the embankment near the Summer Gardens. Malicious tongues assert that it was in precisely these gardens, celebrated by Pushkin, that in autumn they gathered the leaves that became the principal ingredient, or so they say, of the tobacco that we were smoking then, which is why the sailors called it *The Tale of the Summer Gardens*. Other wits, it is true, invented a shorter name for it: *CMS*. We do have *CMS* ships; coastal minesweepers. However, they have nothing in common with this name, since the initials *CMS* when applied to tobacco stand for the words *Crap, Muck and Sweepings*. The lads made fun of the siege tobacco, but they smoked it. It was a blessing that there was enough of it to go round (if only there had been bread in such abundance!).

The 3rd Division with its floating base *Polar Star* had been assigned a place by the Dvortsovaya Embankment opposite the Winter Palace. The 4th Division with its *Oka* was on the opposite bank, where the legendary *Aurora* had now been permanently stationed. And finally, the 5th Division with the floating base *Aegna* had taken up a position on the Small Neva between the Stroiteley and the Tuchkov Bridges.

The submarines' floating bases – big and technically well-equipped ships – were not just our living quarters, workshops and storerooms. They had taken on other functions as well, worthy but fairly burdensome ones. It was not for nothing that the floating base *Smolny* was moored alongside the Admiralty: even though sparingly, she was nonetheless supplying electricity to this huge building, which housed the fleet's administrative headquarters. *Polar Star* was ensuring the supply of electricity, steam and water to the Winter Palace, in whose basement a hospital had been set up. Thousands of paintings had been left in the exhibition halls and it was essential to maintain a constant temperature in order to preserve them.

The submariners formed strong bonds of friendship with the

Director of the Hermitage, Iosif Abgarovich Orbeli, and with his staff. The floating base's engineer officer, Senior Lieutenant A.K. Savostianov, saw to it personally that there was light and warmth in the old scholar's office.

Irtysh, which housed the submarine brigade headquarters, had become the Smolny building's back-up power station. And as long as the Leningrad defence headquarters was not in need of her services, the floating base was both lighting and heating the Librarians' Institute, named after N.K. Krupskaya, where there was a temporary hospital.

The onset of winter was early and severe. The hard frosts began long before any snow fell. Fuel ran low in the city. The wooden houses of Novaya Derevnya were being dismantled for firewood, as were the half-submerged barges in the Neva. People were burning furniture.

The pumping stations came to a halt for want of electricity. The water mains froze up. Even the bakeries were left without water. The sailors came to their rescue. So as not to disrupt the baking of bread, for several days the submariners hauled buckets of water from the Neva to one of the bakeries. In the meantime, submarine engine-room mechanics repaired the waterworks' diesel engines and pumps. The bakeries got their water.

Concerns about electrical power, heating and water on a ship always fall on the shoulders of the engineer officers who are in charge of *Department 5 (D-5)*. In that hard winter the likes of us had a tough row to hoe.

Captain Third Rank Boris Dmitrievich Andryuk, assistant to the Brigade Chief Engineer Officer, summoned the heads of *D-5* on each of the floating bases to *Irtysh* and ordered them to report on how matters stood with regard to fuel. The situation proved to be bleak: stocks of mazout [fuel oil] were coming to an end. 'What are we going to do about it?' asked Andryuk.

A long pause ensued. The first to break the silence was Senior Lieutenant G.P. Kulchitsky, the head of *D-5* on *Smolny*. 'As far as we know, the city's executive committee allowed the dismantling of the wooden seating in Lenin Stadium, in order to provide fuel for the bakeries. Perhaps they would allow us to dismantle the wooden pavements. Their wooden blocks have been thoroughly tarred and would burn excellently.'

Painful silence once more. The wooden pavements were the pride of Leningrad. Made up of neat wooden hexahedrons, they were strong and long-lasting and, most importantly, they muffled sound well.

'The Leningraders will hardly thank us, if we burn the pavements,' Andryuk said. Senior Lieutenant A.K. Savostianov stood up. '*Polar Star* ran right out of mazout. We have already adapted the boiler to run on solid fuel. But coal is also in short supply: we have been saving it just for the blacksmith's forge. My stokers have begun to burn asphalt on the sly. It works, although it leaves a great deal of residue. But asphalt is difficult to retrieve: we are gouging out the streets with crowbars.'

'No, that is not the way out either.'

Senior Lieutenant Pirozhny from *Irtysh* asked cautiously: 'And, as a last resort, may we use diesel for heating purposes?'

'Not under any circumstances! You will save the diesel for patrols! You are answerable with your lives for each kilo of diesel oil. Is that clear?'

'Clear,' the engineer officers replied. 'But what on earth are we to do?'

'Search for coal. Rummage around everywhere, while the snow is still not deep. Think of it as a military operation. We will give it the codename NS. Later on I will reveal what these initials stand for.'

All the *D-5* officers, leading seamen and ratings took part in Operation NS. The searches were crowned with success. Savostianov came upon whole coal dumps. They were found a long way outside the city, near Nevskaya Dubrovka, almost on the front line. The approaches to the coal dumps were within sight of the enemy: you couldn't get through to them in daylight even flat on your belly. The sailors did everything at night. They would drive a truck up under cover of darkness, load it rapidly and drive it away. Quite often, having heard a noise, the enemy would open up with mortar fire. The seamen would interrupt the work only in those instances when the shells began to burst right on top of them.

At one point I couldn't restrain myself and I asked Andryuk: 'Boris Dmitrievich, what does NS actually stand for?'

'Didn't you try to guess it for yourself?'

'We did. We racked our brains together. The sailors suggested

8

a couple of versions: "Necessity's School"; "Necessary to Survive" . . .'

Boris Dmitrievich crinkled up his eyes knowingly. 'Well, the thing is, the sailors almost guessed right. The operation was conceived under the catchphrase "Needs for Survival" and, in practice, it worked out as "Nerves of Steel". But, generally speaking, the floating bases are now supplied with coal for the whole winter. And we got it at a relatively low cost: only two sailors were slightly grazed by shrapnel.'

'Needs for Survival'! How come we didn't guess it straight away? Probably because these three words could have summed up the whole of our work that winter.

The Okhtenskoye Sea

During December the Nazis were shelling the city particularly intensively. I recall one gloomy, frosty day. The shells were landing at very precise intervals. The first one made a hole in the ice some ten metres off the floating base *Smolny*. The second exploded on the granite slabs of the embankment, lopping off the branches of the bare trees with the splinters and covering the walls of the Admiralty with pockmarks. The third threw up a fountain of ice and water between the floating base and submarine *S-7*. The fourth smashed the big wooden barge positioned behind the floating base. In the gunners' opinion, the fifth shell was bound to land directly on the ship, but the enemy unexpectedly shifted his aim towards the middle of the Neva, where the ice went on crumbling under the explosions for a long time still, helping a few hungry daredevils to extract stunned fish. The submarines remained untouched. It was simply amazing: during the whole of the winter not one of them sustained any significant damage. It is true that the external fuel tank on *S-7* ruptured from hydraulic shock. This certainly added to the problems of the boat's crew. But the stokers on the floating base were delighted: with an ingenious scoop they recuperated the leaked fuel from the water and burned it in the boiler furnace.

We were faced with the task of overhauling the submarines using our own resources and getting them seaworthy. N.F. Buivolov, the Brigade Chief Engineer Officer, gathered together

9

all the *D-5* heads on the floating base *Polar Star*. We seated ourselves pleasurably in the saloon, panelled in polished redwood. *Polar Star* was at one time one of the Tsar's yachts. And in 1917 the revolutionary Central Executive Committee of the Baltic Soviets was convened on board. At a later date this vessel became a floating base for submarines. But the Tsar's magnificent saloon had remained intact and we basked in warmth and comfort that seemed like a fairytale in the beleaguered city.

'Working conditions are equally hard on all ships,' Buivolov said, 'but our boats must meet the spring in a state of full combat readiness just the same.'

He made detailed enquiries into the state of repair of each ship. Several engineer officers were severely reprimanded for their poor organization of the work. Difficulties were not accepted as excuses; they were the same for everyone.

And with each passing day the difficulties did nothing but increase. The factories were short of fuel, electricity and raw materials. Although the industries that had remained in the city had switched to round-the-clock double-shift working (and each shift lasted twelve hours!) and the workers didn't go home for weeks on end, taking their rest periods right there on the shop floor, everything got done at an incredibly high cost. People could scarcely stay on their feet. With their ration cards the workers received 125 grammes of bread a day. We fighting men, just a bit more – 200 grammes. The bread was such that quick-witted mechanics advised chewing it with a clearance of one millimetre between the teeth – that way the crunching of sand was inaudible. But the trouble was – there was nothing to chew!

Even with normal feeding, the intensive work in the submarines' frozen compartments might well have been enough to exhaust the ratings and leading seamen, but nowadays they were fading away before our very eyes. But no one grumbled. People were trying their utmost. Anyone who was at the last gasp would just drop down beside the machinery, lie there for five or ten minutes, and then get up again and go back to work. A senior mechanic sent a rating to dismount a valve behind a diesel engine. With great difficulty the latter squeezed into the narrow space, unscrewed the required part, but couldn't get back out afterwards. A second rating clambered in to help him, but lacked the strength to pull his comrade out. They had to put out a call for all hands to report to the diesel compartment. With our combined efforts we pulled both poor devils out into the blessed light of day.

I lost seventeen kilos and then weighed only fifty-three kilos. But I still felt reasonably well. However strange it may seem, the first of us to weaken were the supermen, like D. Ponomarenko, the light-diving instructor, a six-foot giant, whose handshake was enough to bring a man to his knees. The lack of food was particularly telling on his huge frame. Ponomarenko had to take to his bed.

More and more often the doctors were starting to diagnose dystrophy. It is a dreadful disease. The most dreadful thing about it is that you can't build up any immunity to it and there are no inoculations against it.

Alimentary dystrophy – the breakdown of the general nourishment of the organism, basically in consequence of long-term malnutrition . . .

I found this in a reference book. The definition was succinct and comprehensive, but knowing it didn't make me get any better.

The good thing was that we did at least manage to avoid the usual concomitant of dystrophy; scurvy. Every day the doctors treated us to an infusion of pine needles. No-one had to be coerced. Having poured out the bitter-sour fluid, the sailors never neglected the opportunity to clink their mugs and wish one another good health.

There was a brutal frost in the submarine compartments. Only in the control room was there the flicker of a fireplace; a tiny tin stove. The sailors dropped in here to warm their hands. Soot from the fireplace and from the oil lamps had settled on the instruments, a thing unheard of in a fighting ship, where formerly every brass fitting would have glittered like flame.

I collapsed anyway. I spent about a fortnight in hospital, and then lay in a cabin on the floating base. I lay there, angry with myself. It really wasn't the time for this!

Suddenly the door opened, and the sailors dragged an oil pump into the cabin. Dmitri Kanayev, Leading Seaman 2nd Class in charge of the engine room mechanics, explained that they had to decide what to do with 'this stupid thing'. The sailors dismantled the mechanism right there in the cabin. Kanayev showed me the components one after the other. We probed them, measured them and determined whether they should stay in their places or be replaced by new ones.

To our pride, we were the first to get our engines into working order. I.R. Ramazanov, the Engineer Officer for the 1st Division, paid us a visit so as to check for himself the quality of the repair work. The trial start worked brilliantly: both diesels caught, as they say, after half a revolution.

Kanayev was beaming on account of the praises from the Divisional Engineer Officer; the entire engine room crew was radiating delight as well. Meanwhile at headquarters there were games being played. From morn till night the divisional experts were poring over the charts and reference books, making estimates, calculating. The navigators were laying the courses for future patrols. Sasha Ilyin came running to me. 'Listen, my friend, how much time would you need for a full charging of the batteries after an underwater passage to this point?' He pointed with his pencil at the unfurled chart. I dropped all other business, began to draw up a diagram. I provided a ready reckoning. Ilyin ran off, but twenty minutes later was pestering me again: 'And if we were to surface right here?'

Once more we recalculated everything, once more we drew. We checked every figure ten times. We spent a lot of time on it. But I was not put out by my comrade. He was plotting the ship's course. Out on patrol the smallest miscalculation would threaten destruction. And again and again we went over all the possible variations, searching for the most apt. And then Dorofei Vinnik, the Divisional Minelayer, came along. He was working out the manoeuvres for laying mines, a sequence of post-salvo tactics, and techniques for evading enemy depth charges.

The signalmen were working concentratedly, developing a system of coded signals, procedures for radio transmissions. Afterwards all these calculations would be amalgamated by the commanding officers; would be checked out in exercises at head-quarters, and only then would they be shaped into a decision that would form the basis of a military order.

The repair work continued. In their grease-stained padded

jackets, black as sweeps, the sailors swarmed about in the narrow compartments. Now we could all see with our own eyes how tightly the submarine was packed with every possible kind of machinery, and how it all just barely fitted in there! And it all needed checking, adjusting, mending . . .

There was a great deal to be done on the inside of the ship. But all the same this was still not the most difficult area: everything was accessible to the gaze; everything could be touched by the hand. It was worse with the underwater part of the hull. We had no dry docks in Leningrad. All the jobs on the hull were carried out on the spot. Our divers got the rough end of the stick. We hacked a hole in the ice. In the piercing wind, Leading Seaman Piskunov put on his protective suit, lowered himself into the black water. The last that I could see were his fingers, reddened by the frost, gripping the glassy-smooth ice. But then they too disappeared into the ice-hole. Leading Seaman 1st Class Golenko was 'standing on signal'; he straightened the rubber hose and the signal rope. Petty Officer Viktor Yurkevich sat with earphones on his head and a microphone at his lips. Both were freezing cold, blue with it. Not far from them two ratings were rotating the handles of the air pump.

The diver reported that one of the blades of the starboard propeller was missing entirely, while the other two were badly bent, and that the casing of the stern hydroplanes was damaged. Yurkevich ordered him to move over to the port side. Golenko started to carry the hose over there and suddenly he shouted out: 'Watch out, Petty Officer!' 'Don't yell!' the Petty Officer quietened him down. 'You'll scare the diver . . .'

And meanwhile he was already speaking into the microphone as calmly as he could: 'Piskunov, come up. Come up, I tell you.' But his calmness did not last long, and the Petty Officer raised his voice: 'I'm telling you, drop everything! No, no-one's dragging you. It's the hose catching on the ice. Come up as fast as you can. But be careful: keep your eye on the ice!'

The boat moved under the pressure of the ice. The hawsers' steel cables tightened and started to screech. The ice-hole beside the ship was closing up before our very eyes. They scarcely had time to haul the diver up out of it. The commotion brought Ramazanov running: 'Stop work immediately!'

13

For a couple of days he would not allow the divers under the ice. And then once more, taking it in turn, they began to go off into the cold, dark water. They removed the heavy propellers from the shafts. The sailors winched them up onto the deck. The propellers were so warped they were a dreadful sight to see. We began to rack our brains: what could be done with them? There were few spare propellers in the brigade; each one was accounted for.

Luckily for us, at this juncture Osip Grigorievich Briansky, in former days a leading designer at a shipbuilding plant, came to us from the front line. After suffering from concussion, he had a spell in hospital, and was then assigned to the navy, where he was really in his element. Put in charge of the workshops, Briansky, on Ramazanov's orders, set about getting the gas-welding of non-ferrous materials up and running. They got the equipment from a local factory, the carbide from the shipbuilding plant where Briansky used to work, and the oxygen from another local firm.

But for a long time the job did not progress too well. The copper seals turned out to be full of bubbles; fragile. We tried everything under the sun! For the lower layer we tried brick, asbestos, poronite and ceramics. All to no avail. 'Nothing will work without graphite,' said Ramazanov. 'Go and look for some!'

But where were we to find it in the besieged city? We ransacked our own establishment: all the boats and the floating bases. None anywhere. We did the rounds of the neighbouring factories. None there! We found it in a place where it might have been the least expected – in the Alexander Nevsky Monastery. Who could have brought these heavy black slabs there and for what reason? They had evidently taken it to be coal and had wanted to use it for fuel. But it wouldn't burn . . .

The graphite was brought to *Smolny*. The welding went right. The seam came out even and strong. Earlier we had tried to straighten out each propeller blade, no matter how badly warped. Then we plucked up our courage: we simply cut off the distorted part and welded on a new piece. But, of course, there still remained plenty of problems with the propellers. A propeller needs to be rectified against a template, each blade polished, and then given its proper balance. Using files, the ratings were working the intractable copper by hand, until it acquired the necessary shape.

The work was speeded up by the use of pneumatic tools. But this increased the consumption of compressed air several times over. The elderly, rather battered compressors that were available on the floating base were constantly breaking down.

Kulchitsky, the Engineer Officer on *Smolny*, complained to Ramazanov: 'Ibragim Ramazanovich, what on earth is going on? The workshops are using up the compressed air, whereas according to my checklist they are not entitled to air. You know perfectly well that our compressors are intended only for pumping air into the torpedoes. And as matters stand, we are running the wretched machines day and night. The gaskets blow so often that we hardly have time to replace them. We will run the compressors into the ground during the winter, and then when summer comes there will be nothing left to pump the torpedoes with!'

Ramazanov sighed, nodded his head sympathetically, but said something entirely different from what Kulchitsky had been expecting: 'Provide the workshops with air. Maintain the compressors in good working order. Learn how to make fibre gaskets for them yourself. If the compressors fail to work, I will hold you strictly accountable. Just so you know!'

As he left the Divisional Engineer, Kulchitsky was scratching the back of his head and muttering: 'I went in to make a complaint and I come away with a flea in my ear . . .'

Repairing the ships demanded first one thing, then another. On some of the boats the batteries needed replacing. But where could we get them from? We found out that, in the autumn, several wagonloads of batteries were supposed to have been dispatched to the rear. Had they managed to slip through to the mainland? Nobody knew.

The local authorities gave us permission to inspect the lines of wagons left undispatched. Petty Officer Moskovkin, our expert on batteries, was sent off to railway headquarters. The people there 'made his day': 2,177 loaded wagons remained on the tracks. The railway people had no idea what was in them: the paperwork went missing. Captain Third Rank A.K. Vasiliev, representing the submarine department at fleet headquarters, Captain Third Rank N.I. Golenbakov, assistant to the Chief Engineer Officer, and A.G. Moskovkin went clambering in the freezing cold and the blizzard over the railway tracks blocked by snowdrifts, opened up wagons, inspected them and sealed them up again, putting a special chalk-mark on them, so as not to go poking their noses in there a second time. They worked for many days. At times they were collapsing with exhaustion. But they found something just the same. Six new batteries for different types of submarine turned up in the wagons. Hauling the 360 tons of this delicate and cumbersome load over the rails and the snowdrifts was beyond our capability. We put it off until the spring.

Despite the difficulties, the repair work proceeded successfully. We were proud of the fact that our boat was one of the first to get to the end of it. Ramazanov climbed all over the ship. Each mechanism was tested. The Divisional Engineer was left content.

Then we began to concentrate on our military training. But soon the pace of the training programme had to be relaxed: people worn down by lack of food tire quickly. It became clear that putting to sea with such weaklings was out of the question. We joyfully received the news that ten days before they went out on patrol, the boats' crews would be put on a privileged supplementary ration. The sailors hailed this decision with as much enthusiasm as if they had been handed free vouchers to the very best convalescent home.

The sun had barely begun to give out warmth when the Nazis came to life again. During the whole of April they shelled the city incessantly. On building walls there appeared the inscriptions that are unforgettable for Leningraders: 'Citizens! This side of the street is highly dangerous during the shelling!' Nazi aircraft also began to appear in the sky. But, with ever-increasing success, fighter planes bearing the Red Star were intercepting them. The mere sight of them was already enough to raise our spirits.

The increased frequency of the shelling also forced us to move the ships to a safer place. To do this, the bridges had to be raised. A special squad of sailors was detailed. The machinery of the bridges, which no one had laid a finger on since the actual autumn, played up, refused to operate. We never did manage to raise the panels of the Dvortsovy Bridge to their full extent. When the floating base *Smolny* passed under them, she grazed the span with her main topmast. In the darkness (it was only at night that the ships were moved to their new position), the upper part of the huge mast hurtled downwards, shattering everything in its path. Luckily, no one was hurt. I will say straight off that three days

16

later *Smolny* was sporting a new main topmast. It was so resplendent with fresh paint that wags were begging the stokers: 'Make thicker smoke, we need to get some soot over that gilding, or else the Nazis will notice it immediately and all the shells will wing their way here!'

But we feared most of all for the newly-equipped de-magnetizing station. The landing-stage on which it had been positioned was so flamboyantly painted that it dazzled the eyes. The de-magnetizing station was the brainchild of Captain First Rank N.N. Kudinov, the head of the fleet's technological department: his pride and joy. He monitored its operation personally.

We had great expectations of this de-magnetizing station: it should make the submarines impervious to magnetic mines. And it has to be said that these expectations were largely borne out by events.

I happened to look in on Ilyin. The Divisional Navigator was plotting something on a chart.

'What are you up to?'

'I am marking the boundaries of the sea.'

'And what kind of sea could there be here? This is the Neva, when all's said and done!'

'In this area the Neva is no longer a river but a sea, the "Okhtenskoye Sea".'

'Did you think up the name yourself?'

'I thought nothing up. The "Okhtenskoye Sea" is already featuring in our operational bulletins. It's our training area.'

This newly-created sea was a constricted one – it was that section of the river between the Liteiny and the Okhtensky Bridges – furthermore, its shape put you in mind of a hook on the end of a crane. There was a strong current there, an entirely unsuitable feature for a training area, but to offset that, it had depths reaching fifteen to eighteen metres.

Applications to use the 'Okhtenskoye Sea' rained down on brigade headquarters. From dusk till dawn 'minnows' and 'pikes' would plough this puddle, submerge and surface, often with a considerable bow or stern trim – the inexperience of the planesmen and the helmsmen was showing. *M-97* was also put through her paces in the training area. Small, nimble, she would dive and dart up to the surface again, like a duckling at play. Little did we guess then that to precisely this 'minnow', under the command of Lieutenant Captain N.V. Diakov, would fall the honour of becoming the first swallow, blazing the trail out to sea for the rest of the boats.

The submariners were living in the anticipation of major patrols.

Chapter Two

WHITE NIGHTS
OVER THE BALTIC

Let Go Mooring Lines!

I had been given the job of transporting tanks of oxygen to Kronstadt and picking up electrical instruments from there. Our slow-moving *Burbel*, a small steam-tug, frantically furrowing the water with her bow, was proceeding along the Sea Channel when the enemy suddenly opened fire. The shells were falling fairly close by and, with each explosion, I would glance apprehensively at the tanks out of the corner of my eye. All it needed was for a stray shell splinter to land on them and there would be no trace left of either *Burbel* or us. But, never mind, we got through. On the return journey, we were once again escorted by the bursting of enemy shells. We got back to Leningrad unscathed.

And there, as usual, we were up to our necks in problems. We had to load new batteries into the boat. We forged a path to the deserted railway wagons, dragged the heavy ebonite containers out of them, arranged them on the flatbed of a truck with every precaution, then transported them, trembling at each pothole. With block and tackle we then lowered the batteries into the boat. For two days running, the whole crew was working almost flat out. Leading Seaman Pyotr Lyashenko, in charge of the electricians' group, would urge the sailors on: 'Put your backs into it! We'll have a rest at sea!'

When the batteries were in place, I went along to the floating charging-post. This was the famous *L-55* – an English submarine sunk by our seamen in 1919 and later raised from the bottom. She was subsequently fitted out as a floating charging-post. The officer

19

in charge of the 'foreign lady', Senior Lieutenant Alexander Nikitich Chernyshov, having heard me out, thought things over:'The Divisional Commander is busy, there's no getting near him. And without him I can't move my ship.' Then he flapped his hand: 'Well, never mind, let's go for it!'

At low speed *L-55* moved away from the floating base and soon tieu up alongside our boat. I realized that Chernyshov was taking a considerable risk: he really had no right to move the ship on his own initiative. Fortunately, everything went off well. The engineer was giving orders on the bridge like a real commander, and the most difficult manoeuvre – docking – was accomplished brilliantly.

After supper on the floating base I ran into Briansky, the officer in charge of the workshops. He told me that the boat's propellers were in full working order (he had had more than a little to do with this), and he asked suddenly: 'What do you think? If I applied for a post as head of the propulsion group under you, would they fly off the handle?'

'They well might.'

'And how would you view my application?'

'I would support it. Even though you have no specific naval training or sea-going experience, you were a designer in the past, you know ships. And then during this winter I could see for myself that you are a versatile specialist, resourceful and quick-thinking. And, most importantly, we have a well-trained ship's crew. With such people even a novice would soon get the hang of things.'

The boat was already at the de-magnetizing station, ready for the move to Kronstadt, when an excited Briansky came running up to us. 'They've put me at your disposition!' he announced to the ship's captain. Sergei Prokofievich Lisin shook him by the hand: 'That's it then, we'll sail together.' Coming over to me, Briansky confided: 'And I've already studied all the instruction manuals.' 'In that case, everything's under control,' I said jokingly. 'But stick close to me for a while, watch carefully and ask plenty of questions, if there's anything you don't understand. And, Osip Grigorievich, don't be afraid to ask even the leading seamen for advice.'

Three submarines of the first echelon were ready to go. In the twilight we came alongside *Commune*, a big double-hulled rescue ship. Boris Dmitrievich Andryuk, Assistant Chief Engineer Officer, together with the divers, set about inspecting the boat's emergency-rescue equipment. He ordered all escape hatches to be opened. The divers, led by Leading Seaman 1st Class Ponomarenko, tested whether the air hoses fitted the pipe couplings on the hull of our ship. If anything happened to the boat, the divers would be supplying us with air through these pipes.

'Everything's up to standard,' confirmed Andryuk. 'So, Viktor, stay well. Remember that I'll be on duty in the channel on a diving-boat. If anything happens, I will lend a brotherly helping hand.'

'Thanks, Boris. But it would be better if your divers didn't have to search for us on the bottom.'

At 23.00 hours a submarine chaser hurtled downstream along the Neva at top speed. From her bridge, using a megaphone, Captain First Rank Ivanovsky, the brigade deputy commander, ordered the submarines to close up on the Sea Channel and to await the signal for departure.

We let go the mooring lines. Throughout the boat a state of full readiness for surfaced sailing had been declared. The bulkheads had been sealed. On the bridge there were only the Captain, the Commissar, the Navigator and the Bosun; the latter on station at the vertical rudder. The whole crew was at action stations. The emergency team had assembled in the fourth compartment – the lads were already in their diving-suits, the oxygen equipment was ready for use. Everyone understood the need for these precautions: we were about to come under enemy fire.

The submarine was moving along slowly on one diesel at minimal revolutions. From the bridge came the order: 'Record in the ship's log: "Entered the Sea Channel." '

Almost simultaneously with this order the thunderous roll of the opening artillery barrage burst into the control room from above. I knew that it was the cruisers *Kirov* and *Gorki* beginning to adjust their aim. They were firing at the enemy batteries in Ligovo and Strelna, trying to neutralize them in advance, to prevent them from bombarding our boats.

It was silent in the control room. The planesmen and helmsmen were giving occasional glances at the open conning-tower hatch, listening intently to the sounds coming from outside.

'So, the contest has begun. Who will come off best?' I asked. 'Oh, if only we could have a look right now, to see who is firing where, and what the result of it is,' Planesman Lymar joined in.

But from above the angry voice of the First Lieutenant could already be heard: 'You down there! Less noise!'

The diesel had been stopped. Navigator Khrustaliov rushed headlong down the ladder from the bridge, and First Lieutenant Dumbrovsky from the conning tower. They bent over the chart spread out on the navigator's table.

'Where are we?' Dumbrovsky asked. 'We're approaching the burnt-out oil tanks on the portside parapet of the channel. It will start soon. Brace yourselves, lads!' It was the Navigator who was speaking to us now. Grabbing his binoculars, he clambered up the ladder to the bridge once more.

Poring over the chart, the First Lieutenant muttered something under his breath. I was summoned to the bridge. Up I went. The Captain ordered: 'Make ready both diesels. We shall start them simultaneously. No deceleration, no matter what happens!'

I acknowledged the order, while taking a hasty look around. It was as bright as day: it was the time of the 'white nights' in Leningrad. The ruins of Ligovo could clearly be seen ashore. In the port behind us blazed the flashes of the cruisers' salvoes. I could see how columns of fire were sprouting up above Ligovo. These were the shells fired by *Kirov* and *Gorki* exploding. Lightning had begun to flash ahead of us too – the Kronstadt forts had joined the battle. Motor launches to lay down smokescreens scudded past us, trailing their voluminous tails behind them, so as to hide us from enemy eyes in a cloud of smoke. On the starboard side, beyond the earthworks at the very exit from the Sea Channel, I noticed the diving-boats – they were standing by. Ahead of us there were two submarines and a submarine chaser. There were a few more ships behind us. 'Now the Krasnaya Gorka fort will begin to have its say,' the Captain said. 'Beneath its music and under cover of the smokescreen, we will manage to slip through. Go and ask the First Lieutenant to report here.' I went below. I gave out the orders. Four pairs of eyes were trained eagerly on me. In a low voice I described to my comrades everything that I had seen from the bridge.

From above came the order: 'You down there! Record in the

ship's log: "The Krasnaya Gorka and Kronstadt forts are laying down fire. The pivot-buoy in the navigation channel is lit up. The leading submarine has left the Sea Channel. The enemy has opened fire on the navigation channel."'

It had begun! The boat's hull was being shaken by the explosions nearby. The sailors' faces had taken on grave expressions. Both diesels had been started at low revolutions. One minute, two . . . An order from the bridge: 'Full ahead both!'

The ship shuddered under the strain. We reached nineteen knots. The explosions were increasingly frequent and nearer. It looked as though the enemy had turned all his fire onto our boat. Sometimes we could hear shrapnel sliding over the metal of the superstructure. As we made the turn, we felt a slight jolt: we had grazed a sandbank with our keel. The boat's forward movement slowed, but she soon came off the bank; momentum lent a hand. For a few minutes more we squeezed out of the diesels all that they had to give. But then already we heard the command: 'Slow ahead!'

We moored alongside the pier in Kronstadt's Kupecheskaya Harbour. We inspected the surface area of the ship. There were a few holes in the outer casing. Mere trifles!

Fleet headquarters now included us in its schedule. Everything was spelt out on an hourly basis: receiving cargo, clearing the torpedo tubes, loading the torpedoes, detecting and correcting compass deviations, checking the hull's magnetic fields, the final charging of the batteries. We were working flat out again. And once more could be heard: 'Move it, move it! We'll have a rest at sea!'

On the night of 2 July 1942, people gathered on the pier to see us off. The Brigade Commander, Captain First Rank A.M. Stetsenko, the Brigade Commissar, I.A. Ryvchin, and the head of the political department, Captain Second Rank M.Y. Kabanov, were there. My classmate Alexander Mikhailovich Kramarenko elbowed his way towards me through the crowd jamming the pier. Their *P-304* sank an enemy transport in the course of a reconnaissance patrol. Andryuk also found a moment to say goodbye to us.

They clustered round us on all sides. They shook us firmly by the hand. They embraced us. They wished us happy sailing and a victorious return.

The First Lieutenant gave the order: 'Stand by! Let go mooring lines!'

The ships forming the escort were emerging from the mouth of Kupecheskaya Harbour into the Great Roads. The dusk deepened. I heard the Brigade Commander, peering at the horizon, say to our Captain: 'The weather is not on our side. Warn the signalmen to keep their eyes peeled. We could run into enemy motor torpedo boats.'

The head of brigade headquarters, Captain First Rank L.A. Kurnikov, and the commanding officer of the 1st Division, Captain Second Rank Y.G. Yunakov, approached. 'It is time, Comrade Brigade Commander,' said Kurnikov. 'Everything has been done. The notification has been sent out. The minesweepers have begun to sweep ahead for mines.'

Having taken leave of my friends, I hurried to my action station in the control room. Farewell Kronstadt! Till we meet again!

Dumbrovsky's order reached us from the bridge: 'Remove the gangplank!' The last link with the Kronstadt shore had been severed. We picked up speed. 'We have passed the citadel!' the signalman's report came down to us.

The summer night was too short, it wouldn't last long enough for us to get as far as Lavansaari, and it was dangerous for our convoy to move by day. The enemy on both sides of the Gulf would spot it at once and send in the air force. That is why, when we were abeam of the Shepelevsky Lighthouse, the signal for emergency diving was given. We settled on the bottom. The manoeuvre itself was executed well, but it could have been quicker. It would be necessary to have a word with those in charge of the compartments. And then time for a rest. This might be our last undisturbed night. I scanned the instruments. Depth eighteen metres, trim two degrees down by the bow. The rapid-diving tank was full. Everything was in order.

We had dinner an hour before surfacing. We were waiting for a sign from the escort ships. And then with the naked ear we could already hear the signal to surface.

We blew the ballast. Rolling slightly, the boat surfaced. The Captain climbed the ladder. For a long time he tinkered with the hatch release-mechanism; he cursed out loud. Commissar Gusev hurried to his assistance. The two of them pushed at the hatch cover – it didn't give. Air smelling of the freshness of the sea burst whistling into the compartment through the induction valve, but, just as before, the hatch failed to open. I ordered a planesman to open an exhaust vent. A misty wind blew into the control room. The hatch cover folded back unexpectedly easily. The Captain and the Commissar jumped out onto the bridge.

Judging from the orders that we overheard from above, we assumed that our boat had taken its place in the convoy line-up. The diesels began to hammer.

When everything had settled down, Sergei Prokofievich summoned me to the bridge.

'Tell me, Comrade Korzh, do you think that it's a good idea for a submarine to find herself blind for some time after surfacing?'

'No, it's extremely bad, Comrade Captain.'

'So, how would you explain it?'

'By my lack of foresight.'

'How so? And there was I, thinking that it was by the creation of a vacuum.' The Captain smiled knowingly. 'But, just the same, explain the problem to me.'

'There was a powerful build-up of pressure inside the boat. There are three reasons for this. Firstly – the good hermetic seal on all mains, valves and other pneumatic systems, which means that the repairs were admirably done. Secondly – while we were lying on the bottom, there was a marked cooling of the air inside the boat, accompanied by the condensation of water vapour. And finally, the third and, you might say, the most important reason – people had used up part of the oxygen, and the carbon dioxide produced by their breathing dissolved in the water that is always accumulating in the bilges . . .'

'Thank you for the popular-science lecture,' the Captain cut me short. 'I shall know for another time that our chief mechanical man is highly educated. But I would still ask you to bear in mind that, at sea, a theory should be of practical use, and not just to explain away failures.'

'Remember: "Theory is not dogma, but a guide to action",' added the Commissar.

Back down in the control room, I made it my first task to ask

25

the Navigator: 'Misha, my friend, would you please draw up a barograph, and let us find a good place to hang it; here on these pipes, for example. The thing is my nose can't tell the difference between a vacuum and pressure.'

Khrustaliov laughed and promised to install a barograph right in front of my nose.

I summoned Briansky and told him what happened today with the upper conning-tower hatch. Together we thought through how to balance the internal pressure of the boat with that of the atmosphere while surfacing, and how to do this under any conditions, including stormy weather.

At dawn we arrived at Lavansaari, a small island that had become our forward base in the Baltic. Not letting the diesels cool down, we set about charging the batteries. Having made sure that everything was going according to plan, I went up onto the bridge. The Captain was standing on the jetty surrounded by unfamiliar officers. Apart from them, there was no one else nearby. I recalled that there were strict rules in force on Lavansaari. Any movement about the island by day was forbidden. Amongst the officers, my attention was drawn to a skinny man with a stern, resolute face. This turned out to be the base commander himself, Captain Second Rank S.D. Soloukhin. I gave the Captain a report on the work in hand. Sergei Prokofievich asked: 'Is there anything that we need on the technical side? If so, the base command here is offering to help us, in case we have inadvertently forgotten something.'

'We have everything. But some three hundred litres of extra drinking water wouldn't go amiss.'

'Spring water?' asked a short officer in a leather jacket.

'Definitely spring water,' Lisin showed his delight.

Everyone laughed, and I added: 'If some fifty light bulbs could be found to keep in reserve, we would be most grateful.'

'By 06.00 hours everything will be here,' said that same officer.

Looking at my watch, I shook my head in disbelief: we were not likely to get anything here at all.

They all went off down a road leading into some woods. I returned to the boat. On the bridge was a sailor on watch, armed with a machine gun, and Briansky. I advised Osip Grigorievich to go and get some rest, but he replied that he would rather take in the fresh air. And the air that early morning was amazing, imbued with the scents of the sea and the pine needles: the woods on the seashore went down to the very water. The sun had already risen quite high; its rays were piercing through the mesh of the huge camouflage net covering our boat.

At 05.45 hours a vehicle, to which a little bay horse was harnessed, appeared on the road. Driving the contraption was an elderly sailor with a jaunty moustache, dressed in clean, grey overalls. In the vehicle was a barrel and a plywood packing case. Taking the horse by the bridle, the sailor led it along the jetty. Coming to a halt directly alongside the boat, he gave a spirited salute: 'By order of the base commander, I have brought you water and light bulbs. Take delivery!'

'Let me sign for the receipt of the light bulbs.'

'There's no need. I'll sign for them myself at the warehouse later on,' the sailor replied and set the packing case containing the light bulbs down at my feet.

I touched the barrel; definitely cold water from a spring. Skachko, the leading seaman in charge of the planesmen, together with his crew, was already fitting a hose to pump across the contents of the barrel. Briansky went over to the horse, patted its head: 'Nice little brown horse. And how come you weren't eaten during the famine, poor little blighter?'

'And who could do a thing like that?' the old driver was full of indignation. 'The lads were sharing their bread with her. She's such a good little worker!'

And he didn't hang around to talk to us any more. Having waited until the planesmen had taken the water on board, he led the bay off down the road, not once glancing back in our direction.

'Well, what did you want to upset the old fellow for?' I reproached Briansky.

'But I didn't mean to at all . . .'

Lisin and Gusev returned. The Captain ordered Dumbrovsky and Khrustaliov to be woken up. When everyone was assembled, he invited us to a tiny clearing not far from the jetty. We sat down on the sweet-smelling grass, which was still slightly damp from the morning dew.

'I must ask you to listen to me carefully,' said the Captain. 'I am obliged to amend something in the schedule compiled earlier.' He opened a notepad.

'At just these points here our predecessors ran into the enemy. You can appreciate for yourselves that we would do better not to put in an appearance there. We will have to do some of the calculations over again.'

The Captain tore off a sheet of paper and handed it to Khrustaliov. 'Lay a new course.' And to me he said: 'No matter how tough it might be, Comrade Korzh, you and I will have to remain in the control room the whole time we are forcing a passage. We will get some rest later on.' Having given corresponding orders to each of us, the Captain concluded the meeting with the words: 'I ask you to see to it that we cast off as soon as possible. We are not allowed to hang about here: they are expecting an enemy air-attack.'

S.D. Soloukhin, Captain Third Rank M.V. Kapralov, commanding the submarine-chaser detachment, and their staff officers came to see us off. They wished us warm farewells and hoped that we would meet again soon.

The jangling of bells sounded throughout the compartments. We were moving away from the jetty. Bosun Pyatibratov, having passed the control of the helm to Alexander Olenin, a rating, grumbled: 'Spit! What a bind! This is no weather for us! It's endlessly repulsive. If only there would be a nice little Force 4 wind or, even better, sheets of rain, our rain, the real Leningrad stuff, with fog too, so that visibility would be down to zero. And here we have the sun shining and not a cloud in the sky. It's a filthy trick, that's what it is!'

We shared the Bosun's indignation. Our viewpoint on the weather was now quite idiosyncratic: the worse it was, the better it was for us.

The escort ships brought us to the diving point and then set their course for the shore. From here on we would be going it alone. 'Stand by for diving!' ordered Lisin. 'Don't lower the flag!' Over the voice-pipe I ordered: 'Fore! Aft! Cease all movement! Maintain absolute silence!'

Life on board ship resumed its routine round.

A Mine Cable Scrapes Us

Senior Lieutenant Khrustaliov was bent over the chart, thoughtfully twirling his corn-coloured moustache. This was a good sign. It meant that the Navigator harboured no doubts about the course that had been plotted.

Generally speaking, Khrustaliov was a remarkable man. He knew the ship's route at all times, so that he was able to say, without looking at the chart, what the ship's position was, what the depth was like in the area, and how many metres we would have under our keel in a half-hour or an hour. Such expertise on Khrustaliov's part allowed Novikov, who was also strong on navigational matters, no let-up. They openly vied with one another. When Novikov, the Mine and Torpedo Officer, took over from Khrustaliov as officer of the watch, he always set him a searching quiz. Questions relating to sailing directions in the Gulf of Finland came thick and fast. Khrustaliov answered without hesitation. When the Navigator took over the watch from Novikov, the quiz was re-enacted, but this time it was Novikov who replied. He answered with alacrity, but not always accurately. This irritated the minelayer, who was often seen with chart and textbooks in his free time. We were beginning to fear that he was paying more attention to navigational matters than to his own area of expertise. I must confess that I too had become infected with this passion that Dumbrovsky had jokingly christened 'the navigation bug'. However, he was also susceptible to it himself. That's the sort of man our Navigator was, able to pass on to everyone his love for his own sphere of activity.

We were forcing a passage through the enemy's Suursaari minefield – for us the most difficult area. Until we had got through this blasted place, unless there was a dire necessity, not once would we come up to periscope depth even; we wouldn't reset the vertical rudder again and we wouldn't operate the trimming pump: the slightest noise could give us away to the enemy. All hopes were pinned on the skill of our Navigator, on the sensitive hearing of the hydrophone operator, Leading Seaman 2nd Class Lyamin. And, naturally, success was also dependent on how well we had carried out the repairs to the ship during the siege winter.

The watch was changed every four hours in the control room,

as it was at all the action stations. It was only the Captain and I who were never replaced by anyone. The gyrocompass hummed monotonously, and from time to time the rudder movement-indicators would click. An even sound reached us from the stern: a single electric motor was operating at 100 revolutions a minute. After four hours it would be replaced by the electric motor on the other side.

Commissar Gusev, opening and closing the bulkhead hatches with extreme caution, was going through the compartments, chatting to people in a low voice, reminding them time and time again: silence and the utmost vigilance!

Every fifteen minutes the hydrophone operator would report to the control room: 'Horizon clear!'

Only rarely did he give warning of distant propeller noise. You might have thought the Suursaari reaches deserted. But this silence was deceptive. For the moment it was completely calm up above, and in such weather it is extremely difficult for a hydrophone operator to detect a ship lying motionless, whereas the enemy might hear us at any moment.

Time dragged slowly by.

The bulkhead hatch opened soundlessly; Vasili Semyonovich Gusev squeezed through the circular opening. Taking advantage of the open hatchway, the ship's orderly Sukharev peered out, as usual with a rather knowing smile on his ruddy face. He reported to the Captain that the table was laid for tea. Telling me that we would take it in turn to drink our tea, Lisin went off to the second compartment.

I automatically ran my eyes over the instrument dials. Everything normal. What if it stayed like that the whole way! I was intending to go over to the navigator's table. But I was deafened by a hoarse yell from the voice-pipe: 'Mine to port in the vicinity of the first compartment!'

And I immediately heard a slight scraping myself. It was a mine's mooring wire – the fine steel cable that holds the mine up – rubbing against the side of the boat. We were stricken by a kind of numbness. We were simply listening to the scraping, straining our ears.

The bulkhead door folded back; Lisin flew into the control room, red with anger. 'Why aren't you taking evasive action?' he demanded of Khrustaliov.

The mooring wire was already rubbing against the hull in the area of the control room. The Captain yelled to the conning tower: 'Hard a-port!'

Helmsman Volkov executed the order promptly. The gyro-compass repeater-card began to move. But the mooring wire was still sliding along the ship's hull. Only somewhere right in the stern did it tear itself away from the ship's side. The Captain gave the order to resume the previous course.

Having calmed down, the Captain regarded Khrustaliov in silence. The latter was also silent. He adjusted the blue-and-white armband of the officer of the watch on his sleeve. He made no excuses for himself. And what good would it do to make excuses? Our friend lost his head in a moment of panic. I expected Lisin to bawl him out, but not so. Sergei Prokofievich is too tactful to pour out his anger when he can read sincere repentance in a subordinate's eyes.

Lisin's handsome dark-browed face softened. He headed for the second compartment to finish drinking his tea. And with one leg already over the coaming, the high sill of the hatchway, he said to Khrustaliov: 'Another time don't be slow to take evasive action. Otherwise we will get a mine cable wound round a propeller and then – fare thee well, there'll be no trace left of the dead youngsters!'

'Quite so, Comrade Captain!' responded the Navigator, not entirely appropriately. 'I won't stand gaping again.'

'And pass this on to the compartments: they are to report clearly and succinctly – "Mine to port" or "Mine to starboard", not a word more. Is that clear?'

'Clear, Comrade Captain!'

Khrustaliov wiped his sweating brow with the sleeve of his tunic jacket. He bent over his table, to mark on the chart the place where we encountered the mine. And, as if to provide the Navigator with a training opportunity, once more a mine wire slid over the ship's plating. 'Mine to port!' they reported from the first compartment.

This time Khrustaliov was energetic and precise: an order to the helmsman: an order to the motor-room crew, to reduce speed. The manoeuvre was executed with precision, as if on a training exercise. Khrustaliov brightened up. Not so much as a trace remained

31

of his earlier confusion. 'Well done!' the Captain, returning, gave him a brief word of praise.

Peaceful life was at an end. The hydrophone operator reported sounds on a regular basis. Enemy ships were scurrying about on the surface of the sea. Lyamin was reporting propeller noise once more. The Captain bent over the chart; together with the Navigator he refined the bearings. He ordered the helmsman to make a slow turn to starboard, in order to bring the sound of the propellers astern. We got away . . .

Up above night had fallen: time to surface to charge the batteries and ventilate the compartments. The Captain ordered the hydrophone operator to comb the horizon intently. And once he had made sure that there was no danger, he ordered the boat up to periscope depth.

'Come on, Vasili Semyonovich, let's sit in the conning tower, so that our eyes can get used to the darkness,' Lisin suggested to the Commissar. I summoned my assistant Briansky to the control room: let him get some practice in the procedures for surfacing and charging.

We blew the ballast. The boat surfaced in the awash position: only the conning tower and the uppermost part of the outer hull were on the surface. We could very rapidly submerge from such a position. We started charging the batteries. The ventilators forced fresh air into the compartments.

On the bridge were the Captain, the officer of the watch and two lookouts. The Commissar had gone to the radio shack to get the news bulletin from the Soviet Information Bureau. Briansky was at the control panel. He was still not managing entirely confidently; he sometimes needed sorting out. But, for a novice, it was good just the same.

We had been proceeding above water for forty minutes. But what was up? People were spilling down from the bridge like peas. The klaxon was howling deafeningly. Emergency dive! I saw that my Briansky had turned pale. This was the first such skirmish for him. I gently moved him away from the voice-pipe funnel, issued the orders myself. Let Osip calm himself down. In the meantime he would see how you have to act in such circumstances.

The Captain came down last. He gave orders to enter into the ship's log: 'Executed emergency dive, away from ship observed on bearing one-two-zero.'

From the listening post they reported the propeller noise of a high-speed motor launch getting closer.

'Maintain depth at sixty metres,' the Captain ordered the Bosun. And he asked the Navigator to determine the shortest course to the minefield.

Khrustaliov looked at the Captain in astonishment, then at the chart. Lisin explained: 'It's safer for us there.'

The Captain's strategy was understandable: you wouldn't lure the Nazis into a minefield. The Navigator worked out the course. An order to the helmsman. Soon Lyamin reported that the motor launch had come to a standstill. 'They are listening all right, but they won't poke their noses into the minefield.'

Once more the motor launch's propellers began to bore through the water, but they came no closer to us: the enemy was rushing about on the edge of the minefield. Two explosions produced a booming rumble astern. Fairly close. But from the compartments they reported no damage done.

'How are you feeling, Chief?' Gusev asked me.

'I wasn't too fond of the bombing in Leningrad, and for some reason I don't care for it at sea either.'

'Are you being facetious?'

'Well, would you expect me to say that I'm not afraid of being bombed?'

The Captain pulled a face: 'Comrades, this is really not the moment to debate this issue. We all dislike being bombed.'

We had been moving through the minefield for over an hour. Strange though it may seem, at no time did we run up against a mine cable there. True enough, it's more peaceful in the minefield.

At 11.43 hours there was once more the sound of two explosions astern. This meant that there were enemy ships above us again. The explosions were a long way off. It seemed that the Nazi patrol hadn't blundered into us.

With the Captain's permission, I did a tour round the compartments. The boat had become decidedly heavier. I was searching for the cause. In the diesel compartment the starboard gas exhaust valve had sprung a leak; the tiniest trickle of water. I ordered them to measure the rate of seepage. No more than a litre and a half per minute; a mere nothing. But that's already ninety litres an hour and, during the twenty hours that we had been moving about underwater, some two tons had seeped in. This was the reason the submarine was noticeably down by the stern. It made controlling the ship more difficult, but it couldn't be helped. There was no question of starting up the pump: the enemy would hear the noise. We needed to wait for another hour and a half or so.

Evening again. I was at my action station. I couldn't keep my eyes open. I tried to move about more. It didn't help much. As soon as I stopped, I fell asleep standing up. At one point I came to, and I couldn't immediately make out where I was. It turned out that I was standing underneath the conning-tower hatch, clutching the handrails of the ladder with both hands. How did I get there? I could see that Sergei Prokofievich too was fighting a losing battle against drowsiness. He was sitting on a canvas stool and leaning over to one side, about to fall off. No, we wouldn't last out like this. We still had two more days to go.

The Captain opened his eyes: 'At 23.00 hours we are surfacing!'

Leading Seaman Nakhimchuk, the senior planesman, who even during the siege managed to remain plump, was breathing heavily. Already twenty-two hours had passed since the moment when we were forced to submerge. There was really very little oxygen left in the air that we were breathing.

'Could we switch on the regenerator?' I asked the Captain.

Lisin jumped up off the canvas stool, stretched himself: 'No, we'll try to surface before that. We must save the regenerator cartridges for a rainy day.'

'Comrade Captain,' Nakhimchuk made his voice heard, 'don't you worry about us. We can take it. And we will provide those who feel really poorly with a gas-mask and some regenerator cartridges.'

Just the same, the Captain ordered the boat to be taken up a bit. He raised the periscope and hastily lowered it again. In the log appeared the entry: 'Bearing three-three-four: patrol boat in silhouette.'

We dived deep down. It was midnight before we managed to surface. We began to charge the battery. Above the sea, the weather was in our favour: light rain, poor visibility. A moist, cold wind burst in through the conning-tower hatch. We couldn't breathe in too much of it. The drowsiness was completely wiped away. I hastily issued orders as to the charging procedure. We pumped compressed air into the tanks. We dried out the bilges. We threw overboard the tins and other rubbish that had accumulated in the compartments. We came to the end of the first stage of emergency charging. That would be enough, perhaps? No, we wanted to store as much electric power as possible. We continued with the charging. An anxious Briansky came running up. 'What shall we do? The temperature of the second group of batteries is forty-five degrees!'

This was bad; extremely bad.

'We must step up the ventilation of the batteries.'

'Everything has already been done. It doesn't help.'

Should we stop the charging? But when would we manage to surface again? And without electric power the boat would be helpless. I decided on extreme measures: 'Open up the removable deck panels near the radio shack and by the galley, open both of the fourth compartment's bulkhead doors. If we have to, we will even close the shaft providing the diesels with air, so that all the air goes through the compartment to the engines.'

Briansky pulled a long face: this was certainly not the recommended procedure in the instruction manuals. But it was only in this way that we would be able to cool down our new, not yet 'run-in' battery.

Now there was a real gale surging into the control room from the conning-tower hatch. Through the open bulkhead doors it rushed along the fourth compartment, howling as it went; the sailors had to grab hold of the bunks, so as not to be swept off their feet. But still the battery did not cool down. Two hours later, the electrolyte temperature had reached forty-seven degrees. This was dangerous. Briansky was constantly casting glances at me. But I was still biding my time. And only after the battery had been fully charged did I give the signal to stop charging. We closed the deck panels in the compartment. The one most pleased of all about this was the cook, Shinkarenko, because he had been obliged to hover above the open battery pit like a circus performer, risking tumbling into it with his saucepans and ladles.

While the stormy blast had been raging in the control room and the fourth compartment, the diesels had been drawing in all the smells. Now enticing galley aromas were beginning to creep insistently from the fourth compartment. I gave the order for the bulkhead hatch to be sealed as swiftly as possible.

This surface sailing was beginning to get on my nerves. I always feel better in myself beneath the water. In the first place, there are fewer chances of running into a mine there. In the second place, there is no rolling there. And this wretched condition is something I can never get used to. It is true that I have had to endure Force 10 storms on occasion. Many were being thrown off their feet while I was standing watch, but regularly every two hours I would 'pay my tribute to Neptune'. It is a nuisance, though: I have been serving on ships for such a long time – and I can't avoid getting seasick. I used to be awfully distressed about it earlier on. I found out later that even the famous Nelson was unable throughout the whole of his life to get used to rolling. This comforted me to some extent: it means that I am not the only one . . .

After we had finally submerged normally and balanced the trim, Misha Khrustaliov announced ceremoniously to me: 'Chief, hold your head up high! Do you know how much we have done this past night? Thirty-six miles! In the submerged position it would have taken us eighteen hours to achieve this distance.'

'I share your delight. The rain helped. But we could just as easily have run into a mine.'

'In wartime everything has its element of risk.'

'But just the same, if there is an opportunity to do so, it is better not to take risks. As the saying goes: *The more carefully you tread, the further you will go.*'

'I don't believe that at all. In our circumstances, the saying should be amended to: *The more carefully you tread, the longer you will be exposed to attack, and perhaps you will catch it in the neck.*'

'I do believe it, Misha. Today I too was obliged to take risks. I let the battery temperature get as high as forty-seven degrees. And if Alexander Kuzmich Vasiliev had got to know about it, his hair would have stood on end.'

'And what would Vasiliev have done in your position?'

'In my position? I think he would have done exactly the same as me . . .'

For Leningrad!

On the evening of 7 July, we finally heaved a sigh of relief. The Gulf of Finland with its mines and its patrolling ships had finally been left behind. We were in the open expanse of the Baltic Sea. The passage to the sector assigned to us presented no further difficulty. One more day's sailing, and on 8 July we reported to headquarters that we had taken up our position.

The first armed skirmish with the enemy came without warning and from an unexpected quarter.

We were charging the battery. It was a brightly-lit 'white night'. A slight haze was drifting over the sea. At 03.05 hours, when the engines were still operating on propeller-charging, all of a sudden the lookouts, the officer of the watch and the Captain slid down clumsily into the control room. Simultaneously with the resounding clang of the upper conning-tower hatch sounded the signal for an emergency dive. From outside, at that very second, could be heard the loud rapping of bullets and the striking of small-calibre shells. We speedily dived down to the depths. Two belated explosions crashed down in pursuit of us.

When the excitement had died down a bit, the details began to emerge more clearly. The boat was going along in the light haze. A pre-dawn silence was reigning all around, broken only by our diesels' rumbling exhaust. Generally speaking, when you have a diesel hammering at your ear, it is hard to hear anything else at all. But Signalman Alexander Olenin caught a suspicious drone just the same. The Captain immediately gave the order to dive. Already jumping for the hatch, the ratings caught sight of the enemy aircraft. It was flying really low. The fiery tracer of machine-gun bursts and gunfire began to arc from it. Olenin's alertness saved the ship. The Captain announced a commendation for him there and then in the control room.

On the morning of 9 July, the officer of the watch, Senior Lieutenant Novikov, scanning the sea through the periscope, discovered a large convoy. Novikov at once turned the boat onto an interception course with the enemy ships and asked for the Captain to be called to the conning tower. I came running into the control room hot on the Captain's heels. My heart had quickened its beat. The first attack! The shallow waters were a cause of some unease; Navigator Khrustaliov had reported them. But the Captain, after raising the periscope and interpreting the data concerning the movement of the convoy, decided to attack. I made urgent adjustments to the boat's trim, mentally calculating the quantity of water that would have to be taken on board in order to compensate for the weight of the ejected torpedoes.

We moved to intersect with the convoy's course. The Captain raised the periscope periodically. The sea was absolutely still. The water was like a looking-glass. The Captain was fidgety: the bow-wave created by the periscope was probably too conspicuous. But he did not draw back from the attack, he was hoping that a light breeze might still ruffle the smooth surface of the water. First Lieutenant Dumbrovsky had prepared calculation tables. In the conning tower Lisin and Gusev took turns at looking through the periscope. And suddenly an exclamation reached us from there: 'Aircraft!'

I heard the Captain's words: 'If you only knew, Commissar, how disappointing it is for me to let this first convoy go! But I must . . .'

We all understood that it would be dangerous to attack. The boat was running through shallow water, the aircraft would discover her straight away and would set the ships on us. And in shallow water we couldn't take evasive action to avoid bombardment. And on top of that, it would be hard to count on the attack being a success: the water was like a mirror; on the freighters they would spot a torpedo from a long way off and turn away from it.

'But will they understand us back at headquarters?' asked Lisin thoughtfully.

'Five metres under the keel!' the Navigator reported calmly.

'Well, there's the justification for you,' the Commissar said to the Captain and nodded to the sailor on watch. 'Write it down in the log.' And to Lisin again, 'I don't have to tell you, Sergei Prokofievich, that the ability to assess a situation correctly, to weigh up all the pros and cons, is the main component of a commanding officer's skill.'

'Stand down from action stations!' the Captain forced out in anger and bitterness, casting a final glance at the retreating convoy. He came down to the control room in distress.

'There will be other convoys, Sergei Prokofievich,' I offered him in consolation. 'And calm water, although it's an unfortunate occurrence for us, it is nevertheless a rare one in the Baltic.'

We didn't have long to fret. At 15.30 hours First Lieutenant Dumbrovsky could see the smoke of a solitary freighter through the periscope. We manoeuvred for a long time, because we were positioned much farther out to sea than the freighter, which was hugging the coast. A slight ripple on the surface of the sea improved the conditions for an attack, but an abrupt decrease in the reserve depth under the keel forced the Captain to fire a torpedo from a very considerable distance away.

I rapidly pumped the auxiliary ballast across and took water into the stabilizing tank. We counted the seconds, the minutes, but there was no explosion. 'Missed,' the Captain confirmed gloomily, and lowered the periscope.

Having come down from the conning tower into the control room, he scrutinized the navigational chart at length, as if seeking the reason for the miss. I can well see his crimson face with big drops of sweat on his brow. I would have liked to offer him some comfort, but I waited in silence to see what the Captain decided. The sailors were silent. The Commissar was deep in thought. Everyone was cast down by the new setback. It was something of a consolation that in this area of the Baltic Sea the traffic was brisk. There were chances for success. It was actually like going fishing: the more fish there are, the better the prospect of a catch; but if the fish are not there, you won't catch anything in any case, no matter how often you cast the net.

We drew away from the shore again. The sound of the alarm found me in the seventh compartment, where I was talking to Vinokurov, the Party Secretary. I dashed headlong to the control room. The clock showed 16.54, which meant that not so much as half an hour had passed since the stand-down from the previous alert.

On watch as before were First Lieutenant Dumbrovsky and my assistant Briansky. An enemy convoy had been sighted: eight freighters escorted by a destroyer and two patrol boats. Lisin and Gusev were already in the conning tower. Briansky yielded his place at the control panel to me. Our position was very conveniently located in the very centre of the compartment, from where all the instruments could be seen. The movement of their indicators reflected the tension of the moment: the gyrocompass repeater-card swung slowly from one side to the other – the Captain was refining a course for the attack; the pressure-gauge pointers jumped – the torpedomen were preparing the tubes for firing; the depth-gauge needle and the air-bubble in the curved tube of the trim indicator were frozen in one position – the Bosun was leading the ship along as though on a fine-drawn thread. We awaited the final order. But in its place we heard: 'Cancel the attack! Bosun, dive! A destroyer is about to ram us . . .'

No, the Bosun wouldn't be able to manage this all by himself. I ordered them to open the flood valve of the rapid-diving tank. Leading Seaman 1st Class Skachko spun the valve hand-wheels. Leading Seaman Nakhimchuk, anticipating my next order, had squeezed through to the ventilation-tank valves like an eel. Water bubbled, air hissed.

Hydrophone operator Lyamin reported with alarm that the destroyer's bearing was constant. This meant that she was coming straight at us. The noise of the propellers was increasing. And the black depth-gauge needle was crawling dreadfully slowly. The destroyer rushed by above us with a deafening rumble. Instinctively, you duck your head down into your shoulders. Later on we did an estimate and came to the conclusion that the keel of the destroyer was no more than a metre from the periscope standard of our submarine.

All's well that ends well. We had escaped a ramming. But our latest attack had fallen through. When the Captain raised the periscope, the convoy was already far away.

Depressed silence in the control room; a gloomy Captain was looking at the navigational chart. Then suddenly he cheered up: 'You know, it's an ill wind that blows nobody any good. Look where we launched our attacks, Vasili Semyonovich. Note the regularity: it so happens that the enemy is proceeding along the 20-metre contour line.'

'Could it be a simple coincidence?'

'Unlikely. In any event, we will stick close to this 20-metre depth line.'

Relieved of our watch, Dumbrovsky and I made our way to the second compartment. Four alerts in one day; more than enough. Never before was I so tired. I dropped onto the bunk. Above me

Dumbrovsky was noisily settling himself down on his upper bunk.

We slept for no more than a quarter of an hour. Then once more we were dashing to the control room at breakneck speed. Action stations! Doing up my tunic as I ran, I asked the Navigator: 'Misha, what's up?'

'Shh! A straggler slogging along without an escort.'

Lisin and Gusev were in the conning tower. The last of the officers to come running up was the First Lieutenant. His right cheek was scored by a purplish-white scar. 'What happened to you, Alexei Ivanovich?'

He rubbed his cheek: 'I fell asleep on my forage cap. But spare me your idiotic questions. It's bad enough trying to pull myself together as it is. I stood a double watch. Five alerts in one day. It's a madhouse!'

The target was fifty-five cables distant. The time was 18.26 hours. The Navigator marked the position of the freighter on the chart and announced delightedly: 'The freighter is proceeding along the 20-metre contour line!'

The Captain manoeuvred painstakingly and at length. For a whole forty minutes. He wanted to strike without fail. And now came the long-awaited order: 'Fire!'

'Start the pump!' I yelled to the duty planesman.

But we didn't feel the customary jolt made by a torpedo ejecting. 'The torpedo failed to eject: the tail-stop jammed,' Vinokurov, the leading torpedoman, announced through the voice-pipe in a dejected tone.

In the conning tower the Captain groaned out loud. The Commissar, having jumped down into the control room, stamped his foot: 'Fetch Novikov here!'

Such fruity expressions were flying in the direction of the Torpedo Officer that no one could be in any doubt for a future occasion that our Commissar was a thoroughgoing old sea-dog!

Novikov was given no chance to hear this. In the conning tower the Captain rang out in a voice of steel: 'Ready both diesels! Stand by to surface!'

'What are you up to, Sergei?' the Commissar enquired anxiously.

'I can't catch up underwater, and I don't intend to let her go.'

We surfaced at 19.06 hours. The dieselmen produced full speed ahead right away (Well done, Briansky!). After sixteen minutes in pursuit, the Captain fired a torpedo from a distance of no more than four cables (740 metres). For us this was point-blank shooting. A rumble and a powerful hydraulic shock along the boat's hull proclaimed that the attack had been crowned with success. The freighter went to the bottom. Lisin, Gusev, Khrustaliov and Olenin, who were on the bridge, observed her death throes with their own eyes. Dumbrovsky, who had remained in the conning tower during the attack, couldn't contain himself and jumped out onto the bridge as well, but saw only foaming water and a huge cloud of steam and smoke.

The boat submerged. Jubilation in the compartments. The seamen enthusiastically congratulated the Captain and one another. After all, we'd broken our dry spell! The sailors were exultant.

While still in Kronstadt, loading the torpedo tubes, the torpedomen had written slogans on the torpedoes' fat bodies. We now know that written on the torpedo that struck the freighter was: *For Leningrad!*

When the first wave of joy had subsided, everyone felt their fatigue again. Having found a suitable spot, we lay on the bottom. But it was too soon to rest. The torpedomen reloaded the tubes. Briansky and the engine room crew busied themselves with the diesels. Only after all the work had been done did the submariners straggle off to the compartments. An unusual order sounded throughout the ship: 'Everyone off watch to get some sleep!'

The boat was transformed into a realm of sleep. We rested until late in the evening. At dinner – and it was by then midnight with us – the Captain said: 'We used up two torpedoes and achieved one victory. But it might well have been more.'

'You have in mind that freighter that we missed?' asked the Commissar.

'Quite so.'

'But don't you think, Captain, that this would have been a bit too much of a good thing?'

'Two victories in one day?'

'No, not that. Two torpedoes, two freighters. Even on a training exercise, it's rare for such a thing to happen. And if, on top of that, the tail-stops jam . . .'

Gusev gave a sidelong glance at Novikov, bent over his plate. 'Everyone can make a mistake, Comrade Commissar,' the latter responded. 'We will go over the incident with the stops with a fine-tooth comb. And we won't let such a thing happen again, of that you may be sure!'

It was a lively scene at table. The officers were jubilant over the long-awaited success. It was only the Captain who was sipping his tea in silence. He had changed dramatically during the course of the day. He had grown haggard, pale. It was simply incredible that a few hours could have left such a mark. Yes, our Captain had gone through a great deal. One failure after another; even making allowances for the obstructive circumstances, for other people's mistakes. But a crew's failure, whatever the reason for it might have been, is always the captain's failure. He answers for everything. You don't go around explaining to all and sundry how and why an attack came to grief. And, besides, it wouldn't get you anywhere. People inevitably stop believing in an unsuccessful captain. Which is why, in the course of the last attack, Lisin decided to push it to the limit: he surfaced within sight of the enemy, caught up with him on the surface and torpedoed him from a minimal distance. It was just our good luck that enemy aircraft were not in the offing and that the gunners on the freighter lost their heads. Otherwise, he would have caught it in the neck. But the Captain was in need of a success. And not just him – we all were. Right now everyone was full of beans. But the Captain had still not rid himself of the heavy burden of the earlier failures. I knew that he was thinking through his actions over and over again. But even mistakes can be turned to good account, if they serve as a lesson for the future.

Routine Watches

During the night of 11 July we received orders to change position. At dawn the stem of the submarine was already cutting through the water of a different area of the Baltic Sea. At noon Khrustaliov, the officer of the watch, spotted an enemy convoy. The Captain peered intently through the periscope. He held off from attacking: too far away, impossible to intercept. He ordered the Navigator to plot the convoy's course on the chart precisely in order to keep track of where the enemy was going.

Until 16.20 hours everything was calm. The First Lieutenant

was serving as officer of the watch, and my assistant, Briansky, as duty engineer officer. I had remained in the control room, in order to help him with bringing the boat up to periscope depth for the first few times. We were chatting peacefully, when Dumbrovsky yelled out so loudly that we were alarmed. It turned out that he had sighted a huge convoy. He counted sixteen freighters, two patrol boats, a destroyer and several motor launches.

Lisin came running up. The convoy was heading well away to the side, but Lisin decided to attack. Making four knots underwater, we put on a big spurt and set an attack course. With a countdown of only minutes remaining before a torpedo salvo, we heard the controlled voice of the Captain in the conning tower: 'Destroyer! Bearing down on us fast!'

Did that mean it had all been for nothing? The sound of the enemy ship's propellers could already be picked up distinctly by ear and was rapidly closing, reaching a crescendo. But the Captain was biding his time. He raised the periscope and lowered it again then raised it once more. Khrustaliov had his eyes glued to the compass card; two more degrees to the chosen angle of deflection. Well, our Captain certainly knew how to keep his cool!

'Fire!'

The boat shuddered from the release of the torpedoes. 'Dive!' yelled the Captain, jumping down from the conning tower into the control room.

The precision and speed with which the seamen were operating at that moment even robots would have been unable to achieve. Not a single hitch, not a single unnecessary movement, not a single extra word. The depth-gauge needle measured off the metres precisely. Loudly, so that everyone could hear, the Captain warned: 'Now they will depth charge us.'

I took a notepad and a pencil from my pocket. The rumble of the destroyer's propellers and the depth charge detonations fused together. The submarine was thrown from side to side. Like a rag being pulled about by a bulldog. It was impossible to stay on your feet. We virtually flew from one side to the other. With each new explosion it was becoming increasingly dark in the control room: fragments of glass lampshades and light bulbs fell tinkling to the deck. The massive cast iron cover of the signal distribution box fell open with a crash and hit the leading planesman on the head.

44

Nakhimchuk, never taking his hand off the valve handwheel, angrily pushed the cover away with his free hand and rubbed the bruised spot.

After the fourth or fifth explosion, I remembered the notepad and began to take notes. I counted twenty-three depth charges. Nine of them blew up really close to the submarine.

When the destroyer had moved away, we came up to periscope depth again. Lisin asked me into the conning tower and let me look around at the results of the attack. In the thunder of the bombardment we hadn't heard the torpedoes explode. But they had. Debris from the sunken ship was clearly visible through the periscope. There was a second freighter in amongst it. Her lifeboats had been lowered and were picking up survivors. The destroyer, having gone over to the scene of the incident, was also engaged in this task. The remaining ships, funnels smoking, were already seeking refuge beyond the horizon.

We shook the Captain by the hand, congratulated him on the victory. Once we had been stood down, I did the rounds of the compartments, telling people about the new success. I checked for damage. Only minor matters: smashed light bulbs (a thank-you to our Lavansaari comrades, for replenishing our stock!), dislodged instruments. Trifling jobs. Reassured, I returned to the control room and there I learned some disturbing news. The bombardment had left its mark after all. Our underwater listening post – *Mars 1* – was a casualty. The submarine had become deaf. Leading Seaman 2nd Class Lyamin was tinkering about inside the exposed interior of the direct-listening system, but could not make out at all what had happened in there.

For two whole days the Captain waited patiently, but then his patience ran out. He summoned Dumbrovsky, Khrustaliov and Antifeev, the leading seamen in charge of the radio operators. 'I will give you two more days. I shall expect a definitive answer: will our direct-listening system work or not?'

Standing his watch on the morning of 14 July, Khrustaliov saw a freighter through the periscope. Had the direct-listening system been working, we would have detected the enemy a good deal earlier. But now, no matter how hard we tried, we were too late making our move. The Captain lost his temper and said a few harsh words to the Navigator.

Some time later, Novikov reported sighting a freighter too. And once more we had to hold off from attacking: we had spotted it too late.

At 15.40 hours, during Dumbrovsky's watch, we discovered a large convoy. Lisin broke through the protective screen with a daring manoeuvre, but no attack was launched: the enemy caught sight of our periscope, and a destroyer forced us to go deep. And, again, this was entirely due to the 'deafness' of the submarine.

Fed up, the Captain took himself off to his cabin. Khrustaliov came on watch. Taking advantage of the breathing space, he began to transfer to the chart the notes from the rough log that was kept up during attacks by Ignatov, a navigational electrician. Beneath the Navigator's hands the intricate pattern of the boat's manoeuvres was taking shape. I was full of admiration for my friend's work. I tried to talk to him. No way! At such moments Khrustaliov was totally blind and deaf; he was aware only of his chart. But every fifteen minutes on the dot, he went up into the conning tower and ordered the boat to be brought up to periscope depth. He would scan the horizon and briefly report: 'Horizon clear. Sea getting up.' Then back to work again.

We could tell that the sea was getting up from the depth-gauge needle: it was juddering continuously, swinging a whole point at a time. This indicated that there was already a Force 5 wind roughing up the waves.

I glanced into the second compartment. There work was in full swing. Diagrams were spread out on the table. Instruments, components and tools were laid out on big pieces of white rag on the deck itself. To improve the lighting, they had brought in portable lamps from the neighbouring compartments. Leading Seaman Antifeev, the orchestrator-in-chief, was constantly running between the diagrams on the table and the listening post. First Lieutenant Dumbrovsky was there too. He was sitting and observing. He knew the *Mars* equipment inside-out, but he knew even better that outside interference would be of no benefit. Nevertheless, he did put in a word from time to time: 'Don't pull on the wire! Draw it out smoothly, without twisting it! How can you throw an instrument down like that? You have to lay it down carefully. Like this!'

I could see that there was nowhere for me to perch with my notes, so I went back to the control room. The Navigator had completed his work of art. He had already transferred the diagram of the manoeuvres onto tracing paper and now, rubbing his hands with satisfaction, was waiting for the Indian ink to dry in the warmth of the angled desk lamp.

'Is it ready?' I showed my surprise.

'It's ready. I don't like work to pile up. I have a rule: never put a job off until the next day. Do everything straight away and then forget it!'

He carefully removed the tracing paper from the chart.

'Well now, Misha, let's see what the depths are like here.'

We both bent over his table.

'It's all right, we can live with it. It gets a bit worse further on. Can you see?'

After a short silence, he said: 'The sea is getting up. The boat may be thrown up to the surface by a wave at any moment. Keep an eye on it, would you please, while I scan the horizon?'

We came up to periscope depth smoothly. It was difficult to hold the boat steady. The planesman had to hold the ship's nose down all the time.

'Planesman!' shouted the Navigator from the conning tower. 'Come up half a metre, otherwise the periscope keeps getting splashed.'

We came up a bit more, but the lens got splashed by a wave from time to time anyway.

'So what's the horizon like?' I pressed the Navigator, wanting to go deep as soon as possible, since I could see the difficulty the planesman was having in coping with the unruly boat: she would either strain towards the surface uncontrollably, or else burrow down into the deep. To keep her in balance, he sometimes had to put the hydroplanes over almost as far as they would go. 'He's really got the knack!' said Khrustaliov admiringly. 'It's about Force 7, I reckon.'

Scanning the horizon for the second time, the Navigator uttered an incomprehensible exclamation and immediately ordered: 'Helm to starboard!' He added, 'You there, in the control room, report to the Captain that enemy merchant shipping has been sighted. Write down the time . . .' Climbing the ladder to the

47

conning tower, Lisin threw out as he went: 'Bosun to the hydroplanes. Quickly!'

It had already become a routine: at critical moments, Bosun Pyatibratov, our most experienced man at the job, would station himself at the hydroplane controls.

The Commissar was standing beside me in the control room. He was watching the depth gauge and the Bosun's deft hands. Then he approached the opening of the lower conning-tower hatch, glanced into it, said quietly to Lisin: 'It's blowing a storm up on top, Captain.' The latter lingered for a moment and then lowered the periscope.

'You are right, Commissar. In weather like this the torpedoes would be forced off course. Bosun, go to a safe depth!'

'Yes, Comrade Captain!' the Bosun responded gladly. He was already soaked in sweat from constantly manipulating the hydroplanes.

'Weather!' Leading Seaman Nakhimchuk pronounced in meaningful tones.

Sergei Prokofievich came down from the conning tower.

'For some reason we're having no luck today, Commissar.'

Those off watch dispersed to get some rest. At 20.00 hours I replaced Senior Lieutenant Khrustaliov as officer of the watch, for the first time in my life. It was a grave trust. It meant that the Captain did not doubt my capabilities. Lisin was not the sort of man to make rash decisions. Before assigning an independent watch to me, Sergei Prokofievich had been observing me closely for a long time; instructing me, giving me a great deal of advice, and to an even greater extent asking me questions.

Proud and happy, I was fulfilling my new responsibilities enthusiastically. Every fifteen minutes I would bring the boat up to periscope depth, scan the horizon intently. So far nothing had caught my eye, but this did not dampen my zeal. Being an engineer, having almost all the ship's machinery and systems in my care, gave me a considerable advantage. I could carry out all the calculations for surfacing and submerging and deal with charging the battery, by myself. This made the work of the control room more clear-cut. Judging by appearances, the Captain was content. But, naturally, the most contented of all was Khrustaliov, who now had an opportunity to get a good night's rest before the strain of plotting a course at night, when the submarine goes at high speeds and covers significant distances.

Each time I raised the periscope, I noticed that the waves were getting flatter, and the horizon darker and closer. The eighth day of patrolling our combat zone was coming to an end.

I gave the order: 'Stand by to surface!' The deck exerted a slight pressure on the soles of my feet: the boat was coming up. I inspected the horizon through the periscope for the last time. Having made sure that there was no danger, I gave a signal to the planesmen. The boat burst out onto the surface, rocking slightly in the waves. The Captain nodded his head in satisfaction – everything was in good order – and climbed up onto the bridge.

By morning they had repaired the direct-listening system and tested it. It was working properly. When a listening watch was resumed, everyone heaved a sigh of relief. The officers off watch gathered in the officers' mess. We joked, we argued, we recalled various incidents in our lives. 'Comrade Captain, tell us about Spain,' someone suggested.

We enjoyed listening to Lisin. He had something to tell. He was senior to us in both age and experience of the service. He was a volunteer in Spain, sailed in submarines of the Republican Navy, and was already then, in 1936, fighting fascists. Even the inveterate chess players – Novikov, the minelayer, and Shkurko, the medic – set aside the board with a game already begun. The orderly, Sukharev, endlessly wiped one and the same plate. The rating was listening spellbound, he didn't want to leave the mess. And I knew that he would continue to linger there like that as long as the Captain went on speaking.

Amongst the sailors our orderly had the reputation of being the best-read and the most well-informed, and not in the slightest because he read a lot, but because he was around when the officers were talking, and he lacked neither a good memory nor native wit. He had been caught out on more than one occasion, putting forward someone else's ideas as his own. He had been told off for poking his nose into other people's business. But in this respect our orderly was incorrigible.

During the night of 18 July we received orders to change our position again. We were warned by headquarters to observe extreme caution during our passage: there were enemy submarines hunting us.

We were going along surfaced when we received a radio message. Lisin came down into the control room. Splashes were glistening on his leather raglan. He bent over the chart: 'Navigator, calculate the time for a turn here at this spot and plot a direct course for Vindava.'

The Captain climbed back up to the bridge. I went over to Khrustaliov. The Navigator was chewing the end of his pencil. 'Can you get us there?'

'I'll get you there all right, but you see what a discrepancy there is here. I don't know what to do about it. I would have liked to surface near Akmenrags Lighthouse, to fix our position by it, but it's out of the question.'

Khrustaliov had a difficult task. By then we had been sailing for a long time, constantly manoeuvring, and the Navigator had simply had no chance to fix our position with reference either to the coastline or to any lighthouse. He was plotting the course entirely by dead reckoning, relying on his own calculations. And now we would have to travel blind once more for many tens of miles. The smallest error could lead to a large deviation from the set course, and at sea this always threatens disaster, even more so when you are sailing in hostile waters.

'And how is it with you? Everything all right?' Khrustaliov asked me. 'Bear in mind, the way ahead won't be easy.'

'Everything seems to be in order.'

'And how is your vertical rudder shaft?'

'Strictly speaking, that shaft is yours, not mine; it comes within the navigational department's area of responsibility. But it's giving me a lot of trouble.'

We had this shaft under special observation: for some reason it wore down extremely quickly. Several times a day I would measure its thread, estimating how long it would still last out.

I went up onto the bridge. A brisk, cool wind slapped me in the face. It would soon be time to submerge. There was a deep twilight over the sea. Only in the east was a little band of lilac defining the horizon more and more distinctly. The submarine nudged the small waves aside with her hull. The ship's flag was flapping in the wind above my head. Symbol of our Motherland, it was always with us. On patrol we never lowered it from the flagstaff on the conning-tower rail.

Khrustaliov had popped up from the hatchway: 'Comrade Captain, ten minutes' sailing left until the diving point.'

At the appointed time the submarine dived beneath the water. It was as if she had never been on the surface. Silence in the compartments.

Khrustaliov was still chewing his pencil. He abandoned this activity only when the officer of the watch, having in due course raised the periscope, reported that there was a lighthouse in sight, directly on course. Khrustaliov flung himself on the periscope. 'Vindava,' he confirmed in an indifferent tone, but, when he turned to us, joy was simply sparkling from his eyes. As usual our Navigator had worked wonders. He had brought the ship to her destination with faultless precision.

By then we had been cruising in the Vindava area for three days. Increasingly frequently, the Captain would go over to the chart and peer at it at length. He was uneasy. But on the face of it, what was there to fret about? Was it actually our fault that the enemy ships had taken refuge in their lairs and wouldn't poke their noses out? But man is made that way. He is upset by enforced inactivity.

The monotony of life on patrol does not so much tire people out as dim their enthusiasm. Checking the performance of the watch, the diesel crew's leading seaman found Gavrikov, an engine room rating, with a book in his hands. It would have been possible simply to punish the offender. But it was important that others too should learn from this example. I ordered all our department's off-watch sailors to gather in the fifth compartment. I informed them briefly of Gavrikov's dereliction of duty and suggested an exchange of views. The first to ask for the floor was Chief Leading Seaman Mikhailov, in charge of the engine room crew. Normally a taciturn man, today he surprised us. He spoke passionately, bitingly. Gavrikov simply shrivelled. But he is not the type to admit to guilt straight off. As soon as Mikhailov had fallen silent, Gavrikov launched a counter-attack: 'Comrade Leading Seaman, you are wrong to treat me like that. I was reading a book, it's true, but I did not lose my vigilance.'

'What do you mean, you didn't lose it, if you were reading on watch?'

'Here's how. I first of all inspected the bearings and determined which of them was the hottest. I put my hand on it. I know that the hand can stand a temperature of sixty-five degrees. The temperature in the compartment is twenty-five. The permitted overheating of a bearing above the ambient temperature is forty degrees. So that, as long as a hand can stand it, everything is as it should be. So there I was, standing by the bearing and, so as not to waste time in idleness, I took up a book.'

There was laughter and voices in the compartment.

'Sneaky bugger!'

'You've got an answer for everything!'

'He's got breach of discipline down to a fine art!'

'And what if the other bearings had melted down meanwhile?'

Chief Leading Seaman Lyashenko raised his hand, to call for silence.

'Comrades,' he said, 'generally speaking, Gavrikov is a bit thick. He has neither imagination nor inventiveness. Actually, it would have been simpler for him to pull down his trousers and sit on the bearing. In the first place, that particular area is more sensitive than a hand and, in the second, he would not only have been able to read then, but doze as well, until it got too hot . . .'

General guffaws drowned out the Chief Leading Seaman's words. Gavrikov was laughing loudly too. This more than anything incensed Mikhailov. 'You've not really understood a thing, Gavrikov. You should be in tears: you disgrace our whole group, and you are laughing your head off. It's a pity that there is no detention cell on this boat. We could have sent you there for four or five days, to think things over in solitary.'

We began to think about what we should do with Gavrikov. At this moment the Commissar came in. He listened to what the comrades had to suggest, then said: 'But might it not be too soon to reach a decision? Let's first of all inspect the whole of Gavrikov's area of responsibility. It's a fair bet that not everything there is as it should be. And at that point we can have a think . . .'

Gavrikov stopped smiling. He could sense which way the wind was blowing. 'No, no, that's not necessary!' he began to babble. 'I have understood the error of my ways. That's for sure. I give you my word that nothing of the sort will ever happen again.'

'We will inspect his area of responsibility in any case,' said the

52

Commissar, 'and we will postpone Gavrikov's punishment. You can see the man is repentant . . .'

'I am! I am!' Gavrikov grasped the straw. 'I'm speaking honestly!'

Uproar in the compartment: the sailors were laughing. For Gavrikov this laughter was more painful than any penalty. Laughter can drive a lesson home forcefully. I knew that from now on no one on the ship would grab up a book when on watch.

And the enemy still had not shown his face. We roamed around our sector, sometimes on the surface, sometimes underwater; we kept our eyes peeled, the hydrophone operators never took their headsets off; the sea was empty. The Captain even risked penetrating into Vindava's outer harbour. No one there either . . .

I was still keeping the thread of the blasted rudder shaft under continual observation. I grumbled at Khrustaliov for having to spend time on navigational affairs (though, to be honest, I did realize myself that I couldn't simply dismiss the shaft, since an engineer is responsible for this machinery, which is of vital importance to the ship, just as much as a navigator is). Then all of a sudden disaster struck us from a completely different direction than we had expected. A breakdown occurred directly within our sphere of responsibility.

During the night of 29 July, in the course of charging the battery, an engine suddenly stopped. Leaving Leading Seaman Nakhimchuk to take my place in the control room, I ran to the unusually quiet fifth compartment. Smoke was drifting above the lifeless diesel. Briansky reported: 'The supercharger unit has broken down.'

'The gas-turbine ball bearing got ground to mincemeat,' added Chief Leading Seaman Mikhailov.

We started up the starboard diesel, which was in good shape. It rumbled so loudly that it was impossible for us to talk to one another. I took Briansky and Mikhailov to the neighbouring compartment and we continued our conversation there. 'Open up both the gas and the air turbines at the same time,' I told my assistants. 'Transfer the air-turbine bearing to the gas turbine, and a spare bearing to the air turbine. We do have some spare bearings?' 'Yes,' the leading seaman replied. 'We have one and one alone.' It's always like that with Mikhailov. *One and one alone.* But if push comes to shove, a few more will come to light.

Something else was bothering Briansky: 'Why such a long-drawn-out affair? Taking the air turbine to pieces when it is in good working order . . . Simpler to install the spare bearing directly in the place of the damaged one . . .'

'No, it must be done as I say without fail. We will install the bearing that has already been run-in into the gas turbine. You surely know that the temperature of this turbine shaft reaches several hundred degrees. If you put a new bearing in there – one that hasn't been run-in – it could be chewed up and ground to shreds.'

'I would never have thought . . .'

'You would have, if you had ground up a couple of bearings, as has already happened to both Mikhailov and me. Do you remember, Leading Seaman?'

'It's not the kind of thing that you forget,' confirmed the latter.

'Well, let's get on with it quickly now!'

The Commissar arrived. He said that I had been put in personal charge of the repair. I got the message – the Captain wanted the engine operational as speedily as possible.

Replacing bearings in turbines is an awfully fiddly business. You have to be especially careful with the labyrinth seals – it's better if you can avoid dealing with them at sea. We worked all through the night. Cramped, hot and stifled. It was already about ten o'clock in the morning when we tightened the final nut. Briansky and I thanked the tired but satisfied engine room crew. Anticipating a well-earned rest, they all went off to clean their hands. I made my way to the officers' mess, reported to Lisin that both diesels were in working order. At that moment Ignatov poked his head through the hatchway: 'Comrade Captain, a solitary freighter has been sighted!'

'Torpedo attack!' ordered Lisin, and he and I ran to the control room.

Soviet Latvia's Anniversary

The sailors took up their action stations. The Bosun stood at the hydroplane controls, with our second-best helmsman, Alexander

54

Olenin, at the vertical rudder. The Mine and Torpedo Officer, Senior Lieutenant Novikov, a moment ago the officer of the watch, ran headlong to the first compartment. The Navigator was tracing the slender cobweb of the course and swearing under his breath. He reported to the conning tower: 'Seven metres under the keel. Rapidly decreasing depth. Sandbank directly on the bow.'

Commissar Gusev had jumped down into the control room and he too was checking the chart. From the conning tower the Captain asked impatiently: 'Well, what's it like there? Can we get closer?'

'No, Captain, the shallows won't allow us to close up.' Instead of the Navigator, Gusev replied. But the Captain decided to attack just the same. We fired from a considerable distance. We launched two torpedoes nineteen seconds apart. We waited for the explosions. None came. Missed . . .

The Captain came down and joined the Navigator, glueing his eyes to the chart: 'These shoals are enough to drive you crazy. Stand down from torpedo attack!' Lisin tore his gaze from the chart, fell into a brown study for a moment and then pulled on his gauntlet gloves decisively. 'Stand by both diesels!' his voice boomed out. 'Artillery alert!'

Novikov came running into the control room, his binoculars at his chest. Hardly had five minutes gone by, and he had already been through three incarnations. He began as officer of the watch, he became the head of the mine and torpedo department when the signal for a torpedo attack was given and, with the signal for an artillery attack, he was preparing to take charge of artillery fire. I was also performing in a new role: I was now in charge of the action station for ammunition supply. It was my responsibility to give orders to the ammunition store, to check what types of shells were inserted into the slots of the hoist: armour-piercing or fougasse, incendiary or star shells. I recognize the artillery ammunition markings unerringly. 'Fore! Aft!' rang out the order. 'The 100-millimetre-gun crew to the control room!'

'Surface!' the Captain ordered, running up the ladder to the conning tower. We blew the ballast. The deck began to shudder from the diesels working. I kept an eye on the port shaft line on the tachometer. How was the turbo-blower behaving after the replacement of the bearings? It seemed to be working properly. Both diesels were operating at moderate speed.

The Captain and the gunners were already on the bridge. I set up my action station. With the heavy shells in their hands, the ratings were standing at the ready by the ammunition-hoist hatchway. Overhead could be heard hurrying footsteps on the upper deck, loud voices. Novikov ordered: 'Fire!' The din of the gunfire was so deafening that it hurt your ears. The impression you got was that of sitting in an iron barrel which was being pounded might and main by a sledgehammer.

'Above the target,' I caught the lookout's report.

'Down four!' corrected Novikov. 'Fire!'

Another crash, then another . . . After the fourth shot we could hear a sort of crackling and hissing. 'The freighter has been thrown onto the rocks!' Lisin leant in over the upper conning-tower hatch: 'Full ahead both! Prepare to receive the wounded!'

There were two of them. They got down the ladder without assistance and with such joyful faces that, if you had let them, they would have broken into a jig. There and then they began to tell how they had 'beaten the living daylights' out of the Nazis. The medic had to drag them away by force to be bandaged. Their wounds turned out to be minor.

The details of the battle reached us in fragments. While we were firing on the freighter, an enemy escort ship had appeared on the horizon. For this reason, the Captain had abandoned the ship that had been thrown onto the rocks and at full speed had begun to head away from the shore towards deeper waters where the boat could submerge.

'It's a pity we couldn't finish the Nazi off,' said Novikov in distress. 'But we have driven her onto the rocks – which is not bad either. She's bound to have had the bottom ripped right out of her.'

A new problem had cropped up for Novikov. The locking mechanism on the 100-millimetre gun had got stuck. They never managed to close it. At night while the batteries were being charged, the sailors struggled with the gun for a long time. Dawn had already broken, but the lock still wouldn't yield. They had to leave it open.

Once submerged, we made our way to the Latvian coast by the shortest possible course. We had dinner later than usual. Cook

Shinkarenko was beaming: it was a long time since we had eaten with such good appetite. The hours spent out in the fresh air showed. After a hearty meal, everyone who was off watch slept like the dead. It is not for nothing that they joke about submariners that their eyes close automatically with the last spoonful of pudding. But there was no sleep for me or Briansky. We measured the remaining fuel. Now each ton of diesel fuel had to be husbanded carefully, so that there would be enough fuel for the return journey as well.

Briansky and I went from tank to tank. Sleep reigned in the compartments and we envied the lucky ones. But it turned out to be wasted envy. Hardly had we entered the control room when the Captain raised the periscope and gave a delighted whistle: 'The prey is running to the hunter! Enter into the log: "Sighted ships' masts and funnels on bearing one-six-eight." '

'What sort of depth have we got?' asked Gusev.

'Shallow,' sighed the Captain. 'It will be difficult to sneak up, but we shall try.'

The hydrophone operators reported propeller noises. Everybody in the control room burst out laughing: good lads, they've heard it at long last!

In the compartments the klaxon began to sound. The Captain looked through the periscope and said loudly, so that everyone could hear: 'Four freighters moving in single line ahead. For the attack I am choosing the second from the leader – the biggest one. Distance: thirty-five cables. Navigator, estimate where they are heading, according to the chart.'

Khrustaliov, working with a pair of compasses and a ruler, plotted the enemy's course on the chart. 'By the looks of it, to the pivot-buoy.'

'Good, we will wait for them there.'

In the conning tower Alexander Olenin stood at the vertical rudder, concentrated and keen. The Captain ordered him to begin to come about: we would fire from our stern tubes. But we didn't have time to complete the manoeuvre before the hydrophone operators reported that one of the freighters had broken away from the column and was rapidly moving off to starboard. The Captain hurriedly raised the periscope: 'Yes, the leading freighter has changed course, before reaching the pivot-buoy. It looks as though the others will follow her too. And the distance is twenty cables. It's a long way . . . Navigator, what are the depths like here?' Khrustaliov glanced at the echo-sounder dial. The pulse-line was flickering on the figure twelve. 'Ah, hell, these depths are absolutely useless!' said the Commissar, taking his pipe out of his mouth. (Smoking is not allowed on the boat, but Gusev is never parted from his pipe, he holds it between his teeth unlit: 'At least I can sense the smell of tobacco, and I'll settle for that.')

The Captain shook his head: 'There is no alternative, Commissar. We will attack from a surfaced position.' The Commissar hesitated. It was a huge risk. 'Don't forget: there's an observation post in the lighthouse. The moment we surface, they will direct ships here straight away. Half an hour later they will be here and . . .'

'Half an hour is quite enough for us to send one of those tubs to the bottom.' The Captain stood firm in his opinion. The Commissar nodded: 'Go ahead!' Not waiting for orders, I instructed Briansky over the voice-pipe to move from the sixth to the fifth compartment and without further ado to prepare both diesels for a start-up.

The boat rose to the surface rapidly and with each second picked up speed. On the bridge were the Captain, the Commissar and two lookouts. From their comments we could guess that the freighters were trying to make a run for it, but the boat was swiftly catching up with them. We would fire from our stern tubes. The Captain had decided to attack two freighters simultaneously.

Lisin was putting pressure on us, demanding an increase in speed. Both diesels were going flat out. From further snatches of conversation, the Captain's irritability became understandable: a big motor launch had started out from Pavlovskaya Harbour to give assistance to the freighters. I looked at my watch. The chase had already lasted for fifteen minutes. The Navigator switched on the echo-sounder and asked me to report to the bridge that there were seven metres under the keel. Gusev listened to the report in silence and waved me away: there was no time for it right now.

I estimated how much time it would take to get to a deep enough place for the boat to be able to dive. Khrustaliov was evidently thinking along the same lines, because he said to me: 'If aircraft or motor boats attack us in such shallow waters, we've had it.'

The Captain, despite the lack of depth and the fact that the enemy motor launch was getting closer all the time, pressed on with the attack doggedly. The stern tubes were ready for action. The First Lieutenant was in the conning tower and was impatiently awaiting the order to press the lever of the torpedo-firing control system. Bent over the conning-tower hatch, the Captain barked out curt instructions: 'Helm a-port! Stop port diesel! Slow ahead starboard!'

The distance to the nearest freighter was five cables. The submarine heeled over from the sharp turn. 'Fire!' A minute later a new 'Fire!' at the second freighter.

The Captain and the Commissar, commenting loudly to one another, were following the run of the torpedoes through their binoculars. Initially, we got the impression that the first torpedo would slip by ahead of the bow of the freighter, but a powerful explosion dispelled all doubts. The Captain's excited face appeared in the conning-tower hatchway. 'The freighter has sunk,' said he. 'The torpedo struck her astern.'

Watching the second torpedo, the Commissar was confident that this one would hit the target too. But at the last moment the freighter turned away and, having passed along the vessel's port side, the torpedo detonated near the shore.

The order came from the bridge to run both diesels at moderate speed. We were in a hurry to get away from the dangerous shallows. The boat dived at last, having been on the surface for almost forty minutes. The enemy motor launch did not pursue us: they were rescuing the crew of the sunken ship. Taking advantage of this, Sergei Prokofievich, having raised the anti-aircraft periscope and set it to five-fold magnification, invited the First Lieutenant, Khrustaliov and me to take a look at the outcome of the attack. A solitary funnel with two dark-blue bands was sticking up out of the water. The freighter had sunk almost at the very entrance to Pavlovskaya Harbour. It emerged later that she was the German freighter *Kate*, with a displacement of 1,599 tons gross weight. She turned out to be smaller than we had thought at the time. But she was carrying that most precious of cargoes: weapons. That's why sinking her was a great victory for us.

Once more the seamen were celebrating, congratulating one another. The Captain and the Commissar did the rounds of the compartments, thanked the submariners and ordered everyone to get some rest. Only the watch was to stay awake.

It was past nine already. My ears were ringing with fatigue. But I still had to correct the boat's trim, to compensate for the weight of the fired torpedoes. Barely dragging my wooden legs along, I reached my bunk. The last sound that I was still able to take in was the thump of my unlaced boots falling. The pillow attracted my head like a magnet, and in an instant I was lost to the world.

S-7 was en route between Libava and Vindava: familiar places. In peacetime we passed this way many times on our training cruises. I visited Libava and Vindava in the first days of the war: I was sent here after spare parts for submarines. Those were anxious and fearful days. Libava had already been surrounded, and those of my comrades who had been repairing the boats, with no possibility of putting to sea, had scuttled their ships and were fighting on dry land, at the approaches to the town. One of the detachments of sailors was under the command of Lieutenant Captain Fyodor Mikhailovich Oleinik. He made his final stand in a cantonment. Oleinik and the sailors fought there until the end, covering the departure of our forces, which were pushing eastwards. And Petty Officer Ivan Mikhailovich Nefyodov and I loaded onto a frail barge the spare parts taken from an already-burning warehouse, got hold of a tug boat with difficulty and put to sea. Our passage was long and hard, but still we delivered the cargo to Leningrad. It was immensely useful during the time of the siege.

It was the time after dinner when each of us, after the demanding night's work, had earned a long-awaited rest, but the Captain had asked the officers to remain behind. Wearing the armband of the officer of the watch on his sleeve, Senior Lieutenant Khrustaliov entered and reported: 'Comrade Captain, the submarine is passing over the place where S-3 was lost.'

'Attention!' ordered Lisin and added in a low voice: 'I ask you to honour the memory of our comrades with a minute's silence.' One minute. Just sixty seconds; but a great deal flashed through my mind during this time. I remembered my classmates from our cadet days, with whom I studied for five years. Then we did our service together. We became firm friends. Now they were lying at the bottom of the sea. When the enemy reached Libava, the seamen of *S-3* put to sea in their ship, although the boat was not in proper working order and was not able to submerge. This was the place where the Nazi motor launches caught up with her. The submariners joined battle with them. Unequal and hopeless. The enemy motor launches sank the submarine. No one was saved . . . It was here that my best friends met their deaths; Lieutenant Captains Alyosha Tolstykh and Sasha Svitin. The first was the head of *D-5* on board *S-3*; the second had served on *S-1* (they had to scuttle her at the base and her crew transferred to *S-3*). From my comrades' grave faces I could see that each of them had friends on that boat, each of us was sharing one and the same thought. 'At ease!'

We dispersed to have a rest, but hardly anyone was able to get to sleep at such an hour. At 20.00 hours, as usual, I began my stint as officer of the watch. Life on board ship was proceeding with its orderly routine. Half an hour before surfacing, I ordered Senior Lieutenant Khrustaliov to be woken up. He appeared straight away and, clearly, had not slept at all. Silently he took my draft notes and sat down at his table. I watched how he converted the figures into lines on the chart. When the job was done, Misha turned to me and produced from his tunic pocket a folded piece of paper from a tear-off calendar: 'Look what I found in the book I was reading today.' I unfolded the piece of paper. I could see nothing special about it. 'Pay attention: it's the page for August the fifth. It says here that on that day the Latvian Soviet Socialist Republic was taken into the Soviet Union. This was in 1940. This means that tomorrow is the second anniversary. If you bear in mind that we have been fighting off the coast of Latvia for a month already . . .'

'You are right. It is most important. We should remind the Commissar.'

The night passed calmly. At dawn we submerged and sat down for our dinner. At table I produced the page from the calendar and showed it to Gusev. The page caught everyone's interest and passed from hand to hand for a long time . . . Sergei Prokofievich uttered wistfully: 'It wouldn't be bad to commemorate this remarkable date with one more victory. What a pity that we have only one torpedo left, and a "poorly" one at that.'

61

'Yes, it wouldn't be bad at all to send another enemy steamer to the bottom,' agreed the Commissar.

After dinner, everyone struggled to a bunk to 'listen to underwater noises', since, according to our daily schedule, the 'underwater night' began in the early hours of the morning. There was silence in the compartments. Those on watch were protective of their comrades' rest; they tried not to make a noise unless there was some special necessity.

But the Commissar didn't want to waste even these hours. He moved noiselessly from one compartment to another, sat down beside those on watch, showed them the page from the calendar, gave them the short historical note on the back to read, chatted to the sailors in an undertone. He spent an especially long time talking to the political activists: it was they who would lead the conversations when the sailors on the next shift got up. Gradually virtually everyone had heard about the historic date. People were in an elevated mood. And there was just one topic of conversation: 'If only we could strike the Nazis once more today!'

The loud voice of Lyamin, the leading hydrophone operator, roused us: 'Propeller noise of a freighter on its own!' I flew like a bullet to the control room. With a stern trim the submarine was slowly hauling herself the final few metres up to periscope depth. The klaxons were howling out the signal for a torpedo attack. In the bow compartment they were preparing the last remaining torpedo for firing.

The freighter was not a big one. To begin with, the Captain did not even want to touch her at all, but then he decided it would be a sin to let even a target like that escape. We were closing up to the enemy. The Navigator reported anxiously: 'Five metres under the keel. Depth decreasing rapidly!'

'Four metres . . .'

'Three metres . . .'

'Stop port engine!' ordered Lisin. He showed his vexation: 'I'd like to see anyone launch an attack at such a depth . . . Prepare to surface! We will attack in the awash position.'

'Are we near the shore?' asked the First Lieutenant.

'About four miles off . . .'

'Taking risks again . . .'

'There's no alternative.'

Orders to the torpedomen, the planesmen, the dieselmen followed one after the other.

Leading Seaman Nakhimchuk spun the handwheel of the main ballast-blowing pump. There was the sound of air in the ballast tanks. The boat surfaced. The Captain, the Commissar and two lookouts jumped up onto the bridge. The diesels were started up. The chase was on. The fast-moving freighter zigzagged, giving no opportunity to take aim. But the torpedo was nevertheless racing towards the vessel. It seemed that it would unfailingly hit her broadside on. But the freighter turned sharply away and left the torpedo astern. It passed about thirty metres away from her. The Captain ordered: 'Artillery alert!' We had one 45-millimetre gun in working order. Some weapon!

Led by Novikov, in charge of the firing, the gunnery ratings clambered up the ladder. The last to hurry by, puffing and panting, was the cook, Shinkarenko. When there is an artillery alert, his place too is by the gun.

I set up my action station for the supply of ammunition. The whole of the control-room deck, from the ammunition storage area to the ladder, was being laid with straw mats, on which cases of shells were being set out. From the bridge sounded the ringing report of the gun-crew's leader, Subbotin: 'Gun ready to fire, Comrade Captain!'

'Fire!' ordered Lisin. The firing was carried out at the maximum rate of rapid fire. We barely had time enough to open the cases and supply the shells. Lisin leant over the hatchway. We had difficulty hearing him in the din of the gunfire: 'She's on fire! She's stopped moving!'

Mostly by guesswork we entered into the log: 'Freighter on fire, movement ceased. Artillery fire proceeding. We are circling around the freighter.'

Gusev tumbled head-over-heels into the control room:'Camera! Where's my camera?'

They fetched the Commissar's camera from the second compartment. Snatching it up, Gusev vanished. The Captain shouted from the bridge: 'Enter into the log: "Freighter giving off steam. Two lifeboats lowered into the water. Crew abandoning ship."'

I was summoned to the bridge. I ran up the ladder. For only the second time during the entire patrol I was seeing the sky. It was densely overcast. The coastline could be seen in the distance. The burning freighter was dirtying the sky with black smoke. The lifeboats were hurrying to get as far away from her as possible. The Captain asked me: 'Do you have everything ready for an emergency dive?'

'Yes, everything.'

'Then feast your eyes on this scene. Such occasions do not occur often.'

The bridge was shrouded in smoke from the gunfire. The semi-automatic gun was firing non-stop. It fired sharply, piercingly – it hurt your ears. The paint on the barrel blistered and smoked. The gun grease was boiling on account of the prolonged firing. Burning splashes would burst through the sealing, land on the gunners' hands and faces. The seamen didn't seem to notice the burns; they didn't have time to wipe the grease, mingled with their sweat, from their cheeks. They toiled stubbornly and tirelessly. With each shot the seamen were exacting revenge for Leningrad, for the suffering of their loved ones, for all the hardships that the enemy had visited on our land. Gunlayers Kulochkin and Lukash stayed glued to the gun's rear sights, even though with each shot the rubber eyepieces struck them painfully in the face.

The Commissar had been clicking his camera so enthusiastically that he failed to notice when he ran out of film. And now, when we were virtually on top of the freighter, there was not a single frame left on the roll.

The freighter was ablaze. It seemed that the very metal from which she was constructed had been transformed into combustible material. From the water pouring in through the numerous holes (even though they were small in size), the vessel was noticeably listing by the stern. Suddenly there was the most frightful cracking inside her. The vessel started to sink rapidly, listing to starboard. The bow rose up higher and higher, with the stern already under water. Now the freighter was almost standing on end; you could hear it when the stern struck the bottom. She stayed like that for a few moments and then disappeared into the water, to the sound of hissing. There was nothing but seething, dirty foam left on the surface of the water. The wind carried away a cloud of black smoke.

The radio operators were reporting intensive radio traffic in German. Nazi ships would be here at any minute. The Captain ordered: 'All below!' The gunners tumbled down through the hatchway with their reddened, sweaty faces, sooty, splashed with grease from head to toe. They were feeling like birthday boys.

'Vasya, how did it go?' Ignatov asked his friend Subbotin, the man in charge of the 45-millimetre gun, when the latter was the first to set foot on the deck of the control room. 'Fine! We gave them a hell of a pounding!'

The submarine dived deep. We had stayed surfaced for almost an hour. It is not that easy to sink a freighter with a 45-millimetre gun. We fired off almost 300 shells. But, be that as it may, an enemy freighter was now on the bottom. The little gun, which we had previously treated with disdain, had immediately acquired stature in our eyes.

In the second compartment, Shkurko received everyone coming down from the bridge with eager enquiry. The medic, as he should during an artillery alert, had transformed the officers' mess into a sickbay, which he proudly referred to as his operating theatre. Everything in it was gleaming with snowy-white cleanliness, Shkurko himself and his sickbay attendants were arrayed in white overalls. The dining table had been covered with a white sheet – it was now an operating table. Beside it on a little table surgical instruments shone. To our doctor's disappointment, this time, too, he turned out to be jobless: there were no wounded, and the gunners pay no attention to bruises, minor burns and grazes, so that, as far as our doctor was concerned, the battle turned out to be no more than another exercise in setting up an action station. The fact is, the medic treats such exercises with total seriousness. He remembers how on exercises once the Captain found fault with our medical service. At that time, Shkurko had trimmed down all his preparations for battle to spreading a clean cloth on the table and laying out the medical bags on the sofas. The Captain stopped by, inspected everything and asked the medic whether he knew what his duties were in the event of an alert. The latter reeled off his instructions without the slightest hesitation. The Captain was not satisfied with this. He suggested a scenario: 'I have a shrapnel wound in my left arm above the elbow. The shrapnel is embedded in the soft tissues. Carry on!'

And so it began! The sickbay attendants knew everything by the book. In practice, however, they looked absolutely helpless. On top of that, they were also clad in dirty overalls. The instruments turned out not to have been sterilized. The medications were arranged in such a way that the medic himself was unable to make sense of them. Since this shambles, Shkurko had run the sickbay attendants ragged with training exercises. They endlessly carried in and bandaged the 'wounded' (the medic himself most often acting the part of the 'wounded'). Nowadays during the alerts everything in the medical department was as it should be.

Shkurko grabbed hold of Novikov and persuaded him to describe in detail what had been going on up there. Novikov needed no persuading; he liked to talk, especially when he had before him such grateful listeners as Shkurko and his sickbay attendants, amongst whom was the orderly Sukharev. The Senior Lieutenant, having settled himself into an armchair as comfortably as possible, began his tale: 'After the first shot I look through my binoculars, but I don't see a splash. Well, I think, we've overshot the target. I order: "Down four!" Second shot. Now I see a splash – halfway to the target! The Captain is cursing. And I also realize myself that we are not shooting too well. But by now my gunners have become acclimatized to the Force 4 swell and have begun to fire directly into the side of the steamer, like driving in rivets. The fifth shell slammed into the wheelhouse, where smoke appeared – not much at first, but then increasingly dense. Gunlayer Valentin Kunitsa is saying: "Brothers, look, it looks as though we have made a direct hit on an oil-lamp!" '

'Grisha,' I interrupted Novikov, 'watch your tongue! Kunitsa is one of my best men, and you are making him out to be a talkative fool.'

'There is a time for everything, Chief. During a battle a witty word can be very timely. If you want to know, Kunitsa helped a number of ratings with his joke. The lads cheered up, picked up their pace.'

Medic Shkurko was looking at me beseechingly: 'Viktor Yemelianovich, I beg of you, don't interrupt Grigori Alexeievich. It's all very well for you, you saw it all with your own eyes, clearly this isn't interesting for you . . .'

'Hey, doctor, he could tell you tales till the cows come home, and you'd believe him too . . .' But, really, why did I butt into this conversation? If you don't like it, don't listen, and leave the liar be . . . I busied myself with my own affairs. Grisha went on with his tale, but now he tried not to stray away from the truth: 'When the freighter came to a standstill, we went right up close to her. We were firing point-blank. At that point my orders were no longer necessary: the gunners were managing by themselves. You just have to load and fire, there's no way you're going to miss. But what's going on? We fire and we fire, but she's not sinking. Generally speaking, the holes that our shells make are small. "Fire below the waterline!" orders the Captain. We started seizing the moment when the swell would subside and expose her side a little. But just the same she doesn't sink! The whole of her side is riddled with holes, but she doesn't sink! What's going on? I peer more closely and I see that some of the holes have been plugged from the inside with something. There is a fresh hole. Something is spilling out of it. Potatoes! They went on and on spilling out, but then – plop! – a big potato has plugged up the hole . . . Perhaps you are going to say that this didn't happen either?' the storyteller asked me aggressively.

'It did happen, I agree. But, listening to you, you might think that the freighter was loaded with nothing but potatoes.'

'But I haven't finished telling the story yet . . . So that's how it was, I order the firing to be shifted to the stern. A shot, another shot, then all of a sudden such a bang! An explosion!'

Dumbrovsky's menacing shape appeared in the bulkhead hatchway: 'Comrade Senior Lieutenant, do you really think I will stand your watch for you, while you are making a speech about battles at sea?'

'I'm off, I'm off at the double! My watch is a bit slow. Its guarantee period expired just before war broke out. Would you be kind enough to chalk these few minutes up to the Germans' account, please?' Having straightened his tunic and adjusted his peaked cap, Novikov hurried to the control room to take over the watch from the First Lieutenant. The medic sighed and set about clearing away his sickbay: the officers' mess needed to be freed up for supper.

And in the compartments there was rejoicing. After all, we did mark the anniversary of Soviet Latvia with a victory! People of various nationalities were gathered together on the boat. To take just the officers seated at the dining table – the Internationale personified! Lisin and Khrustaliov – Russians, Commissar Gusev – a Buryat, First Lieutenant Dumbrovsky – a Pole, Briansky – a Jew, Shkurko and I – Ukrainians. True, there was no Latvian on our boat – not one. But did this really matter? For any one of us, Latvia was a part of our huge Motherland. And that is why the anniversary of that republic was our common festival, and we were glad that we had bestowed our modest gift on it.

Nautical Astronomy

During the night of 8 August we were charging the battery not far from the shore. Without ammunition, there was now nothing for us to do in the enemy shipping lanes. In the daytime we would carry out reconnaissance, and when darkness fell we would put further out to sea, to do the charging without interference. As usual during surfaced sailing, I was in the control room. Now and then I would go over to the navigator's table to watch how dashingly Khrustaliov was drawing the curves of our tacking on the chart. Everything was jogging along nicely, but then Leading Seaman Antifeev, in charge of the radio operators' group, appeared in the control room and asked permission to report to the bridge that a radio message had been received.

When Khrustaliov and I were alone, I asked him: 'Misha, what do you think the radio message says?'

'I reckon, permission to return to base. We've no ammunition, so why should they keep us at sea?'

There is a rule on board ship: apart from the Captain, the Commissar and the radio operator, no one knows what's in the dispatches. But no one is forbidden to have a guess. However, we were not given long to discuss this issue. The bulkhead hatch crashed open. Pale as death, Briansky blurted out: 'Calamity! The starboard diesel's cooling pump has totally disintegrated. The engine is overheating. I don't know what to do . . .'

Leaving Briansky in the control room, I ran to the diesel compartment. Leading Seamen Lyashenko and Mikhailov were already there. Lyashenko and one of the electricians were taking the pump's electric motor apart, while Mikhailov, lying flat on his stomach on the deck, was shouting to a mechanic down in the bilges how to adjust the valves so that the surviving port-engine circulation pump would supply water to both diesels. I went down into the bilges and checked that the adjustments had been correctly carried out. Everything was as it should be. When the temperature of both engines had begun to equalize, I joined the electricians. Lyashenko handed me a portable lamp. The sight that greeted my eyes gave little cause for optimism. The electric motor's manifold had fallen to pieces, the armature winding was ruined. Damage like that cannot be put right at sea. 'There's no way we can even think about a repair job,' I said to Lyashenko. 'You had better take the circulation pump on the port side under your personal super-vision – all hope rests on it now.'

'I understand, Comrade Engineer. We will do everything we can to haul her back to base.'

The effects of the bombardment: you can't see them all first off. You can hardly take each individual mechanism apart, after all! A brush-holder was knocked loose by some blow. We didn't spot it at the time. And now the brush had fallen out, causing a short circuit. In answer to my enquiry as to the causes of the calamity, Chief Leading Seaman Lyashenko did not give an immediate response: 'I don't want you to think badly of the section leader, Samonov. He's an excellent specialist.'

'I've no quarrel with that. But in the given circumstances he shares some of the blame. We must monitor the machinery even more vigilantly.'

The technology doesn't stand up to the constant overloading. And people have got tired. I must confess I was somewhat to blame as well. I hadn't given much thought to the personnel. Was it really necessary to sail submerged for days without regenerating the air? I was being stingy with the regeneration cartridges and the oxygen, saving them in case the enemy drove us to the bottom for a long time. So far, such a circumstance had not arisen. And, as it turned out, people were stifling for hours, and here we were, carrying unused cartridges back to base with us. And what about the drinking water? We were economizing on that with all our might too, we even cooked dinner mixing sea water with fresh. And we did actually have water purifiers. But we didn't make any use of them: it's a long-drawn-out process, besides which the summer nights are short – we reckoned we wouldn't have enough time to run the purifier and, on top of that, it guzzles a lot of power. But if we had wanted to, it could all have been done. We simply did not pay any attention to minor matters, although it is as a consequence of such minor matters that people have become excessively tired. No, in future we must give more thought to it all. And when we return home, I will tell my comrades on the other boats, so that they won't repeat my mistakes.

I returned to the control room. I reported the calamity to the Captain.

'Will the one pump supply both engines?' he asked.

'Absolutely.'

'Mind you, we are going to need both diesels. We have received orders to return to base.'

The glad tidings flew swiftly around the compartments. I was a bit afraid that people might lapse into carelessness in their joy. I instructed the leading seamen to explain to the ratings that the way ahead was difficult and dangerous; it was too soon to drop our guard.

The rainy August night helped us to enter the Gulf of Finland unobtrusively. The boat dived an hour before dawn. We would be forcing a passage underwater through these most dangerous defences. By evening we had already reached the Helsinki meridian. There was still a long time to go before surfacing for recharging. The off-watch ratings were resting lying down: that way oxygen is used more sparingly, and there is also less noise.

Through my sleep I heard a little hooter begin to wail. I woke up. I tried to recall where this alarm was installed. A bulkhead hatch clanged open. Dumbrovsky shouted: 'Electrician Ignatov – to the control room!' So that's which hooter it was: the gyrocompass temperature had risen! That was not my area of responsibility, I could go back to sleep. I could hear Ignatov fumbling about behind the bulkhead, muttering under his breath. But then came his anxious exclamation: 'The gyrocompass has gone off the meridian!'

Further sleep was out of the question now. The Captain came out of his cabin, calling as he went: 'Navigator!' Khrustaliov leapt up as if on springs. We ran to the control room together.

'Navigator, check the magnetic compass!'

'It has been out of order since the last bombardment.'

'I know. But we must have at least an approximate idea of where the ship is heading . . .'

'The magnetic compass isn't showing anything at all, Comrade Captain. If time doesn't allow us to surface, we'd be better off lying on the bottom . . .'

'Lying on the bottom in the navigation channel is equal to committing suicide.'

Lisin was beginning to fret. He ordered: 'Step up the listening watch! Bosun – to the hydroplanes! Surface to periscope depth, without going off course or changing speed!' Having scanned the sea through the periscope, Sergei Prokofievich ground out through clenched teeth: 'Too early, too bloody early . . . But there is no alternative. We shall have to surface.'

We surfaced and started the diesels. The Navigator consulted the chart and flung himself up on the bridge. A minute later he came back down to his table again – and then headlong up on top once more. And so he ran up and down, like a squirrel on a tree trunk.

We were proceeding in the awash position – only the conning tower was above water. The boat is less conspicuous that way. The Captain was in a hurry, he ordered both diesels to full steam ahead. Not for the first time, we were running flat out. You only had to let your eyes wander for a moment and you'd wind up with a damaged piston. Having summoned Briansky, I ordered him to stand by the starboard diesel control panel in person. Mikhailov could deal with the port one, while Nasin, the section head, was to remain in the bilges and with his own hands regulate the supply of water from the one and only functioning circulation pump. I summoned Chief Leading Seaman Lyashenko to the control room, to help Ignatov repair the gyrocompass.

The diesels had been working for ten minutes and were beginning to get hot: water for cooling was in short supply. I ordered Skachko to shut off from the circulation pump everything in the sixth compartment that consumed water – the thrust bearings, the main electric propulsion motors, the air coolers and so on. We would provide water to cool this machinery using the trimming pump.

The abnormal pressure on the engines was making itself felt.

Worried reports were coming into the control room, whether from the diesel room, the electric motor compartment or the shaft lines. Gases were leaking from the starboard diesel's turbo-driven supercharger, the port engine's fifth-cylinder safety valve wasn't holding and 'blew' incessantly, the temperature of the starboard thrust bearing was rising uncontrollably, in the sixth compartment the rubber seal had broken loose from the mains flange. The whole of D-5 was on its toes. I kept shuttling the ratings from one area to another. They hardly had time to report to me that one disaster had been dealt with before new weak points came to light. So it went on for two hours. At last we crossed the Tallinn-Helsinki shipping lane. The Captain ordered a reduction in speed and a switch to the propeller-charging mode.

In the control room Lyashenko and Ignatov were gutting the gyrocompass and checking the integrity of the power supply and the windings. Sweat was pouring off both of them, although the temperature in the compartment was no more than eighteen degrees.

'Stop! There is no contact . . . Let's do it one more time. Hurrah! This is where the break is!' Lyashenko shouted joyfully. Ignatov rubbed his brow in puzzlement: 'So how come I didn't work it out earlier that the whole problem was in the lower blowing coil . . . ?'

But locating the damage is only half the battle. You still need to be able to repair it, to adjust the highly complicated mechanism and get it going again. The gyrocompass involved a lot of fiddling about. And Khrustaliov meanwhile was running up and down the ladder like a squirrel. 'Why are you rushing about?' I asked him.

'I am busy with nautical astronomy.'

In our time we were all taught how to determine the cardinal points – the main points of the horizon – with the aid of a compass, by the sun, the moon, or the stars. We had no compass at the moment; the sun doesn't shine at night and there was no moon. What remained were the stars. Fortunately, the sky was clear. Khrustaliov had locked onto the Pole Star. Having chosen his place on the bridge, he aligned the star with the antenna mast and stayed rooted to the spot for a long time, giving out orders to the helmsman. The helm was in the reliable hands of Alexander Olenin. Whenever Khrustaliov ran down to the navigator's table in the control room to calculate the time to turn to a new course through the minefields, Sergei Prokofievich would take his place. Coming up onto the bridge with a report, I caught sight of the Captain, fixed in place like a statue beside the conning-tower rail. His stance was an uncomfortable one; he had to lean over the side to see the star at a certain angle. And, so as not to be a nuisance to him, I compressed the report and came below as soon as I could.

The medic Shkurko appeared in the control room and asked me: 'May I go up to the bridge?'

'What for?'

'To ask permission to cook the dinner.'

'You know, I imagine that, right now, no one is giving a thought to dinner. But you are doing the right thing, Doctor, to take care of us. I take full responsibility on myself. By all means cook the dinner. And the tastiest you can. Have a think about the menu with Cook Shinkarenko and Quartermaster Senokos. The only thing I ask is that you don't get in our way in this hellish cramped place; if, God forbid, a screw should go missing, we will eat you alive!'

Ignatov and Lyashenko had assembled the gyrocompass. All that remained was to fill it with a special mixture. They had got the spirits, the glycerine and the other components of the solution ready. But what could they mix them in? The galley crockery was not allowed to be used for such a purpose. 'Suppose we took the lampshade from the officers' mess?' suggested Lyashenko. A minute later they brought in the capacious crystal bowl. I had to hold it in my arms while Lyashenko and Ignatov concocted the solution and stirred it with a glass rod. To be on the safe side, I picked out a place to set this concoction down, if the order for an emergency dive should come. It would, of course, have been possible to summon a rating and have him hold the shade. But this would have meant losing precious time. So I patiently cradled this fragile vessel in my arms, and kept an eye myself on the conning-tower hatchway opening. The sky was getting lighter; it was increasingly difficult to make out the stars. And what was most important – with the dawn the danger that the enemy might detect us was growing. We had to hurry. The solution was ready. With extreme precaution Ignatov poured it into the instrument. The current was switched on. The low buzzing, which we had got so used to in the control room in the course of the patrol, was once more to be heard. A few minutes later Ignatov reported: 'The gyro-compass has regained the meridian.' The emergency diving klaxon sounded like music to our ears. The 'nautical astronomy' amongst the minefields was done with. Now we could sail confidently again both on the surface and underwater.

We sat down to dinner at four in the morning. A marvellous mood; we shared our impressions of the difficult night. It turned out that, while navigating by the stars, we had sped almost 100 miles. And not once did we run into a minefield. Our Navigator is a magician! By now in an atmosphere of calm, we reviewed different means of finding our bearings in a given locality. One person recalled that the northern side of stones gets overgrown with moss. Another asserted that a tree growing in isolation is the ultimate compass: on the southern side it is always more thickly covered with leaves. Someone suggested determining the south by the ring layers on tree stumps. But none of these signs is of any use at sea. And to be at sea without a compass – it's a lethal affair.

At dawn Novikov, the officer of the watch, saw the saddle of Suursaari Island through the periscope. The Captain took the bearings; the Navigator entered them on the chart and proudly announced that there was a discrepancy of no more than three miles. With a smile, Lisin admitted: 'I never thought that an antenna mast could serve as such a precise astronomical instrument. To rush around for seven hours with constant changes of course, using just this instrument, and not make a sizeable error . . . You will tell your friends about it – they won't believe you!'

The Captain issued orders for our onward sailing. We would be going by dead reckoning alone, never once raising the periscope. The most strict regime in the compartments: no noise at all. 'Slither like a grass-snake!' We all understood: there were enemy ships every step of the way here. Extreme stealth and caution were necessary. 'Slither like a grass-snake' the Captain required; meaning noiselessly and unobtrusively. This was not so simple. Although the diminutive word 'boat' is used to describe our ship, the reader should bear in mind that this is a boat over seventy metres long; it weighs more than 1,000 tons, has more than fifty people on board, hundreds of machines and instruments. To achieve the silent running of such a behemoth was no light matter.

And we had to keep it up, not for ten minutes or so, but for hours on end.

At 14.00 hours on 10 August we turned southwards, and at 17.00 hours, having carried out the last underwater turn of the patrol, lay on a direct course to the point of rendezvous, where our ships were to await us. The last night on patrol was passing. Worn out by lying on our bunks for so long and having slept enough for a week in advance, we were no longer able to close our eyes. Each one was occupied with his own thoughts. I admit in confidence that there was nothing in the least elevated in my daydreams. Hot baked potatoes, pulled straight out of the bonfire . . . I was eating one with spring onions and salt, stretched out on the tender green grass. Or a hunk of fresh rye bread, spread with creamy butter that melted in the warmth and gleams in the sunshine, and I was sitting under a huge pine tree on slippery fragrant needles and rejoicing in the twittering of the birds and the tranquillity . . . There was a distant dream too – the reunion with my nearest and dearest. But this, I know, would not happen soon. Will I even see all of them again?

At dawn on 11 August the Captain came out of his cabin and asked the Commissar quietly: 'Vasili Semyonovich, are you asleep?'

'Fat chance of sleep! I'm lying here tormenting myself, like the whole crew is.'

I moved aside the heavy plush door-curtain.

'And you're not asleep either,' the Captain smiled. 'Let's go along to the control room. We might manage to inspect the horizon.'

The three of us entered. The Captain ordered the listening watch to be stepped up. A few minutes later the hydrophone operator Lyamin reported that the horizon was clear. Sergei Prokofievich ordered Bosun Pyatibratov to come up a bit. I took up my position under the conning-tower hatch, opposite the instrument panels. If something happened, I would give orders for the electric motors to increase revolutions, to help her go deep more quickly. And now after almost a full twenty-four hours of moving blind underwater, the Captain raised the periscope. With a practised movement he unfolded the handles, rapidly rotated the periscope around its axis. Then he aligned the lens directly along the boat's course, peered intently and said joyfully: 'They're already waiting for us at the rendezvous point. And there is Lavansaari. You could say we're home . . .'

Lisin lowered the periscope: 'Bosun, resume previous depth!'

'Have we still got long to go?' asked the Commissar.

'A couple of hours.'

'No sign of the enemy?' I asked.

'No, none. Would you like to know if we could stand down from the strict regime?'

'I would, Comrade Captain.'

'I think we might.'

In the compartments everything immediately came to life. The ratings jumped up from their bunks. In the first compartment the gunner Vasili Subbotin opened a barber's shop. Clicking the scissors loudly, he trimmed his comrades' locks. 'Who's next?' There were many coming next, so, as an exception, Subbotin sat me down without me having to queue. Patiently I tolerated the tweaking of the blunt scissors.

'Shall I shave you?'

Not likely! Better to do it myself. Thanking the amateur barber, I went to my place in the second compartment.

A hydrophone operator reported noises on various bearings. Cautiously we came up to periscope depth. At last the long-awaited order sounded: 'Blow the central group!' Leading Seaman Nakhimchuk blew generously, no longer economizing on high-pressure air. The upper conning-tower hatch was flung open, the Captain and several ratings jumped out onto the bridge. They transferred the megaphone to there – a tin loud-hailer, unused by us for a long time now.

Around us were minesweepers and submarine chasers. We were ordered to follow strictly in the wake of one of the minesweepers.

I was acting mainly on my own initiative, not waiting for instructions from the Captain, who was up to his neck in it. I blew the main ballast. I ran up onto the bridge several times, to estimate from the ship's draught whether the ballast tanks had completely drained.

All of a sudden everyone on the bridge began to talk loudly, to bustle about, pointing with their arms in one direction. I looked there too. Following in the wake of our convoy, the periscope of some submarine could clearly be seen.

So that's why our hydrophone operators had heard noises on different bearings! And no one had paid any attention to their report in all the joyful bustle.

The signalmen on our escort ships had also noticed the suspicious periscope. Red rockets soared up into the sky. Three motor boats darted away to attack. I could see *MO-107* rushing at full speed towards the fully-extended tube with its glass eye. The exploding depth charges rumbled resoundingly. The enemy submarine was taking a pasting!

Our boat moored at the jetty. A small group of officers was already waiting for us. Here were Yevgeni Gavrillovich Yunakov, the Commander of our 1st Division, who had come in to Lavansaari with the submarine *S-9*; Captain Third Rank A.I. Mylnikov, the commanding officer of that boat, Captain Third Rank Safonov and Lieutenant Captain Vinnik, the divisional minelayer. I also knew another officer by sight; the base commander on Lavansaari Island. They all greeted Sergei Prokofievich Lisin noisily, congratulated him on his success. They provided a gangplank, and we fell into our friends' hearty embraces. Safonov squeezed my shoulders tightly: 'How are you, then? You look a bit thinner, brother, even though you've been on submarine rations.'

'We shall see if you manage to get fatter on them.'

But, joking over, we immediately got down to business. I advised my friend to take all our rubber bags that had contained distilled water and fill them with drinking water – it would stand them in good stead on patrol. I told him about our breakdowns and damaged items, I asked him whether they had the necessary spare parts.

The ratings were camouflaging the boat with netting. They were working with such enthusiasm that even Dumbrovsky was satisfied: 'Smart; not just a makeshift effort. The lads have really been longing for some work out in the fresh air.'

The visitors toured the ship. They examined lengthily the rusty, warped plates of the outer hull. An army gunnery colonel asked me to show him our disabled 100-millimetre gun. He inspected the gun, felt it all over, stamped his foot on the steel deck in a professional manner: 'Yes, you have special conditions. You can't dig yourself in here.' With regard to the gun, he said briefly: ' Nothing can be done about it. It will have to be replaced. It hasn't stood up to it . . .'

I thought: it's not just the gun that didn't stand up to it. You could see that the entire hull of the boat was crumpled and riddled with holes. And how many times did the machinery break down . . . ?

Engineers have a term 'reserve of strength'. It denotes the capability of a metal or a machine to withstand loads higher than normal, rated in advance. When a submarine is under construction, the designers are careful to assign to its hull and to all its machinery an enhanced reserve of strength. And yet it still happens that the most hardened steel gives way. But people . . . ? People will withstand anything. If only we could learn how to provide metal with just such a reserve of strength!

On the island a siren began to wail. White rockets soared into the sky. A large-calibre machine gun began to stutter. I followed the lines of fire of its bursts. Three black crosses appeared very high up. The anti-aircraft guns hidden in the woods began to hammer away. White puffs popped up in the path of the aircraft. One of the Junkers turned aside. The others passed over the island. Three bombs fell into the water, raising high white columns, a fourth exploded on the shore not far from the jetty.

We left Lavansaari at dusk. We were escorted by several minesweepers and submarine chasers: a hefty escort for one submarine!

I won't describe in detail our reception at Kronstadt. It was ceremonial and noisy, with a band and deafening hurrahs! Each of us was embraced and congratulated by A.D. Verbitsky, a member of the Fleet Military Council. The commander of the shore base presented us with some clean, rosy piglets – the traditional gift to submarines returning victorious. The piglets, failing to appreciate the ceremonial nature of the moment, squealed and struggled to jump out of our arms.

Boris Dmitrievich Andryuk and Alexander Kuzmich Vasiliev broke their way through the crowd to greet me. They showered me with questions. I begged off: 'First you tell me what's new in Kronstadt and Leningrad. We've been away for a month and a half, you know . . .'

'We'll tell you everything later. Right now, show us your ship.

Show us everything just as it is, while nothing has yet been scrubbed or painted.'

They clambered through the compartments and cubicles, examined each piece of machinery. I escorted them patiently, showing, telling, even though with all my heart I was longing for the shore. But no, I was not irritated by their painstaking inspection and was not accusing my friends of callousness. They were doing an important job; they wanted our experience to be of help to others, those who were getting ready to go out on new patrols.

Chapter Three

AUTUMN STORMS

No Time for Relaxation

In Leningrad again. We had still hardly recovered from the patrol and from the boisterous reunions that our friends had organized for us when I was summoned by Y.A. Veselovsky, the new Brigade Chief Engineer Officer.

'Viktor Yemelianovich, have you by any chance forgotten your official title?'

'No, I haven't, I still have it in mind.' Officially, I was supposed to deputize for the Divisional Engineer Officer. But, in point of fact, I had not had the opportunity to exercise this function. Out on patrol I was the Engineer Officer for the boat, and by now everyone had got used to seeing me in that role. 'Take these documents.' Yevgeni Alexandrovich handed me a folder. 'You are to be in charge of the transfer of the boats to Kronstadt.' I leafed through the contents of the folder: drawings, descriptions. The boats were all familiar to me. Their engineers were my friends. I headed for the ships straight away.

By dusk I had been round them all. My comrades had made their preparations conscientiously. Darkness had already fallen by the time I reached the diving-boat, hidden away behind the outer sea wall at the mouth of the Sea Channel. Petty Officer Yurkevich and I examined the channel from behind some shrubbery. The Gulf of Finland gleamed peacefully in the reflection of the setting sun. We knew for a fact that there was danger here at every step of the way – the enemy had clogged this confined space with magnetic and acoustic seabed mines. The Nazi guns were trained on it. To counter them, gun batteries, camouflaged with green-splotched netting, had been sunk into the channel walls. Hidden away, two gunboats and some smoke-laying motor launches were standing at the ready.

I knew that everything that we had experienced when we set out on patrol in the spring would repeat itself. It's just that on that occasion I was observing it all from on board my ship, whereas this time I was watching from the wings. But I was no less involved because of that.

The opening barrage began. On the Neva one of our ships (probably the battleship *October Revolution*) opened fire. Three bright little tongues of flame flashed periodically: the triple gun-turret was firing. So far the enemy was silent.

The submarines made their appearance. Their black silhouettes moved along slowly and soundlessly. Overtaking the boats, a submarine chaser glided past. On board was the leader of the operation, Captain First Rank L.A. Kurnikov, head of brigade headquarters. I could see the megaphone gleaming in his hands. Then he put it to his lips and said something. Four smoke-layers moved off immediately and one gunboat got under way. High in the sky above us two of our *U-2* aircraft flew by. They couldn't be seen in the darkness, just the noise of their engines carried. 'But what are they doing here?' Puzzled, I put the question to Yurkevich, who was by now no novice at overseeing the passage of our boats. The Petty Officer chuckled: 'You will soon see for yourself.'

The gunboats, having emerged from the Sea Channel, opened fire at the shore. The enemy was silent. 'Leading boat stand by!' Kurnikov's command could be heard through the thundering of the barrage.

One of the submarines pulled out ahead. As soon as she had left the exit from the Sea Channel behind her, a searchlight lit up on the shore and illuminated the submarine with its beam. Immediately multi-coloured tracer began to stream through the sky from the aeroplanes' machine guns. The searchlight went out, but four guns opened fire from the shore. Soon afterwards a blue beam began to skim over the water once more. Then this search-light too was swiftly extinguished by the streams of lead from the *U-2s*. The 'crop-dusters' kept on hovering above the enemy. As we watched they put out a third searchlight. The enemy did not even attempt to light them up again. They began to fire star shells. After the next salvo over the Gulf, 'chandeliers' – bright lights, slowly descending on little parachutes – began to shine. It became fully light. But the leading submarine had already plunged into the dense smokescreen laid down by the motor launches. Following in her wake, the rest of the boats darted inside it too.

Kurnikov was letting them out at staged intervals. The enemy had undoubtedly detected them, but they were moving so fast that the Nazi gunners did not have time to take aim.

The barrage was still thundering away. But by now the enemy could exert no effect. The regular routine of the boats breaking out from Leningrad had been successfully accomplished. When the salvoes had died down, the sound of their engines became audible in the darkness. Amplified by the megaphone, the sound of Kurnikov's voice reached my ears: 'Comrade Korzh, you may proceed to *Commune*.' Yurkevich and I sighed with relief. That meant that all the submarines had slipped through the danger zone undamaged. We could relax.

A few days later Ramazanov, the Divisional Engineer Officer, said to me: 'Tomorrow morning you will head over to *S-13*. You are to examine Dumbrovsky's performance of Task Number Two.'

'Dumbrovsky? But he could just as well be examining me,' I replied, adjusting a brake on our bicycle (this was our personal vehicle, which we took turns to use, to get round the boats).

'Viktor, don't quibble over the words. You know perfectly well that you won't be examining Dumbrovsky himself on the task, but his ratings and leading seamen. And be demanding.'

I went off to *S-13* and conducted training exercises. The ratings did a fine job. You could sense that the ship had an outstanding engineer officer. No sooner had I returned to the floating base than Ramazanov gave me a new assignment. 'On *S-12* the main ballast tank isn't venting. Give Gagarin a hand.' I had already visited *S-12*. Indeed, there was something the matter there with a non-return gas valve. When the diesel was started in order to blow the ballast, black clouds of smoke surged into the compartment.

'The valve assembly should be taken to pieces, but this would take several days.'

'No one is going to give us as long as that. From one moment to the next the boat could be given the green light to leave. Go and have a think about what might be done.'

Mounting the 'personal vehicle', I rode over to *S-12*. We took the boat out to the 'Okhtenskoye Sea', dived and surfaced. Each time we blew the ballast with the diesel working as a compressor, the fifth compartment was filled with pungent smoke. But the diesels were running like clockwork. I made an entry in the log to the effect that the small defect in the valve would not hinder the patrol.

Senior Lieutenant Y.I. Gagarin muttered discontentedly: 'If you had to go on this ship yourself, you would never have written that.

'If that's what you think, you're mistaken. I assure you that you can live with valves like that. Do you agree with me?' I asked Viktor Sorokin, a broad-shouldered, rosy-cheeked young man, the head of the propulsion group. He shrugged his shoulders. I could see that he agreed with me but did not wish to contradict his superior officer. He said to me jokingly: 'You should come with us on patrol, Viktor Yemelianovich, out there you could teach us how.'

'I'd be delighted,' I quipped back. 'I've already had a breather and, besides, I'm fed up with wandering from one ship to another like this . . .'

We had a new Brigade Commander – Captain First Rank A.M. Stetsenko. He and I had not known one another before, and I was surprised when, on meeting me, he immediately invited me round. The conversation was exceedingly brief. 'Comrade Korzh, I know that you have only just returned from a very tough patrol and deserve a rest. But a combination of circumstances has compelled me to ask you to put to sea again.'

Taken aback, I wasn't immediately able to find the right words. Then I replied: 'I am ready to go. On which boat?'

'On *S-12*.'

Well, how about that!.

'But she already has a head of *D-5* on board . . .'

'Senior Lieutenant Gagarin is seriously ill. He has been concealing the fact that he has tuberculosis. Tikhon Alexeievich Kuzmin, our brigade doctor, has explained it all and has categorically forbidden that he should be sent to sea.'

It had now become clear why Gagarin had grown so morose and irritable lately. I felt sorry for the poor chap!

'When does the boat put to sea?'

'In four days' time. In view of the difficulty of the forthcoming voyage, we are trying to beef up the complement of officers on board this boat. Divisional Navigator Lieutenant Captain Ilyin and Lieutenant Captain Loshkariov will be on her. You know both of them.'

'They are friends of mine.'

'That's all to the good.'

I recalled how, in the winter, we had gone to *La Traviata*. We were already dreaming then about sailing together one of these days. It seemed an unrealizable dream, but now here it was, coming true.

'Go to your new ship, Comrade Korzh,' the Brigade Commander said in farewell. 'I wish you success.'

After supper the commanding officer of *S-12*, Captain Third Rank Vasili Andrianovich Turayev, asked me to stay behind in the officers' mess. He invited me to play a game of chess. He was not a brilliant chess player, but he enjoyed playing. I realized, however, that on this occasion the chess was a mere pretext. Moving the pieces, we conducted an unhurried conversation.

'Evidently, the present patrol will be a very short one,' said Turayev.

'What makes you think so?'

'It is autumn. It will get cold in no time. I think that we will be at sea for some twenty days, not more.'

'It's not realistic. In that amount of time we could do no more than get out into the open sea, sail as far as the southern Baltic coast and come back again.'

'That may be so, but I am hoping that, even within that time-slot, we will chalk up some successes.'

We discussed the crew's state of combat readiness. I knew that it still left a lot to be desired.

'Tomorrow we will spend the entire day in the "Okhtenskoye Sea",' said the Captain. 'We will practise emergency diving. I would ask you to be a hard taskmaster with the crew.'

So there we were, heading for the middle of the Neva. I was getting the measure of my new comrades. No, it was by no means *S-7*, where everyone understood everyone else with no more than half a word. It was noisy in the control room: a lot of unnecessary

1. Viktor Korzh when serving as Senior Engineer Officer on *S-7*.

2. Lieutenant Captain Alexander Alexeievich Ilyin (Sasha), Divisional Navigator and also Navigator on *S-12*.

3. Lieutenant Captain Lev Alexandrovich Loshkariov served on *S-12* and was later promoted to Captain Third Rank and put in command of *P-318*.

4. Senior Lieutenant Georgi Petrovich Kulchitsky, head of *D-5* on the floating-base Smolny.

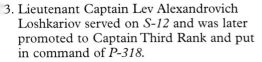

5. Ibragim Ramazanovich Ramazanov, Divisional Engineer.

6. Captain Third Rank Sergei Prokofievich Lisin, Commanding Officer of *S-7*.

7. Chief Leading Seaman Pyotr Lyashenko, head of the electricians' group on *S-7*, with members of his crew.

8. Captain Lisin with cadets of the Leningrad Higher Submarine School.

9. Seaman Alexander Olenin, a helmsman on *S-7*.

16. Seaman Valentin Kunitsa, (second from right) a gunlayer on *S-7* and a political activist, leading a political discussion with other members of the crew.

17. One of the divers working on the hull of a submarine in the icy waters of the Neva.

18. Senior Lieutenant Nikolai Sergeievich Dolgopolov, head of *D-5* on *L-21*.

19. Captain First Rank Alexander Yevstafievich Oryol, Divisional Commander, sailed with *L-21* and later became Commander of the Baltic Fleet.

20. Captain Second Rank Sergei Sergeievich Mogilievsky, Commanding Officer of *L-21*.

21. Rear Admiral Valentin Stepanovich Kozlov, the author of the foreword.

22. Captain First Rank Viktor Yemelianovich Korzh (Vitka), author of *Red Star under the Baltic* at the time of its publication in Russian in 1966, under the title *Reserve of Strength*.

orders, explanations. Petty Officer Kazakov, in charge of the planesmen's group, knew his stuff, but he was nervous too. At each command he would rush headlong to the action station manned by Paravoy, one of the planesmen's section leaders, and help him to sort out what to close, what to open. I wrote my first 'verdict' in my notebook: to replace the section leader – it was too late to be teaching him.

After the first round of diving and surfacing I gathered together the leading seamen of our department in the control room. I told them: 'We are in far too much of a muddle. Man your stations and observe how it should be done.'

I manipulated the valves and the Kingston valves' pneumatic systems; I explained why you had to operate in exactly this way, and not in any other. Then I made each one do precisely the same thing. I explained what each member of the watch had to do at his action station. We repeated emergency diving and surfacing several times like that; we adjusted the trim. Only when I was satisfied that the leading seamen had mastered the techniques did I bring the training session to a close. I suggested conducting such exercises with each rating at his action station. Fewer words, more practical demonstration!

The Captain was in complete agreement with me. He gave the orders for diving and surfacing over and over again. The 'Okhtenskoye Sea' is shallow and confined. We kept on the go in this narrow space; we dived and leapt up to the surface again. Though it was really poor to begin with, by evening it had gradually started to come together.

When we had returned to the shore, I told Ramazanov that the planesmen's section leader had to be replaced. The Divisional Engineer Officer agreed without further ado: 'I will assign Zmienko from S-4 to you. There's no better man for the job!' I knew Able Seaman Ivan Zmienko. It was impossible to imagine a better candidate. So this action station of ours would be absolutely reliable.

Each day we went out to the 'Okhtenskoye Sea'. By the end of the day the sailors were half-dead with fatigue, but no one complained. They understood that we wouldn't be able to cope without the stepped-up training.

The group leaders were fired with enthusiasm. The leader of the electricians' group, Petty Officer Anatoli Vasilievich Lavrikov, said to me: 'When you're doing a worthwhile job, and particularly one on which your own life might depend, there's no question of slacking off. When the work is pointless, it's a different matter altogether, something along the lines of that favourite old naval saying: "If it's flat, roll it along; if it's round, drag it." ' But I ordered them to moderate their zeal. Otherwise we would exhaust the men completely. And we had a patrol ahead of us, where there would be no rest.

On 15 September a meeting took place on the floating base *Smolny* at which the head of brigade headquarters acquainted us with the plan for the departure of the boats from Leningrad. Two boats, *S-12* and *D-2*, would set off on patrol. I learned that Captain Third Rank Rim Yulievich Gintovt, the neighbouring Divisional Engineer Officer, would sail with *D-2*. For some reason, an unusually large number of divisional specialists would be taking part in this patrol! One might have judged from this alone that the voyage would be a difficult one.

This time the passage to Kronstadt was relatively calm. The darkness and the rain helped. The Germans did do a bit of firing, but not one shell so much as grazed a ship. Our smoke-layers provided them with sufficient cover.

We spent a few days in Kronstadt, loading ammunition, fuel and provisions. Every now and then the enemy fired on the city. Fortunately, not one shell fell within the precincts of the submarine base. But somewhere on the outskirts, a huge column of smoke arose; from the look of it, a shell had landed on a fuel storage tank. The fire was soon put out.

On the evening of 19 September our friends said their goodbyes to us.

The First Step is the Hardest

Mooring lines cast off, gangplank withdrawn. We took up our position in the convoy. Submarine chasers and minesweepers accompanied us. Life on board the submarine 'turned through 180 degrees'. Night would be day for us from now on, and day night. Kozlov the cook was ordered to prepare dinner. On the boat

Kozlov was always addressed as Vasili Nikolaievich, evidently as a sign of especial respect for his action station.

The port diesel was being used to charge the battery; the starboard one for the propeller. From the very first moments, trouble set in for the engine-room mechanics. The minesweepers crawled along with their sweeps at a speed of eight knots. Using just one of our engines at low revolutions gave the ship a speed of ten knots. If the engine-room crew decreased the revolutions, the diesel started to run erratically. The revolutions had to be stepped up again. At one moment the boat would be running up onto the sweep, then would fall back and be in imminent danger of encroaching on the stem of the ship following along behind. The engine room crew were constantly manipulating the levers of the manual cut-out, under pressure all the time. They couldn't take it for more than ten minutes at a time; then they had to be relieved. By two in the morning they had pushed themselves to breaking-point and were asking for quarter. Senior Lieutenant Sorokin reported to the control room and asked me: 'Viktor Yemelianovich, how much longer is this farce going to go on for the engine-room crew?'

'Let's ask the Navigator.' Ilyin turned round, irritated, his nerves on edge.

'I don't understand what you are doing with that diesel of yours, I can't figure it out, not even with the aid of the integral calculus. But we will get there about two hours from now.'

My assistant grimaced, as though he had bitten into a lemon: 'By that time, we will all be off our heads.'

'Stay in the control room for a while,' I said to Sorokin, 'and I'll go up on the bridge and see what's going on up there.'

'Look for all you're worth,' Ilyin responded. 'It's dark up there, like under a barrel in a cellar at midnight.'

I climbed the ladder. For the first few minutes I really couldn't see a thing. Gradually my eyes adapted. I began to make out the ships' stern lights and the silhouettes of the minesweepers ahead of us.

'Vasili Andrianovich,' I said to the Captain, 'for some reason we are changing speed more often than usual today. The engine-room mechanics are absolutely worn out.'

'It can't be helped. New mines are turning up. So the

87

minesweepers have to clear their sweeps. What can a submarine do about that?'

Ahead of us a light flared abruptly, a huge pyramid of water heaved up, lit from within. A hydraulic shock struck the boat's hull, and it was only afterwards that the boom of the explosion reached us. My forage cap was torn from my head, and it fell down into the control room. 'Stop diesels!'

Fortunately no one was hurt. It was a mine that had exploded in the sweep of one of the minesweepers. The broken sweep was replaced and we resumed our onward way.

I went below. The sky was beginning to turn grey in the opening of the upper hatchway. Soon it would be dawn. The order came from above to stop the diesels. Everyone came down from the bridge into the control room. The Captain sealed the hatch, ordered the boat submerged for trimming. At first everything went as it should. I monitored the instruments, let water into the trimming tank and pumped it through. But I sensed something untoward in the boat's behaviour. She couldn't maintain herself on an even keel at all. 'Loose air bubbles in the fuel tanks' the suspicion struck me. In the fuel tanks, as the diesel fuel is expended, it is replaced by water. Evidently, what had happened with us was that some air had got in there. I reported to the Captain and requested permission to surface in the awash position. 'Only briefly. It is already dawn!'

We blew the central tank. The Captain and I jumped out onto the wet bridge. I kicked my boots off, ran to the hatch in the deck that covered the supplementary venting valve of one of the portside tanks. There was only a moderate sea running, but the swell was rolling over the low deck just the same. The water was dreadfully cold and, when I was almost up to my ears in water out on the casing, I felt like yelling. I opened the valve. There was almost no air. I closed the vent, wound wire round it. I moved over to starboard. No air there either. But from the third tank air hissed out noisily. I held the valve open for a minute, then another. Impatiently, the Captain asked: 'How's it going, down there?'

'About one and a half cubic metres have come out already.'

'Get a move on!'

My teeth were chattering by then, but the air kept on coming out. Eventually diesel fuel came out of the valve. I checked the other tanks. There was no more air in them. With an effort I wound the slippery wire round the last valve and battened the hatch with a wrench. I ran to the spar ladder, but my hands, smeared with fuel oil, slipped on the handgrips. Vasili Andrianovich grabbed me by the collar and helped me climb onto the bridge, muttering his apologies for such an unorthodox means of assistance, and we both dived down the hatch. 'Open the central tank vents!' I ordered, with blue lips.

With a faint sigh of relief, the submarine dived to periscope depth. The remainder of the trimming took less than ten minutes to complete. After that, we settled smoothly on the bottom. In the diesel compartment they poured warm water over me, I had a soapy wash, changed into dry things. The cook fed me with hot cabbage soup, and the medic, G.Y. Kuznetsov, treated me to some fiery potion. After that I was as warm as toast.

Everyone lay down to rest for about an hour and a half. At 06.00 hours we were roused by the order: 'Duty watch stand by to take her up'. I went to the control room. The duty mechanic was the planesmen's group leader, Petty Officer I.A. Kazakov. He was behaving confidently, giving clear orders to his subordinates. I didn't interfere with his instructions. The submarine detached herself smoothly from the bottom and, at a depth of forty metres, set a course for Suursaari Island.

At 18.45 hours three powerful detonations thrust the submarine upwards. I rushed headlong to the control room. I got there in time to put the submarine into a dive by filling the rapid-diving tanks, with the depth-gauge showing no more than three metres. The boat settled heavily on the sandy bottom at a depth of forty-seven metres. Fragments of glass crunched under our feet: the lamp-shades and light bulbs had been shattered by the explosions. Petty Officer Kazakov and I checked the sea outlets together. Everything seemed to be in order, if you discounted the fact that a fine-tuning valve on a trimming tank had opened by itself from the vibration. We closed it.

The Captain ordered the hydrophone operators to do a blanket sweep around the horizon. Leading Seaman 2nd Class Syomin reported that the apparatus was not operational. This was really bad news. On top of that, it came to light that the bilge trimming pump couldn't be started. Its automatic starting-switch had been damaged.

'Malakhov to report immediately to the control room!' I ordered. The leader of the second compartment came running at the double and announced himself with full formality: 'Leading Seaman 2nd Class Malakhov reporting for duty as ordered!'

'In a combat situation you could shorten it a bit,' I broke in. 'Get going on the automatic starting-switch straight away.'

An enemy aircraft had spotted us, when we had come up to periscope depth to fix our position with reference to the Upper Suursaari Lighthouse. The Bosun had failed to maintain the boat at periscope depth, and the conning tower had appeared above the surface of the water. The Nazi pilots had taken advantage of the situation. It was not bad enough that they had dropped their bombs fairly accurately. They were now in a position to summon enemy motor boats here too, and we had no possibility of evading them; the underwater listening apparatus was on the blink. This was what a mistake made by one member of the crew can lead to!

The leader of the radio operators' group, Chief Leading Seaman A.S. Yermolayev, sent the head of the radio unit, G.M. Metreveli, to Syomin's assistance. Fortunately, they managed to locate the defect swiftly and repair it. 'The underwater listening system is working!' – the report reached the control room. And then straight away a new report: 'Two motor boats heard approaching.' Turayev was anxious. I understood him: such headaches at the very beginning of a patrol!

Malakhov had dismantled the automatic starting-switch. It turned out that a little ratchet, making a connection to a resistor, had broken. I ordered a similar component to be removed from one of the diesel cooling-system's circulation pumps and to be installed there. Ten minutes later the bilge trimming pump was up and running. The engine room mechanics would have to cut a little ratchet by hand, to replace the one removed. 'Where are the motor boats?' the Captain enquired. The hydrophone operators replied: 'The motor boats are on the move, but they're not closing on us.'

The Captain and I exchanged glances. Silently he nodded his head. Equally silently, I made a sign to Able Seaman I.P. Zmienko, the planesmen's section leader. He switched on the bilge trimming pump to drain the stabilizing tank. Five minutes later we switched it off. The hydrophone operators combed the horizon. It seemed that the enemy had not heard us. We started the pump again, to pump out extra ballast.

At 19.27 hours we silently detached ourselves from the seabed. And – a new mishap – Petty Officer N.A. Balakirev reported that the stern hydroplanes had got stuck.

We attempted to switch over to manual control. The Bosun applied his full strength but the wheel did not turn. Leading Seaman 1st Class B.A. Zviagin, the leader of the helmsmen's group, hastened to his assistance. The two of them together overpowered the recalcitrant wheel. For nearly a mile they coped with it manually. Then suddenly the wheel began to move easily, as though some wire that had been holding it back had snapped.

When everything in the control room had gradually returned to normal, I again sent for Malakhov, who had been absent in the fifth compartment for a long time. 'Well, what's the word on the ratchet?'

'Engine-room Mechanic Osovsky will make it, if Petty Officer Lavrikov doesn't find a spare one. He says that he had one hidden away somewhere, but he doesn't know whether it will be the right size.'

'And so what kept you away so long?'

'I was helping the electricians to put the propulsion systems in order. When the explosions took place, the casings there fell to pieces; it was about to cause a short circuit. We had to replace the circuit-breakers.'

'Go to your compartment. Measure the conductivity of the battery casing right away.'

Two explosions erupted some distance astern. The hydrophone operators reported: 'Having picked up speed, the motor boats are moving away.'

The Captain's expression brightened up. 'We've outfoxed the Germans. They're used to our submarines going via the southern navigation channel or across Narva Bay. That's why they made up their minds on this occasion too that we had gone south. Whereas we will try to pass through the northern channel.'

The northern channel? I was calling to mind what I had heard about it. It was extremely difficult for submarines: narrow, like a cleft in the mountains, and in one area absolutely shallow; it's not for nothing that the navigators called this place 'the pass'. This channel went past the northernmost tip of Suursaari Island and was vigilantly defended by the enemy.

Malakhov reported from the second department that not only was the battery undamaged, but that it had even dried out a bit and its insulation improved, which meant that we were back in business!

We crawled through the pass on our belly. I supervised the planemen's work myself. The utmost care was called for. Otherwise we would break the propeller blades or the vertical rudder on the rocks. Even so, we scraped against the rocks on three occasions, fortunately with the bow section of the hull. At last, at a depth of seven metres, we passed over the saddle of the underwater ridge. The depths began to increase. It was over! Good old Ilyin! Not even the bombing had prevented our Navigator from carrying out his precise calculations. That's how we managed to pass so successfully through such a narrow place.

At midnight in the deserted Suursaari reaches we decided to surface to charge the battery. We would be charging it hove-to: there were minefields around.

Even Bombing Can't Be Blamed For Everything

We were blowing the ballast. As soon as the boat had broken the surface, the Captain, the duty officer M.I. Bulgakov and the signalmen Karpov and Bondarenko had gone up onto the bridge. Commissar Fyodor Alexeievich Ponomaryov had stayed behind in the conning tower.

Everything was going according to plan. Then I suddenly noticed that the pointers of the tachometers indicating the propeller shafts' rotation speed were standing at zero. From the electric motor compartment they reported that the automatic control unit for the first group of batteries had cut out. What should be done? The submarine was neither fully surfaced nor in the awash position. We had either to complete the surfacing or dive again and find out what the matter was when submerged. I decided to continue blowing the ballast, since the time for charging was all too short.

And at this point the second compartment's bulkhead hatch

swung wide open and Orderly Danilin's contorted face appeared, amid clouds of black smoke. He shouted: 'Fire! The batteries are on fire!' A choking cough prevented him from further speech. The fire alarm resounded throughout the ship. The emergency team headed by Senior Lieutenant Sorokin came running into the control room. 'You stay here,' I told him. 'Don't blow any more ballast. Charge only the second group of batteries. And I will go with the emergency team.'

Captain Third Rank Turayev came hurtling down from the bridge. I reported to him about the decisions taken and, with his permission, went to the second compartment. It was pandemonium in there. The ratings were throwing the furnishings out into the first compartment. The planking removed from the deck was being transferred there too. Malakhov had laid asbestos mats over the two batteries, from which acrid smoke was still pouring. It was impossible to breathe. The compartment was in semi-darkness. It was such a sight that my hair stood on end beneath my forage cap. I felt the touch of someone's hand on my shoulder. I turned around. Commissar Ponomaryov. He was there already. And, as ever, he proved to be the person you most needed: composed and energetic. Already his mere presence seemed to keep confusion and panic at bay.

'Nothing dreadful, Chief,' he said. 'Report to the bridge that there is no open fire any more.' The tone of the Commissar's voice was even. On his lean face not so much as a muscle twitched. 'Go and tell people what to do next.'

At that moment I was imbued with the deepest respect for Ponomaryov. That's just how a genuine officer should be. No matter how dreadful the combination of circumstances, be calm and active, so that not the slightest doubt arises in your subordinates' minds as to your competence or your self-control. I pulled myself together completely. I tried to issue orders cheerfully, confidently. And the ratings took heart. There were even jokes to be heard. 'Isn't it about time to give the all-clear?' asked the Commissar. He was referring to the fire alarm. So long as it had not been turned off, the whole crew felt on tenterhooks.

The Commissar might well be right. Now that the danger of another flare-up had been removed, there was no point in keeping people on edge for nothing. I called the control room on the voice-pipe, ordered a request to turn off the alarm to be passed on to the Captain. A minute later the all-clear sounded throughout the compartments.

I examined the battery. We were in for masses of work. Why on earth did all this happen? Was it due to the bombardment? But Malakhov had checked the battery before the charging began, everything was in order. I instructed him to measure the insulation again. I saw him taking the voltmeter. He connected one of its terminals to the battery's return wire; he touched one of the ribs of the framework with the other. He shrugged his shoulders. Then he connected the terminals to the two battery clamps; and went white. 'Comrade Captain Third Rank,' he shouted to me, 'the voltmeter isn't working!'

Another one was fetched. It showed what the electricians call a 'full earth'. A short-circuit! Which is why, when we switched on the current, the battery caught fire. Even so, we were let off lightly. There might well have been an actual explosion!

Malakhov was looking at me in guilt and dismay. I was absolutely seething inside. You have to be a hopeless ignoramus to put your faith in a dud voltmeter.

'Viktor Yemelianovich!' The Commissar drew me aside. 'Get a grip on yourself. Malakhov's mistake can be dealt with later on. What matters now is to salvage the battery.'

Little by little I cooled down. There were indeed more important issues than a few words with Malakhov. We had to make a decision swiftly. Nothing could be done about the broken-down battery yet; we would deal with it when we were lying on the bottom. And in the meantime we would charge the second group of batteries, housed in the fourth compartment.

I climbed up to the bridge, to ask the Captain's advice.

It was impenetrably dark over the sea. The boat was hove-to. The diesel was throbbing resonantly, charging the battery. I peered around in vain – it was as if Indian ink had been spilt over everything. Then suddenly, a long way off somewhere, seemingly on the peak of Suursaari Island, the beam of a searchlight blazed. Having made a smooth descent to the horizon, it glided evenly over the sea. At any minute it would touch the bow of the submarine, but at the very last moment it lifted higher up, swept over the bridge and died away in the distance beyond the stern. This was repeated several times. Apparently, there on the peak of the island, something was preventing the searchlight from deflecting its beam lower and spotlighting the submarine.

Gulping in the fresh night air, I reported to the Captain everything that I had seen in the second compartment. 'Is this the result of the bombs from the aircraft exploding?' enquired Vasili Andrianovich.

Well, yes, generally speaking, it could all be put down to the bombing. It would take the blame for everything. The batteries' ebonite tanks cracked from the concussion. The voltmeter with which Leading Seaman Malakhov measured the insulation was put out of action by the concussion. But I was dead sure that such a mistake would not have occurred on S-7. No, not even the bombing could be blamed for everything. If people had been better prepared for testing times, the battery fire would not have happened. I told the Captain this too. He listened attentively, not interrupting.

'What do you suggest?' he asked.

'When the second group of batteries has been charged, we must lie on the bottom and there, without haste, do everything that we can.'

'But we can't lie on the bottom here.'

The Commissar backed the Captain up: 'With the dawn there will be such a free-for-all here that you would hardly be able to take it. We have already been detected, although we haven't actually been seen. They will be searching for us without fail.'

'All the same, we must lie up.'

Bending over the hatch, the Captain shouted into the control room: 'You below! Divisional Navigator to the bridge!'

Alexander Alexeievich Ilyin didn't keep us waiting long: 'At your service!'

'Choose a convenient place where we could lie on the bottom. The kind where no one would disturb us.'

'There is an enemy minefield on our course. It seems to me that this would be the most peaceful spot. The enemy will hardly poke his nose in there.'

The duty officer, Lev Alexandrovich Loshkariov, liked this idea. 'As the old seadogs have it,' he said, 'For a cushy life on the ocean deep, another man's cabin is where to sleep.'

'Another man's cabin is one thing, but another man's minefield – that's something entirely different,' laughed the Captain. 'But we shall give it a try. And now don't let me distract you from your duties.'

Having finished charging the surviving group of batteries, we submerged and, diving beneath the minefield, settled smoothly on the seabed at a depth of fifty-eight metres.

I assembled a team of nine ratings and leading seamen and led them to the scene of the incident. A tenth man was the cook, Vasili Nikolaievich, who, although he was not part of our team, was nevertheless working for us, heating up the mastic for the battery on his electric stove. The orderly, Danilin, was serving this hot 'dish' to us in the smashed-up officers' mess.

It was only then that it was possible to appreciate fully the consequences of the incident. Out of sixty-two battery cells, thirty-two were damaged. Thirteen of them had chunks of ebonite knocked out. Four tanks had been cracked right down to the base, and there was a constant leakage of electrolyte from them. We worked right through until evening. We repaired everything that we could. But six cells had to be switched off – their plates had welded together. The same number of cells had to be switched off in the second group too – to maintain the balance.

There were some hotheads to be found, like the orderly Danilin and the electrician Makhankov, who suggested dragging three undamaged cells from the fourth to the second compartment. Attractive. But, as the saying goes, 'it looked good on the drawing-board, but they forgot about the pitfalls'. It was impossible to drag the cumbersome and weighty tanks (each weighing 645kg.) through the narrow bottlenecks of the bulkhead doors.

The Captain looked in on us in the compartment several times, asked how the repair work was coming along. He didn't hurry us up, didn't urge us on, he could see that we were sweating over the work as it was. The Captain understood better than we did that the important thing now was not so much speed as quality and reliability.

When the basic jobs were done, the Captain invited me into the leading seamen's mess in the fourth compartment. This was where all the ship's officers who were not busy on watch in the control room were now taking refuge. Vasili Andrianovich asked how much damage, all in all, we had clocked up after the bombing. I replied that, as well as the battery, more than forty different damaged items had been discovered, beginning with such trivialities as the broken porcelain basins in the washrooms, and ending with the anti-aircraft periscope's broken braces and the speed-indicator and the gyrocompass, both of which had been put out of action.

'A bit much for the beginning of a patrol,' sighed the Captain. But it was the battery that worried him most of all.

'How reliable would you say your glueing of the battery tanks was?'

'Reliable to the extent that, if we were put to a similar test again, other tanks would crack, but not the ones that we glued together.'

I had a fit of coughing. The air in the compartment was saturated with the fumes of the mastic that the cook had heated up for us. The smell is not very nice, it stings your throat and nose, but it's excellent mastic, it glues ebonite together hard and fast.

'Will the battery lose much of its capacity?' the Captain voiced the question that was troubling him particularly.

'About nine per cent. Consequently, at a speed of three knots we will be able to go 132 miles, rather than 145.'

'And at full submerged speed?'

'At a speed of nine knots we will be able to go for fifty-four minutes, rather than an hour.'

The Captain smiled: 'We can go to war!'

At night, when we surfaced, the repaired battery was put on charge. No problem; it operated normally. We were charging until morning, and then continued our onward course submerged.

The work of putting right the various malfunctions went on. There were so many of them. Sorokin was keeping a detailed account of them. The blade of the main portside electric propulsion motor's cooling fan had jammed. Six manometers were broken; the glass of the control-room depth-gauge had shattered. Six ammeters were out of action, one of them burnt out. The flange of one of the torpedo tubes had got a crack in it and was letting water through. The upper conning-tower hatch had warped. Fourteen lampshades were broken; forty-nine electric-light bulbs had torn filaments. After reading the note about the light bulbs, I reproached Sorokin: 'You still can't steer clear of trivialities, Viktor Tikhonovich!'

'That's some triviality – fifty light bulbs! If it goes on like this, we will have to grope our way home.'

'And is the emergency lighting intact?'

'All intact. We can be thankful that they put in special shock-absorbers!' It is indeed a great thing, shock-absorption. If only the designers and we ourselves put more thought into it, a great deal of damage could be avoided during even the bitterest of bombardments.

Sorokin and I were chatting, while at table in the officers' mess the usual light-hearted exchange of fire was going on. As usual, the instigator was the medic, Senior Lieutenant Kuznetsov. He was heatedly maintaining that caffeine not only dilated the blood vessels, but was also a stimulant, and was therefore a very effective aid against fatigue.

'All right, doctor,' said Loshkariov, 'it's time I got ready for my watch. We'll continue our scientific debate later. But tell me, if I drink a glass of coffee now, will it compensate me for the lost hour of sleep?'

'Absolutely. But the caffeine won't enter the system until four hours later.'

'Thank you for the consultation. That means that when I come off watch I shall feel full of beans and won't want to sleep?'

'Now that we are on the topic of sleep,' I joined in the conversation as well, 'allow me to tell you a true story. At naval college, the most trying night watch – the 'dog-watch' as we called it – was being stood by my friend, and I had to relieve him at four in the morning. He agonized and agonized, but then he could hold out no longer and woke me up: "Vitka, Vitka, do please finish sleeping quicker, because you are on watch in half an hour's time." At first I was annoyed with my friend, but then I laughed and relieved him before the appointed time.'

I loved those friendly conversations in the mess. They brought people closer to one another. Had we been together for long? Already it seemed to me that I had known each one of them for a long, long time.

In the Nets

At noon our Navigator Ilyin invited me to join him in the control room, where he and Komissarov, a navigational electrician, were trying to find the break in the distance-indicator's electrical circuit. We were absorbed in the task and didn't notice the time. Suddenly, four explosions sounded at the bow, one after the other. From the first compartment they reported that they could hear the screech of some kind of metal cables.

Petty Officer Balakirev was fidgeting on his revolving stool: the boat was not responding to the rudders. Turayev, Ponomaryov and Loshkariov came running into the control room. At that moment the boat's stern shot sharply downwards. The Captain ordered the engines reversed. The boat remained where she was. The electric motors were switched to ahead: the result was the same. The explosions were relatively mild. We were of one mind – these were not mines.

The boat was twisting slowly to starboard. Lieutenant Captain Loshkariov was the first to put forward the conjecture that we might have run into an anti-submarine net. Now our bow was stuck in it, and the side of the boat was being held against the net by the current. From the first compartment they continued to report the screech of steel cables on the bow. What could we be caught up by? The bow hydroplanes? But, in that case, the screeching would be either on the starboard or the port side of the first compartment. Still, no matter what had got caught, the main thing was that we were unable to tear ourselves loose.

So as not to have our side pushing against the net, on which were hung canisters containing sixteen kilos of explosive (it was these that exploded off the bow), the Captain ordered the electric motors to be operated in opposite directions: port ahead, starboard astern. But this was only a temporary measure. A way out had to be sought.

We got stuck in the anti-submarine net at 13.35 hours, and at 13.55 hours the hydrophone operator reported a ship closing on us. The detonations of the very first pattern of depth charges all but thrust the boat up onto the surface. And to expose ourselves then would have meant certain death. Without pause for thought, I filled the rapid-diving tank. The Navigator had determined from the chart that the depth of the sea here was thirty-five metres. I recalled that, when the Navigator had called me into the control room, the Bosun was already at that time maintaining a depth of thirty metres. That meant we had very little water indeed under our keel. Fearing for the integrity of the screws and rudders, I ordered Able Seaman Zmienko to let the water flow of its own accord from the stern to the bow trimming tank.

Amid the din of a new pattern of depth charges, I gave the order to draw water from the outside into the stabilizing tank. The depth of the dive increased rapidly. The depth-gauge needle was already on the 45-metre mark when the bow touched bottom and was sharply flung to port, as though it were sliding over a slippery inclined plane.

From the first compartment Lieutenant Captain Bulgakov reported that the cable had torn free from the bow. But we had no time to feel glad about it. The boat was so heavy now that she could no longer maintain her position afloat. She was falling ever deeper. At last, at a depth of sixty-seven metres, she bumped her hull on the stony seabed.

The sound of a depth charge being fired from a ship could be heard distinctly. Here it comes, somersaulting, gurgling, getting inexorably nearer to us. It banged against a rock, banged once more, and then everything was blotted out in the uproar. The boat was thrown so hard to port that few were able to keep on their feet. Crunching, cracking, ringing, banging . . . From a cubicle not far from me came the sound of a deafening hissing; fog was belching out of there. 'Hole in the cubicle!' shouted Petty Officer Kazakov and hurried there with the emergency wedges and bungs.

The cramped control room became even more cramped – ratings, pushing and shoving, were running to their places. With difficulty, I fought my way over to starboard; I yelled, trying to make myself heard above the din: 'Block up that hole!'

'Non-essential personnel clear the control room!' ordered the Captain and somewhat unceremoniously drove Ilyin, Bogdanov, Loshkariov and Ryzhkov off to the second compartment. A concentrated jet of water was spurting out of the cubicle, smashing against the piping. I took a closer look: no, it was not a hole, it was simply that an outboard valve drive lubricator had been knocked out. But it was a powerful jet; the cubicle was already full of water. Kazakov and I attempted to reach the opening. Impossible: the pipes got in the way. A broom caught my eye. I broke off its long handle, sharpened the end of it with a knife. I endeavoured to drive it into the opening. Not a hope! The jet threw the broomstick off. Like it or lump it, the pressure at a depth like this was more than six atmospheres. Eventually, with three people hanging onto the broomstick, we drove it into the hole. It became quiet instantly. The three of us kept holding onto the pole. And above our heads once more the propeller noise of an approaching ship. There was an audible splash, after it another. A few seconds later, two explosions thundered. Kazakov, Zmienko and I, plus the pole, were thrown off to the opposite side. I barely managed to grab hold of a ladder, to stay on my feet. A heavy lead sledge-hammer fell from the conning tower, almost hitting me on the head. Water gushed out of the cubicle with renewed force. Soaked to the skin, we flung ourselves at the opening again. For a long time we were unable to synchronize our movements so as to get at it, besides which, it was by now hidden beneath the water.

Water had already filled the bilges and begun to appear over the deck planking by the time we accidentally drove the sharp end of the broomstick into the hole. Clutching onto the pipes, we kept hold of the broom handle.

'Hold it tighter!' I said to the sailors. 'We'll try to brace the pole.'

They found some wire, and with it they bound the broomstick tightly to the pipes. But, not trusting to the wire, the sailors took turns holding the pole in their hands, keeping watch all the time that the bindings didn't slacken during the next set of explosions.

'Petty Officer, part of the water should be diverted into the fifth compartment's bilges, since it is already seeping towards the gyro-compass,' I said to Kazakov, when we had calmed down a bit.

This was not as simple as it might seem. Valves had to be opened in both the control room and the fifth compartment. Kazakov did everything according to the book.

A few minutes later the water had retreated to below the deck planking, leaving rags, wood shavings and fragments of glass on it.

Zmienko was lying on the deck, never taking his eyes off the blocked-up hole, and Leading Seaman 2nd Class Komissarov was collecting the rubbish in a bucket.

Petty Officer Kazakov returned with an electric heater. We were extremely glad to have it; we switched it on at once. Kazakov stripped to the buff, wrung out his tunic jacket, his trousers and his underwear, put them back on damp and tenderly embraced the electric heater. Steam poured out in a cloud.

In turn we all did the same. About forty minutes later, the sound of depth charge explosions reached us again. But not so near now. 'It looks as though our baptism of fire will end up happily,' I said as cheerfully as possible, although my lips had gone numb with cold and were totally reluctant to move. 'Throw salt over your left shoulder!' laughed Able Seaman Zmienko.

Having cautiously pushed the bulkhead hatch ajar, Loshkariov squeezed himself into the control room. He said that the Captain was at the hydrophone operators' booth. Judging by the sounds, the enemy ships had lost track of us. A rising wind was preventing them from continuing the search.

We had noticed ourselves that the depth-gauge needle had begun to quiver. That meant that there was a swell getting up on the surface.

'Lev Alexandrovich, how do you explain that, according to the chart, the depth at this spot is thirty-five metres, whereas we, as you can see, are lying at almost twice that depth?'

'We have evidently fallen into some particular ravine that hasn't been marked on the charts yet.'

'But the enemy knows about this ravine . . .'

'Undoubtedly. The charges were definitely detonating at precisely this depth. Could you feel that?'

'I could,' I replied, rubbing the bruise on my left shoulder under my damp tunic jacket. 'But why is he bombing so inaccurately now?'

'It is already dark over the sea: the sun set half an hour ago. There is a strong coastal current here. Add to that the wind factor. Clearly, in such conditions, the enemy ships have lost their points of reference.'

As if in confirmation of Loshkariov's words, another single explosion rumbled about 100 metres off the starboard beam. If they continued to bomb us like that we had nothing to fear. We even had a slight advantage: we knew where the enemy was positioned, and we were monitoring him, whereas he was dashing about blindly. Now the most important thing was not to give ourselves away.

In came Turayev. He smiled wearily. 'Well, how are you getting on here? Were you awfully scared?'

'The same as everyone else, I expect,' I replied. 'I won't lie. It was rather frightening.'

'You can say that again! Thirty-two depth charges in our immediate vicinity. But that's it for now. The Germans appear to have gone. Or it could be that they have run out of depth charges. We are going to wait for a while and then we will make our way out of this trap.'

We waited for a while longer and started the pump to drain the bilges. We would pump for ten minutes, then listen intently for ten minutes, in case there might be enemy ships about.

Having restored the trim, we took off from the bottom and left this godforsaken hole. The Captain made the decision to surface in between two minefields, which intersected almost the entire Gulf of Finland in long strips. There was a heavy swell. The boat was rolling violently. We carried out the charging hove-to, in constant fear that either the wind or the current would drive us onto the mines. Having replenished our supply of electricity, we submerged again at 02.48 hours and, virtually hugging the very bottom, we went on our way.

Two days passed without incident, although the hydrophone operators occasionally reported propeller noise. There were enemy ships and motor boats galore here.

On 25 September we heard a powerful screeching. We had touched a mine's mooring-cable. We turned to the side, manoeuvred about, but we could feel that the mine cable was not tearing itself free. What were we caught by? We manoeuvred once more. Eventually the cable tore itself loose and slid along the hull. We hardly had time to recover from this encounter before we brushed up against a mine cable again. And, according to the chart, this was a clear area. It followed that the enemy must have laid a new minefield. The Navigator marked on his chart the points where we made contact with the mine cables. We transmitted these coordinates to headquarters.

We found out later that in the course of our passage we had left in our wake forty-seven of our own minefields and fifty-one enemy ones!

On 26 September the Captain congratulated us on the completion of our forced passage through the Gulf of Finland. We were in the open sea! At night, for the first time in the whole patrol, Chief Leading Seaman A.S. Yermolayev's men – the ship's radio operators – were given work which drew directly on their special expertise. The boat reported our emergence into the open sea to headquarters. Radio operators Galperin and Metreveli received a short report from the Soviet Information Bureau; the latest news of events both at home and abroad. As the ship's Party Secretary, Yermolayev hastened to make this material available to the political activists.

The ship's commanding officer was aware that the crew was in need of at least a brief rest period. We moved to a calm area of the sea. Needless to say, the 'rest' was only relative. We repaired the damage and conducted training sessions, which some of the seamen needed badly. This was especially true of the planesmen: they were never able to hold the boat steady at periscope depth.

The uninitiated reader will not believe me when I say that controlling a submarine using the hydroplanes is 100 times harder than controlling a car. When you are driving a car, you know that it will respond immediately to each turn of the steering wheel. In a submarine, however, the planesman makes an adjustment to a rudder, but the boat responds to this only five, or sometimes even ten, seconds later – depending on the running speed. Just imagine a driver's state of mind if his control of the wheel operated with similar delays. Supposing he had returned the wheel to the neutral position, and after that the car still went on turning to the right or to the left for a ten-second period . . .

I apologize for the crude illustration, but I wanted to explain more simply the difficulties facing the planesman. A good planesman on a submarine has a genuine talent; he is an artist in his own line of work. Not everyone can become a good musician, nor can every sailor become a good planesman – not by a long chalk. But every other man can become a car driver, after a modest amount of instruction.

Bosun N.A. Balakirev is an experienced seaman, not bad at teaching the ratings. And yet a turn of duty at the hydroplanes seems to be beyond his capability. It is quite another matter when it comes to his crewman, Leading Seaman 1st Class Boris Zviagin.

Loshkariov, the officer of the watch, giving Zviagin instructions, unobtrusively nudged me with his elbow. Even before that, I could not take my eyes off this skilful fellow. The boat was amazingly docile in his hands. The pupil surpassed his teacher by far. The Bosun should have been delighted. But Balakirev was down in the dumps. We could take a guess at his state of mind. A teacher is always likely to be a bit put out, when he can see that his pupil is coping with the matter better than he could himself.

If at First You Don't Succeed . . .

On 28 September, continuing our passage in the propeller-charging mode, the submarine submerged at 06.00 hours at the western edge of our quadrant, in the vicinity of the Akmenrags Lighthouse. We roved about all day in search of the enemy. By evening we found ourselves on the southern edge of our sector, abeam of the Uzava Lighthouse. We had encountered no enemy ships. We circled around in our allotted area equally fruitlessly the following day as well. Only late in the evening did the duty officer, Lieutenant Captain Loshkariov spot the enemy. The Nazi ships were forty cables away from us.

We sounded the general alarm. We discontinued charging. Equipping himself with the night sight, the Captain began combat manoeuvres to establish the enemy's course and speed. The poor visibility, which earlier had been our ally, had now turned into an enemy. We were chasing after the ships' lights for a long time until we revealed ourselves. One of the ships suddenly turned sharply and, picking up speed all the time, hurtled towards us. It was a destroyer, escorting a freighter. We had to get underwater urgently. The attack came to nothing. We had no alternative left to us but to lie on the bottom.

At 15.30 hours on 30 September, when we were just off Libava, the hydrophone operator Leading Seaman 2nd Class Syomin reported propeller noise to the officer of the watch, Lieutenant Captain Bulgakov. Beginning to manoeuvre into a combat position before the Captain arrived, the officer of the watch gave orders for the boat to be brought up to periscope depth. Three of us came running into the control room – the Captain, the Commissar and me. Turayev went up into the conning tower, I to my usual place, beneath the lower conning-tower hatch; the Commissar stayed in the control room too. A few minutes later we heard the Captain's voice: 'A battleship! Now there's a catch for you!'

The battleship *Schlesien* was escorted by destroyers. So far none of us had had to deal with such a target as this. We were all thrilled. The signal sounded for a torpedo attack. The Captain took a bearing and summoned Loshkariov to the conning tower. Senior Lieutenant Ryzhkov rapidly got the tables ready. In the control room I couldn't hear what was being said in the conning tower. The winch hummed: the periscope was raised a second time. But then Loshkariov's words reached our ears: 'They've all made a sharp turn. They are zigzagging to avoid torpedoes. The attack will not work.'

Turayev once more changed course to get into a position to attack, but twelve minutes later was finally convinced that, with the enemy ships going at such a speed, not to mention the zigzagging, it would be impossible to attack them, and he ordered: 'Stand down from action stations! Weapons to original status. Dive to a safe depth.'

Having come down into the control room and gone over to the navigator's table, Turayev and Loshkariov for a long time afterwards mulled over their own manoeuvres and those of the German battleship. It hurt to let such a catch slip away.

This area of the Baltic Sea had become extremely lively. Anti-submarine patrols were scurrying back and forth the whole time. We had to evade them, altering course and diving deep.

During the night of 4 October when we, after a change of tack, were carrying out battery-charging, the signalmen caught sight of the lights of a convoy of three ships through a veil of fine rain. The Captain immediately changed course. We closed in on the enemy at a sharp angle. The bad news was that we were positioned in the brighter area of the horizon where the enemy might detect us. But there was nothing we could do for the moment to change that.

The composition of the convoy became clearer: a freighter with an escort of two destroyers. It was heading in the direction of

106

Libava. The Captain increased the speed to full ahead, so as to shorten the approach time. All of a sudden the rearmost destroyer made a sharp turn and bore straight down on the submarine. We swung round onto the opposite course, not diving. The situation remained unchanged. The destroyer did not open fire. Loshkariov hazarded a guess: 'The rain is drenching their gun-sights.'

About fifteen minutes later, the destroyer turned back. So did we. The Captain had decided to attempt to catch up with the convoy (our speed being considerably greater than that of the freighter). We kept on a parallel course for two hours, barely able to distinguish the silhouettes of the enemy ships against the background of the coastline. The rain intensified. The Captain decided to turn this to our advantage. At full speed we followed a course that would intersect with the freighter's. But we were once more dogged by misfortune. The leading destroyer changed course and headed for us. 'Helm to starboard!' Turayev ordered the helmsman, P.A. Zhulin. Again we saved ourselves by taking to our heels. Ilyin hurried over to the chart, with Bogdanov close behind him. They were measuring something off, arguing about something.

'Sasha, what are you conjuring up over there?' I asked Ilyin.

'We are choosing a position.'

'A position for what?'

'The Captain wants to outsmart the three enemy captains.'

'Hasn't he given up on the attack?'

'Not yet.'

'I haven't understood a thing,' I confessed.

Senior Lieutenant Bogdanov smiled. 'Viktor Yemelianovich, do you remember the saying: "The wolf is fed by his legs"?'

From the gyrocompass repeater, buzzing away beside me, I could see that we were once more taking a course parallel to that of the escort. I envied the Captain his tenacity and I waited to see what would happen next, still not understanding what kind of manoeuvre I needed to be ready for.

We went on for one hour and then another. Then we turned sharply towards the coast and twenty minutes later submerged.

From the conning tower Turayev was keeping up a constant exchange of comments with Leading Seaman 2nd Class Syomin. It was dark on top, all our hopes rested on the hydrophone operators. Time moved dreadfully slowly. A double torpedo salvo had been set up in the bow.

At 02.40 hours the leading destroyer passed by us. At 02.51 hours the order: 'Blow central tank!' sounded.

From the dark conning tower the Captain, the Commissar and Loshkariov jumped out onto the bridge. From the exclamations coming from the bridge, I surmised that the Captain's plan had succeeded: we were still lying in wait for the freighter. But it was raining cats and dogs. Turayev could not make out the luminous dots on the night sight at all. 'Fire!' the order sounded at last.

The First Lieutenant moved the handles controlling torpedo fire. The submarine shuddered twice. I looked at my watch. It showed 02.55. 'Helm to port! All ahead half!'

In the control room everyone had gone quiet. We were waiting for the torpedo detonations. The appointed time passed. No detonations . . . The Captain came down to us, visibly ruffled: 'We've kicked up quite a rumpus here. The Germans are most likely under the impression that there are three submarines on the go. Let's go back to the south, towards Memel.'

But on our way we ran into the enemy again. At five in the morning the signalmen noticed lights. No question of passing them up! We turned towards them. To make the boat less obvious, we switched from the cruising to the awash position.

The Captain, the Commissar and the officer of the watch were on the bridge. Everyone took up his station for a torpedo attack. The Navigator was rushing down the ladder from the bridge to the navigator's table, over to the echo-sounder and back up to the bridge, sometimes shouting to the bridge directly from the control room: 'Shallows ahead!'

We had to stop the engines. For over an hour we idled virtually motionless, waiting for the enemy to close on us himself. The lookouts scanned the dark horizon, making sure that no one attacked us from the side or from the rear.

The distance to the enemy was lessening. It was difficult to judge accurately how distant an object was in the dark, and even more difficult to do so on the water. In the control room we could hear comments from the bridge: the signalmen were having an argument as to how many cables away the target was.

Time: 06.23. Distance: three cables. 'Fire!'

A torpedo ejected. But there was no trace of it. It had sunk! They had turned out the lights on the freighter, and she was hove-to. The Captain ordered: 'Electric motors: starboard – full speed ahead! Port – full speed astern!' The gyrocompass repeater-card turned through 180 degrees. 'Ready stern tubes!'

Distance: three cables. Time: 06.26. 'Number five tube. Fire!'

A torpedo ejected. It ran straight at the target. It went under the freighter. No explosion followed.

At 06.32 came a new order to fire, and once more we waited in vain for the explosion. I had gripped the handrails of the ladder so hard that the palms of my hands were on fire. Why weren't the torpedoes exploding? It was possible that the ship drew a very shallow draught, so that they were passing beneath her, not touching the bottom of her hull.

'Artillery alert!'

Alarm bells jangled loudly in the compartments. Lieutenant Captain M.I. Bulgakov, supervising the firing, came running into the control room, after him came Leading Seaman 2nd Class Smirnov, in charge of the 100-millimetre gun, together with his gun crew. One after the other they clambered up the ladder.

On the upper deck the stamping of feet, the clanging of metal. Eventually Bulgakov's order could be heard: 'Fire!' Not a shot. 'Fire!'

The gun was once more silent.

The stamping of feet; the crew tumbled head over heels down the ladder. From the bridge came the order to run both diesels at full speed. The last to come down from the bridge into the control room was the gunnery officer, Lieutenant Captain Bulgakov. 'Mikhail Ivanovich,' I asked him, 'why did you put up such a poor fight?'

'You have to understand, both ready-service lockers had got damp. And there was no time to change the shells: two patrol boats had appeared to the south.'

'Yes, there must be a general hubbub over the air-waves right now. We don't seem to be having any luck at all, do we, Mikhail Ivanovich, eh? Your torpedoes don't detonate, the guns don't fire. We're just scaring the Germans for nothing . . .' Offended and muttering harsh words in all directions, the Lieutenant Captain went to ground in the second compartment.

An emergency dive with the diesels shut down brought this

whole turbulent episode to a close. We had lost several torpedoes for nothing and also a couple of dozen shells, which had got damp (they had to be thrown overboard). But this was not what stuck in our craw. What did was that the men might feel disillusioned, lose faith in their own capabilities. I remembered that it was like that on *S-7* too: we had an unbroken run of bad luck to begin with; everyone was already beginning to throw in the towel. How did this come about? Most likely from the lack of combat experience. *S-7* was putting to sea for the first time after the siege winter. And *S-12* was a new boat, the majority of her crew had not taken part in war patrols at all.

The three of us got together – Ilyin, Loshkariov and I. We discussed the current situation and made up our minds to help the Captain in this trying circumstance. It was essential to talk things through with our subordinates, to convince them that bad luck could occur in any context, but that our expertise was increasing with each passing day and success would come without fail. Commissar F.A. Ponomaryov, having become involved in the conversation, warmly approved our idea.

When the submarine was lying on the bottom and the torpedo-men were getting on with reloading the tubes, I gathered the engine room crew together at their action station in the diesel compartment. The Commissar was present there too. I began a conversation about the matters that concerned us:

There were some difficulties during our passage through the Gulf of Finland. We overcame them successfully. It was an opportunity to learn a little something. And we did. Now we must provide the Captain with anything that he might think up for his manoeuvres. So, from a practical standpoint, what can we accomplish? By starting up the diesels in choppy weather conditions the engine room crew flooded the engines with water. From the outset, Seaman Nikolai Ivanovich Arakcheyev admitted to making such a blunder (animation in the compartment). It would seem that everyone could have learnt from his lesson. Not so. The very same blunder was repeated by Nikolai Ivanovich Drozdov (even more animation). Do you think that this was the end of it? No, it was not. Even Able Seaman Konstantin Grigorievich Tavrovsky decided not to be outdone by them (laughter, joking). As a result, the ship found herself without surface speed three times in an hour and a half. And all this solely because some of our comrades simply will not learn to open the upper exhaust valve at the right time. The planesmen are having a laugh here, but the fact is that not everything went smoothly for them either, not by a long chalk. Comrade Senior Planesman Alexei Nikolaievich Kopylov, what happened to the mesh filter for the bilge trimming pump?'

Red to the tips of his ears, Kopylov stood up: 'I didn't do it on purpose.'

'That's all we needed, for you to throw the most precious components overboard deliberately! But, just for the record, how did this come about? Tell your comrades, so that they may benefit from your bitter experience.'

'I was ordered by the leading seaman to clean the filter,' Kopylov began bashfully, 'I removed it and placed it in a bucket. The sailors were taking it in turns to have a smoke in the conning tower. My turn came too, and I climbed up the ladder. And then they were tidying up in the control room and piled rubbish on top of the filter. I hear them saying on the bridge that we are about to dive shortly. I quickly grabbed the bucket – and up I went. Once it had been emptied over the side, it was by then too late. But I did make a new filter . . .'

'You made an extremely poor filter, Comrade Kopylov,' Sorokin broke in. 'It lets all kinds of dirt through, and the valves are now constantly clogged.'

Commissar F.A. Ponomaryov took the floor. He spoke sincerely and reassuringly. In conclusion he said: 'Comrades, you can see how many blunders have already been allowed to occur and, in fact, each one of them could have led to disaster. Do you imagine that there have been no blunders in the other departments? No, they have made them too. And, it goes without saying; each of them affected the running of the ship to a certain extent. We must do a better job, faultlessly meeting our own responsibilities. Only then will we be able to count on success in combat with any certainty.' Yes, we had to do a better job. And we all had something to learn – from the ratings to the Captain. We were convinced of this over and over again.

At 17.05 hours, while on passage to Memel, First Lieutenant Ryzhkov sighted a freighter. He turned the boat onto an interception course. But he had to abandon the idea of an attack: close to, the vessel seemed so small that it would have been a shame to use up a torpedo on her.

Having discharged the battery reasonably well, we were running on a single electric motor, doing fifty-five revolutions a minute and, not to put too fine a point on it, dragging out the time until evening.

The next day, 8 October, at 14.37 hours – for the umpteenth time – the klaxon sounded its insistent call throughout the compartments: 'Torpedo attack!'.

The officer of the watch, Mikhail Ivanovich Bulgakov, had spotted a lone freighter through the periscope. This time the catch seemed certain. Everything was running on greased wheels. The triangulation for the torpedo attack had been calculated. The boat had been set on a combat course. The Captain, having made sure that everything was just so, lowered his periscope, intending to raise it again a moment later. But at that instant the boat suddenly dipped her bow and, failing to obey the Bosun, could not be levelled off for a long time. By the time he had managed to raise the periscope, the Captain could see that the moment for a salvo had irretrievably passed. Once again an attack had fizzled out.

I remembered with chagrin the conversation that Turayev and I had had on board the floating base *Smolny*. He was sure then that the entire patrol would last no more than twenty days. We had now passed the twenty-fifth day, and our success in battle was still at rock bottom.

To balance things out, our troubles were on the increase. The lid of the cylinder housing the high-pressure air compressor's final stage blew off unexpectedly. There was no spare lid. I asked the engine room crew's section leader, Leading Seaman 2nd Class Georgi Petrov, to try and turn it on our lathe. It didn't work. While they were busy with the first compressor, the lid blew off the second one as well. By now this had developed into a disaster. We now had no way to replenish the supply of compressed air. And, without it, we couldn't blow the ballast or prepare or fire the torpedoes. I swiftly imposed the strictest limitations on the consumption of compressed air. I ordered the diesels to be started only by the main electric motors and the outboard and ventilator valves to be opened and closed manually. The submarine's heads (the toilets) were closed off, so that compressed air would not be consumed in using them, either. Measures that were all very well, but not enough by themselves to get us as far as Kronstadt. And as for forcing a passage through the Gulf of Finland on the surface; exactly like trying to bash through a brick wall using your forehead. Something had to be done.

At my request the Captain took the boat to the sort of peaceful area where no one would disturb us and force us to take shelter underwater. The mists and the rain lent themselves to this. While we were rolling about in the swell, I tried all possible means of reinstating the lids. We tried welding. Able Seaman Zmienko employed various electrodes and different kinds of flux. It didn't hold, so that was that! A short-circuit put an end to the matter. Zmienko scorched his arm from wrist to elbow; I myself got my throat and forehead fairly well-grilled. Zmienko had to put himself in the capable hands of Senior Lieutenant Kuznetsov of the medical service; I made do with a bandage.

An attempt to heat up the massive lid with a blow-lamp to the melting temperature of brass wire didn't work either. Then I decided to switch from empirical methods to calculations. These showed that the temperature which was created in the compressor chamber, where the final stage of compression took place, could not be withstood by either tin or lead. But what if the pressure were reduced a little? Apparently, tin withstands pressure up to 120 atmospheres. We might still be able to manage with air at such a pressure.

The attention of the entire crew was now riveted on the seventh compartment. Here Leading Seaman 2nd Class G.F. Petrov was turning a lid coated with welded tin on the lathe. Chief Leading Seaman Ivan Vasilievich Kononov, the head of the compartment, had blocked the hatchway with his gigantic form and none of the would-be spectators could get in. Petrov coped with the task magnificently. Late at night he handed the lid, still warm from the cutting, to Petty Officer Kazakov, who began to reassemble the portside compressor along with engine room crewmen Kopylov and Karpov. We checked it. We cranked it up and started it running on idle through the distributor. It worked.

'Connect up the empty group!' I gave the order and was aware myself that my voice was trembling. Thirty minutes later the pressure in the cylinders had risen to twenty-five atmospheres; an hour later – to fifty atmospheres. 'Stop!' I shouted, drowning out the din of the compressor.

At that very moment came an enquiry from the control room: 'What happened?'

'Everything is all right. We will dismantle the lid to make sure.'

We took the lid off and examined it. It was holding together. We took the pressure up to 100 atmospheres. The lid held. We pumped it up to 130 atmospheres. We dismantled the compressor once more. In two places the tin had started to melt, which meant we'd overdone it.

'You can't bamboozle theory,' I said to Petty Officer Kazakov and I gave orders that the pressure should not rise above 110 to 115 atmospheres. The compressor functioned to the very break of day, replenishing the stock of compressed air, without which a submarine turns into a substandard surface ship. Only after this did I report to the Captain that the compressor had been restored to use and that we could continue with our combat operations.

I rapidly shaved, washed, put on my 'best' uniform jacket and did the rounds of the compartments, to thank all those who had taken part in the repair of the compressor. I still had enough strength left to get as far as my bunk where I collapsed. Three days and nights without sleep is enough to flatten anyone.

Three Victories

Roaming over our assigned quadrant underwater, we began with ever-increasing frequency to hear strange noises in the water. We racked our brains for a long time as to what it might be. Eventually we worked it out. It was the Germans sweeping the whole extent of the 20-metre contour line with hydro-acoustic anti-mine sweeps. The impressive number of ships which the enemy had lost during the summer of 1942 had forced him to strengthen not only his anti-submarine, but also his anti-mine defences – once bitten, twice shy. So the Germans were doggedly sweeping the sea with ordinary, magnetic and acoustic sweeps. We rejoiced in the successes of our friends, for arousing such fear among the Nazis. And we envied them. The fact of the matter was that we still did not have a single victory to our credit.

We dived at dawn on 21 October abeam of the Pape Lighthouse. Right up until sunset not one of the officers on watch had had the good fortune to spot a freighter or an enemy convoy.

I came into the control room, in order to change places with Petty Officer Kazakov, for whom it was time to start getting our precious compressor ready. We had already got used to the fact that the pressure in our cylinders was lower than normal, and experienced no unease on that account. Only two pressure gauges in the control room were showing 200 atmospheres as they used to. These were the so-called 'captain's' group of cylinders, whose air was expended only in exceptional circumstances, on the direct order of the ship's captain himself.

Senior Lieutenant Ryzhkov was standing watch. He had just come up to periscope depth, in order to scan the sea. The horizon was clear.

Ilyin came in, asking for the periscope to be raised once more – he needed to take a bearing on the lighthouse. Having fixed the boat's position, Ilyin began to examine the horizon out of curiosity. To port it was empty but, having turned the periscope to starboard, the Divisional Navigator froze and then shouted out: 'Smoke! Report to the Captain!'

I felt a slight tremor under my heart; the way it happens to an angler, when he sees the float begin to bob in the water from a bite. The Captain came running in. Peering into the periscope, he gave his orders: 'Comrade Ilyin, adjust our position for an attack, taking into account the depths hereabouts. And do it so that we can manage to hold the position until darkness falls.' The Navigator bent over his table. A few moments later he invited the Captain over to the chart.

'See, here is probably the most suitable spot. The enemy will reach here at 18.00 hours precisely. At that time there will still be excellent visibility.

'Good,' the Captain approved and added, turning towards Bogdanov:

'Warn Leading Seaman 1st Class Zviagin that he will be manning the hydroplanes.'

'The Bosun will be offended.'

'He is not well. Let him stay in the fourth compartment.'

'But . . .'

'Do as I say,' Turayev cut in calmly.

The composition of the convoy became clearer: three freighters under the protection of a patrol boat, a minesweeper and two big motor launches. The Captain decided to attack with the stern tubes, which the leading torpedoman, I.V. Kononov, was warned about in good time.

The 'Torpedo attack!' signal pealed out. The submarine did a slow underwater U-turn, settling on the combat course. I was keeping my eye on Zviagin. He was noticeably strung up, but he was working well, the boat was moving along evenly. At 18.00 hours the Captain gave the signal to the torpedomen. 'Torpedo away!' announced Chief Leading Seaman Kononov. And, indeed, we felt a powerful recoil. The Captain raised the periscope again, in the nick of time. Simultaneously with the explosion we heard his joyful exclamation: 'Explosion in the bridge area!'

The Captain yielded his place to Commissar Ponomaryov, and then to Loshkariov. 'That's it! She's gone down!' confirmed Loshkariov.

The Captain took over the periscope again. At 18.12 hours he once more gave the order: 'Fire!' Another freighter's turn. On the patrol boat they had obviously spotted the track of the second torpedo. The enemy ship dashed furiously in our direction. We got under way using both electric motors, thanks to the boat having turned around in the sea and the depths here being suitable. We listened tensely – but no, the torpedo explosions never came.

At 18.30 hours the first depth charge crashed down behind the stern. The explosion was fairly close, but did not pose a danger for us. Seventeen minutes later there was a new explosion from behind and slightly to starboard; by now a considerable distance away, which meant that we had evaded the pursuit.

The Captain, smiling broadly, came down the ladder into the control room. Everyone there rushed up to him, stretched out to shake his hand, to congratulate him. 'Let's swing the Captain up!' someone shouted. 'Now, now, we're still on alert!' warned the Captain. However, he needn't have worried. It was so cramped in the control room that with the best will in the world you wouldn't have been able to swing a man in it.

We stood down from action stations. The Captain and the

Commissar made their way to the seventh compartment, to thank the torpedomen.

The sailors were larking about like children. Off the cuff, someone had already composed a fairly scabrous little ditty: 'To Akmenraki Light we come, and boot the Jerries up the bum . . .' Ilyin was indignant. His navigator's penchant for accuracy could not be reconciled with that kind of poetic licence. 'We sank the freighter by the Pape Lighthouse. And there is no such thing as the Akmenraki Light. It is the Akmenrags Lighthouse!' But no one was listening to him. The ditty had gone winging through the compartments. 'Don't upset yourself,' I calmed my friend down. 'Let the lads have their bit of fun.' It must be said that the little ditty was swiftly forgotten. Such is the very nature of art; it, too, does not tolerate any deviation from the truth.

We roamed the sea for another week. We had calculated the consumption of fuel and lubricants. There was not all that much left in reserve. At night we worked on the upper deck, fastening down everything that we could, because after the bombardments, when we were cruising submerged, our outer hull had begun to rumble like a cart going over potholes.

In response to a request from the medic, the seamen were allowed to wash themselves in warm water. The water-distiller worked throughout the night for this purpose. It wasn't such a great 'bath' – three litres per man, but, on the other hand, it was not just ordinary water, but distilled water. The lads absolutely deserved such a comfort, and Petty Officer Kazakov and I felt in generous mood.

On 27 October, as usual, we were resting during the daytime. The klaxon woke us up. Torpedo attack!

Five seconds later I was already in my appointed place under the lower conning-tower hatch, replacing Sorokin. Bulgakov who, at the sound of the alarm, had been transformed from officer of the watch into gunnery and torpedo officer, before running off to the first compartment, whispered loudly in my ear: 'Five huge freighters on the move. Heavily protected. Brace yourself, Viktor Yemelianovich, it will be a real war!'

I turned back towards the bilge trimming pump, to give the order to level up the trim a bit, and I caught sight of Able Seaman

Zmienko. Having guessed that I would set about throwing him out of the control room straight away, he forestalled me: 'The Petty Officer said I could. The bandages will not hamper me. Let me stay at my action station.'

There was no time to argue, so I gave him the order: 'Use the natural flow from outboard to put fifty litres into the bow trimming tank; and into the number one stabilizing tank – a hundred litres.'

I watched the sailor manipulate with his burnt hand; just a blur of bandages. Well, I thought, Kuznetsov's manganese lotion has helped wonderfully, whereas I had always heard before that burns were slow to heal.

The Captain's voice reached us from the conning tower: 'Write down in the log: "Protective screen: a patrol boat, two minesweepers and two escorting motor launches."'

The submarine dived to the maximum possible depth for the shallow waters thereabouts. As before, we maintained a speed of four knots. Soon one of the escorting motor launches passed by behind the stern.

Hydrophone operator Leading Seaman 2nd Class Syomin was constantly reporting the whereabouts of the enemy ships. So far we were closing on them blindly. The patrol boat rushed by above us at high speed, evidently having noticed something suspicious.

'Speed three knots!' the Captain ordered and for a few carefully calculated seconds stuck the periscope up in the foam left in the wake of the patrol boat. A huge motor vessel with a displacement of 15,000 tons was selected for attack.

We reduced our speed to two and a half knots. It was very difficult to steer the ship at that speed. But it was all right, everything was working normally. It showed that the trim was perfect. The noise of a ship's propellers distinctly reached our ears. Time stood still, the hands on the clocks didn't move.

'Speed two knots!'

'Comrade Captain, at this speed I won't be able to hold the boat steady after the salvo,' I said.

'We're only four cables away. We don't have room for more speed. Do everything possible . . . Fire!'

'Start the pump in the bow trimming tank! Prepare bow tanks for diving!'

'Torpedo away!'

Time: 14.35.

'One degree to port. Fire!'

'Torpedo away!'

Time: 14.36. I just had time to catch my breath and yelled in a voice not my own: 'Fill the rapid-diving tank!' Zmienko hastily switched the valves over. Petty Officer Kazakov dashed over to help him. The depth was by then less than six metres. In spite of all the steps that had been taken, the boat's lightened bow lifted upwards. 'Hard a-port!' reached my ears from the conning tower, amid the roar of the air that was bursting into the compartment from the rapid-diving tank. 'All ahead half!'

The noise of the air rushing into the control room was replaced by the gurgling of water. It was streaming into the hull, flooding the bilges. I deliberately allowed it to make the submarine heavier, but the circular movement and the two-torpedo salvo combined to create a stern trimming moment. Operating at half speed accelerated the upward thrust of the submarine towards the surface.

I mistakenly took an enormously powerful hydraulic blow on the starboard side for a depth charge exploding, but I realized at once that there were no enemy ships close to us. 'The motor vessel is sinking!' shouted the Captain from the conning tower.

Lev Alexandrovich Loshkariov seeing that, according to the depth-gauge, the submarine had risen to three metres raised the second anti-aircraft periscope at the exact same moment that a second explosion thundered out.

'There is a second one sinking too!' yelled Loshkariov.

For a good ten seconds all the harmony and coordination of the crew's actions was shattered by triumphant exclamations and joyful laughter. But I didn't feel like breaking into raptures. The boat had finally gone towards the depths. The trim was slowly shifting to the bow. The depth-gauge needle was creeping inexorably to the right. On the six-metre mark I ordered: 'Stop the pump! Blow the rapid-diving tank!'

In the conning tower they lowered both periscopes. With considerable effort I managed to hold the boat steady two metres from the bottom. Our underwater speed was brought up to six knots. You could hear how all the ships of the escort were rushing to the place where only recently our conning tower had been jutting up from the surface of the sea, with its periscopes sticking up like two telegraph poles.

But it was not so easy for the Nazis to pull themselves together after the destruction of two of their ships, which went to the bottom in the space of a single minute. The first depth charges did not rumble behind our stern until twelve minutes had elapsed since our salvo. We counted forty-three depth charges in all. This was substantially more than had been launched at us in the anti-submarine nets in the Kalbådagrund area in September. But right now these explosions didn't scare us: the enemy had lost our boat and soon called off the pursuit.

And then the Captain got it into his head that a single torpedo was not enough for a motor vessel of 15,000 tons. She had to be finished off.

At 16.15 hours we again turned towards the Akmenrags Lighthouse. Lieutenant Captain Loshkariov armed himself with a camera, in order to photograph the results of our work. A considerably softened Vasili Andrianovich invited each of us to look through the periscope. We had come so much closer that with five-fold magnification it was already possible to get a good view of the motor vessel lying on the coastal rocks. Not far from her, the funnel and masts of the 10,000-ton freighter were sticking up out of the waves.

While we were admiring this scene, we were very nearly punished for our curiosity. When there remained no more than seven or eight cables to the motor vessel, an escorting motor launch leapt out from behind her half-submerged superstructure at full speed. She rushed at our raised periscope. Grasping the situation instantly, the Captain ordered us to dive and to take the opposite course. The launch did not pursue us for long and did not throw off a single depth charge. The ratings were cracking jokes on this account: they said we were pressing so closely to the bottom at full submerged speed that we were throwing stones up from the seabed to the surface with our screws, and that it was this that was preventing the launch from getting close to us.

Joking aside, I think that the launch simply had nothing left to throw at us – she had used up all her depth charges earlier on – otherwise she would have shown us by now where the crayfish go in wintertime . . .

We never did manage to finish off the enemy motor vessel, but nature herself took care of the matter. The rising gales dealt such final blows to the wrecked ship that we did not have to use up an additional torpedo.

Sinking three big ships on one patrol was an excellent outcome. But we couldn't wait to increase our combat tally. Over and over again we ploughed the sea. But fortune had turned her back on us: nothing else came our way.

On 7 November, the day that nowadays commemorates the October Revolution, we received the order to return to base. We took a northern course. Both diesels were operating on propeller-charging. In spite of the stepped-up ventilation of the battery, there was a strong smell of sulphuric acid in the compartments. I went up to the bridge to breathe in some fresh air. The night was so dark that, no matter how hard I looked, I could not even make out the bow of our ship. 'Lookouts! Don't shelter from the wind! Keep your eyes peeled!' Hearing this stern yell from the First Lieutenant, I couldn't help smiling. Just you try to make something out in this!

All of a sudden a powerful blow shook the boat. She tilted sharply to port. Further blows could be heard beneath the keel, heading towards the stern, then the boat began to vibrate: the screws had been affected as well. We peered over the side – total darkness, impossible to make anything out. I jumped down into the control room, gave the order through the voice-pipe: 'Fore! Aft! Look around in the compartments!' The Captain hurtled on to the bridge. On his heels Loshkariov came running. Before climbing up the ladder, learning that I had only just come down from the bridge, he asked: 'What did we run into?'

'There was nothing to be seen. A patrol boat, perhaps?' Lev Alexandrovich shook his head disbelievingly. 'To tilt the boat to that extent, what would the displacement of a motor boat have to be? Do you remember, back before the war, *S-101* accidentally ran into a Finnish sailing-boat, with a cargo of salt? She had a displacement of 500 tons. There was no listing at all. But even on the bridge there were splinters.'

'Perhaps there might be splinters on our deck, too?'

'We'll check it straight away.'

Loshkariov climbed up onto the bridge. Viktor Sorokin, my

assistant, came into the control room at the double: 'Everything is all right in the aft compartments. I'm afraid that the screws have suffered. The portside screw in particular has begun to howl a bit. What was it? What do you reckon?'

'I don't know.'

Lieutenant Captain Loshkariov came down from the bridge. He said that they had checked the whole of the upper deck. They hadn't found anything anywhere. 'We should go back and do a sweep round with a searchlight; we might pick someone up, perhaps. Then it would be clear who it was we sank,' I suggested.

'Not on your life! That way we would shine so much light that someone would take the opportunity to ram us themselves.'

'For some reason I have the impression that it was a submarine . . .'

'Could be.' An anxious Captain, coming down from the bridge, put a stop to this conversation: 'Guesswork is pointless. Our results are not bad as it is. Let's not ascribe this mythical submarine to ourselves as well.'

But I was to recall this conversation again many years later. A list of the German submarines sunk in the Baltic came into my possession. *U-272* featured among them; she sank following a collision in November 1942, possibly on that selfsame night that we experienced the impact, as a result of which one and a half metres of our forged stem was torn out.

Antenna Mines

On 8 November we crossed the northern edge of our latest patrol area and headed for the Ristna Lighthouse at full speed, because the Captain assumed that the Nazis would turn it on for their own ships in the stormy weather.

The rolling was brutal. At one point a huge wave enveloped the whole of the aft superstructure; the diesel, having sucked water into two cylinders, stopped dead. It took Leading Seaman 1st Class Dogonov's engine-room crew two hours to get it started again.

The fierce northerly winds brought the cold with them. The curtains of rain were abruptly replaced by snow flurries. It never stopped raining inside the submarine either: moisture, condensing on the deckhead, fell on us in big, cold drops. The bedclothes were damp. The woollen blankets didn't keep us warm any more. 'Papanin's team in the Arctic had it ten times better than this,' complained Loshkariov, pulling on his hat with ear-flaps and his kapok jacket, before lying down on his bunk.

The electric heaters, turned on in the first and the seventh compartments – the coldest ones – didn't help very much, and the sailors were literally shivering with cold. On top of that, our rations had grown meagre, too. The provisions were coming to an end. We had been without porridge and sugar since as far back as 20 September, after the bombardment off Suursaari, when all our reserves were found to be waterlogged. And it is well known that a hungry man feels the cold more intensely.

I ordered all the heaters to be distributed to the end compartments. It was still more or less bearable in the second and the fourth compartments: they were warmed by the batteries and by the various appliances burning the hydrogen emitted by the batteries.

The cosiest of our compartments was now held to be the sixth; the electric-motor compartment. Earlier on, everyone had fled from there because it was too hot. But now everyone off watch clustered in it. It was the only compartment whose ceiling didn't drip.

And the famous 'King of England's fur coat' had made its appearance in the control room. This was the name given to the detachable beaver-lamb lining of Lieutenant Captain M.I. Bulgakov's raglan, which he removed because he couldn't get the raglan on over his kapok jacket. It was extremely warm in this fur lining and the water droplets sparkled like diamonds on its satiny-black surface in the bright light of the control room. 'Even the King of England never in his life went around in such a stylish fur coat!' said Mikhail Ivanovich Bulgakov, giving out this treasure for the general use of the officers on watch. The 'King of England's fur coat' was handed on from watch to watch, and its temporary possessor was the envy of all.

We came up to the Ristna Lighthouse. We waited in vain for it to be lit. Having pottered about in this area for a whole hour, we decided to head for the Tahkuna Lighthouse. It was really essential for us to fix our position.

I went up onto the bridge. Waves were tumbling over the

conning-tower shield with a roar, drenching all who happened to be on the bridge with icy spray. Now and then the moon would break out from behind the black clouds. Then the sea would be absolutely dreadful to see: all seething and frothing. 'A hundred and forty degrees to port – enemy submarine,' reported a signalman, in a voice straining against the wind.

The moon lit up a low, black silhouette. The boat passed by on the opposite course from ours. It was a smaller boat than ours, and was being shaken about even more roughly than we were. 'In a sea like this, neither one of us can do the other any harm,' said Vasili Andrianovich calmly.

Twenty minutes later the flashing lights of the lighthouse came into view. The navigators applied all their expertise to fix our position accurately. The Captain allowed the boat to be turned head-on to the waves for a while, taking advantage of the safe channel through which the enemy submarine had only just passed. The rolling diminished somewhat and the navigators were able to take the bearings with tolerable accuracy. After that we immediately submerged: the rolling had exhausted everyone.

At 13.00 hours on 11 November the Navigator reported that the spot where we got stuck in the nets on 22 September was off the port beam. Animatedly we called to mind the difficult hours that we went through at that time. We remembered them jokingly. Past disasters are soon forgotten. The tragic things disappear from the memory, while the comic things remain and are remembered for a long time. Submariners are incurable optimists.

At 14.00 hours near the island of Naissaar, eight miles from Tallinn, the Captain decided to come up to periscope depth, to fix our position. The collision in the night was still telling on the propellers and now, even with the electric motors making exactly the same number of revolutions, the boat was developing a different speed. In connection with this, the Navigator had to introduce a correction into his calculations, otherwise it would have been impossible to guarantee the accuracy of the courses plotted.

The visibility was excellent; the Captain was even able to make out a herd of cows on the shore through the periscope. But he also saw something else: two Arado seaplanes were circling in the sky. 'Take her down to sixty metres!' he ordered without hesitation, lowering the periscope.

I went over to the navigator's table and had a look at the chart over Sasha Ilyin's shoulder. The depth here was eighty metres. That suited us fine, we could hide further away from the surface our loosening, rumbling 'externals', as Bosun Balakirev called the ship's superstructure, as distinct from its 'internals' – the contents of the compartments. This area also had two other advantages. First, the enemy did not lay seabed mines at depths of over fifty metres; and second, it was easier at such depths to manoeuvre between the cables of electro-contact mines. But there was one consideration that we had failed to take into account and we soon paid dearly for that.

Having satisfied ourselves that everything in the control room was as it should be, Vasili Andrianovich and I went to the officers' mess to warm ourselves up with some tea. This was something we did often nowadays. But as we had had no sugar since the first day of the patrol, we used raisins instead.

The orderly, Danilin, gave us each a glass of scalding tea and a few rather damp raisins on a saucer. Unhurriedly we sipped the burning-hot, faintly yellowish liquid (we had to be economical with the tea as well) and discussed our affairs.

An explosion of shocking force threw me up to the deckhead, then down onto the deck, and piled furniture on top of me: there was total darkness in the compartment. Icy streams were lashing in whirlwinds of roaring air, bursting out from the damaged main, sweeping fragments of lampshades and crockery from the deck.

Floundering in the streams of water pouring from the deckhead, I quickly satisfied myself that, apart from bruises, I had suffered no other damage. Spluttering and groping around with my hands, I found the valve and shut off the high-pressure air main. The roaring ceased. There was the sound of frightened exclamations all around, which I had difficulty making out through the bells ringing in my ears.

Bumping into the overturned furniture, we rushed to the control room. Turayev, drenched from head to toe, ran into the room the same time as me.

There was semi-darkness in the control room. Beneath the constant downpour gushing from the deckhead, Sorokin, Kopylov and Bulgakov were closing the valves that had come open and the ventilation-shaft mushrooms. I switched on the emergency lighting. My first glance was at the depth-gauge. Having lost all her way, the submarine was slowly sinking to the bottom.

From the first compartment they reported water coming in. Having opened the bulkhead hatch from the fourth compartment, Leading Seaman 2nd Class Vasiliev also reported that the compartment was filling with water. I gave a general order: 'Block up the holes! Prepare the compartments for drainage!' And I myself, with the Captain's permission, ran to the electric-motor compartment. She had to be got under way – at any cost; even with only one of the electric motors. Otherwise – certain death!

In the fourth compartment water was pouring in a broad swathe from the warped upper hatch. It was sparkling frighteningly in the rays of the one light that had remained intact in the far corner. You could have imagined that a real waterfall was flowing inside the boat. The ratings were toiling in the compartment, dragging in the emergency-rescue equipment. I ordered Vasiliev to look sharp and let the water out into the fifth compartment's bilges, so that it didn't spill over the batteries.

In the electric-motor compartment, in the aisle between the main propulsion stations, the detachable casings of the knife-switches and the armature cut-outs were lying in a heap. Petty Officer A.V. Lavrikov, in charge of the electricians' group, was lying belly-down on the deck, his head and shoulders inside the opened casing of the starboard main propulsion motor's manifold. In a similar position, Seaman A.V. Denisov, an electrician, was tinkering about inside the port electric motor.

The electrical measuring instruments were in the most lamentable state. Some of them were hanging helplessly on their wire; others had been smashed to smithereens. Broken glass crunched underfoot. Hearing my footsteps, Petty Officer Lavrikov raised his head: 'The armature cut-outs failed,' he reported, 'the brushes went out of whack.'

'Have you reinstalled them yet?'

'Yes, sir!'

'Keep an eye on the armature, I will try to get her under way. Be careful.' I turned on a knife-switch. I rotated the handwheel of the shunt rheostat. In vain! The armature of the electric motor didn't budge. 'Check the first group's automatic battery controls!'

126

I gave the command to the control room. I turned on the knife-switches once more.

'It's rotating!' rejoiced Lavrikov. This was already excellent. The boat hadn't even had time to lose her momentum and now she had got some way on again. I reported this to the Captain and went over to the port propulsion station, pushing aside the casings with my feet. Here, too, switching on the automatic controls and the knife-switches produced no results to begin with. I had to give instructions for the second group's automatic battery controls to be switched on. Once more I did the switching over. There were sounds of clanking, screeching, grating. I folded back the handles of the knife-switches. We took a look, to see what the matter was. It turned out that a protective casing that had broken loose from its place had got squeezed between the shaft and the side. We prised it out using crowbars and sledgehammers. Torpedoman Fedorenko, Helmsman Komarovsky and Gunner Krylov really put their backs into it. They pulled out the warped plates. Now the second electric motor was rotating unimpeded too.

The ratings were restoring order to the compartment, so I hurried off to the control room. Ilyin and Bogdanov were tipping water off the charts. Leading Seaman 2nd Class K.P. Komissarov, a navigational electrician, and Petty Officer I.A. Kazakov were rigging up something rather like an awning, to protect the navigator's table from the water. The rain in the compartment was ceaseless: almost all the rivets around the perimeter of the conning tower were loose.

In the second compartment the detachable plate for loading the batteries had vibrated; in two places a gasket had been dislodged. Leading Seaman 2nd Class M.S. Malakhov and Seaman N.K. Danilin, directed by the medic G.Y. Kuznetsov, had suspended a piece of oilcloth and a canvas hammock on some bandages. Water was streaming through the open bulkhead hatch, down the makeshift gutter into the first compartment's bilges, although there was no lack of water in them without this extra. In the first compartment the recess of the torpedo-loading hatch had been forced out of shape. The leakage there was comparatively minor, but it was powerfully disturbing for the ratings in the prevailing darkness. The bilge trimming pump, the upper part of whose engine-bed had cracked in two places and whose ammeter was out of order, was nevertheless managing to cope with the water entering the pressure hull. Both groups of batteries, including the tanks that we had glued together, had withstood the blow. And the force of that blow could already be judged from the fact that we counted thirteen dents in the pressure hull's 20mm-thick plating!

But everything seemed to be well in hand now. Having calmed down a bit, we began to speculate as to what, after all, had actually happened. We reached a unanimous opinion: the boat had struck an antenna mine. This is a treacherous device: it hangs in the water, with its slender tentacles – its antennae – spread out. A boat just barely grazes against them and the mine explodes.

We had not had time to gather ourselves together when our boat was again flung downwards and sideways with such force that not a single man in the control room was able to stay on his feet. I was hurled onto the main drainage pump. How I managed not to break my neck and ribs on the numerous valves and levers of the water mains, I marvel to this day.

No more than an hour had passed since the first explosion. The ratings, busy struggling with the damage and with the water entering the pressure hull, had not even had a chance to change into dry underwear. Everything still in one piece jangled, smashed and split apart. Everything not yet smashed to pieces fell down and broke. Virtually the whole episode was repeated all over again, except that the emergency lighting didn't go off. We could hear large mine fragments falling on the upper deck with a noise like thunder. The next mine cable in line was moving along the plating, clanking; it caught on some protruding parts, stretched tight with a clanging noise and, having pulled itself loose, trailed along the ship's hull once more.

The submarine had lost all her way again, but this time she didn't sink. She was trimmed to zero buoyancy, and the incoming water was constantly being pumped out.

In the fourth compartment the upper hatch had again vibrated out of position, but this time it had been dislodged to the other side, and the flow of water had stopped.

In the sixth compartment all the knife-switch and armature cut-out casings had flown off again. Petty Officer Lavrikov was checking the brushes. Without having to be prompted, the leaders of the electricians' groups had switched on the automatic battery controls.

We got under way using the port main electric propulsion motor, then the starboard one. Everyone said that the explosion this time was weaker than the first. But that was not much of a consolation. The gyrocompass had been put out of action. The electrical measuring instruments that had escaped destruction until now had broken down. The fuel tank inside the pressure hull had cracks in two places, and the replacement water (the fuel had come to an end) was leaking from it into the battery pit. The Bosun was complaining that the boat had begun to respond sluggishly to the hydroplanes.

We forged straight ahead, using conspicuous depths as points of reference. We chose a relatively shallow place and at 15.47 hours we settled on the bottom.

Bogdanov and Komissarov set about repairing the gyrocompass. Having instructed Sorokin to watch the battery like a hawk, I accompanied Petty Officer Lavrikov to search for a suitable ammeter to fit on the bilge trimming pump. We dismantled the ammeter from the distiller for this purpose and the gyrocompass was successfully repaired.

We officers had commandeered the leading seamen's mess again. Having spread the wet chart out on the big table, Turayev, Loshkariov and Ilyin were bent over it. They were attempting to solve an insoluble problem – what the position of the field of antenna mines was, given that we had already been blown up on them twice. Could we possibly be blown up again?

At 19.00 hours we lifted off from the bottom and continued on our way. I was not leaving the control room any more now. The leading seamen and the ratings were also all at their action stations and were putting all their efforts into restoring order to them, making things fast, clearing away the shards of glass, smartening up or simply tying up this or that instrument with emergency binding wire, just to prevent it from dangling.

I was watching over the propellers as though they were the apple of my eye. It would have been easier than ever to damage them now, given that the boat was going along with a predominantly stern-down trim, in order to have at least the opportunity of an increase in speed to change the depth of the dive. The bilge trimming pump was constantly getting blocked up, because the water, working its way through all the crannies in the bilges, was scouring them out, carrying the filth and rubbish along with it. Every ten minutes we stopped the pump, took it apart, cleaned it out and put it back together again.

The Captain, shaking his head in dismay, said to me: 'We are going to have to go along in this manner for at least another three hours.'

'I am afraid that making a noise with the pump the whole way we will attract the enemy's attention.'

'That's what I'm afraid of, too. But we cannot possibly surface.'

Clutching the ladder with my numb hands and wobbling on my buckling and aching legs, I clenched my teeth, to stop them from chattering: I felt feverish. The sea water, like acid, was eating away at the countless cuts and scratches on my body. I realized that I was not the only one in such a state. The Bosun had also worn himself to a shred. There had already been more than one occasion when he had been unable to hold the boat with the rudders, and she had fallen to the stony seabed, scraping the hull.

Five hours had passed since the first explosion. According to Turayev's and Ilyin's calculations, we had already passed the far edge of this newly-discovered enemy minefield of ours.

At last the Captain allowed us to come up to thirty-five metres. The rain in the control room slackened at once: the outboard pressure had decreased. It had become easier to hold the boat on an even keel. It was now no longer necessary to start the pump so often to drain the bilges.

Darkness had fallen over the sea. It was raining. We decided to surface.

'Blow central ballast!' Petty Officer Kazakov rotated the valve handwheels. So far everything was proceeding normally. Just one of the outboard valves jammed. With difficulty they managed by hand to get it just halfway open.

The diesel had been started to blow the main ballast. But now something unexpected occurred. For a while the boat lay there, rolling on an even keel, and then she heeled over to port, ever more so with each passing moment, in spite of Petty Officer Kazakov's efforts to right her by blowing the side ballast tanks.

Four minutes later the listing ceased. We began to correct it a little at a time.

Having summoned Sorokin to the control room, with the Captain's permission I was concentrating on charging the battery. This was not such a simple matter now, because we had almost no measuring instruments left. I set up extra working positions in the battery pits. I ordered the ratings not only to watch attentively, but also to be on the alert for smells. This constituted a problem too, at the time, since almost all of us had blocked-up noses from colds in the head and it was easier for us to sneeze ten times than to identify a smell just once.

Petty Officer Lavrikov hung on the instrument panel a portable voltmeter with a range of 300 volts, the only undamaged one that we had. Using it, we measured alternately the voltage of the generators, then of the battery. With the utmost caution we switched on the knife-switches. With equal caution the engine room crew loaded the diesels. The machinery yielded reluctantly to the crew's persistence and, having put up a token resistance, surrendered. The charging began.

When everything had settled back into its normal routine, chains of ratings hauled pails and old ship's-biscuit tins filled to the brim with broken glass, rags, splinters and other rubbish from the compartments to the bridge.

And on the upper deck an absolutely crucial and dangerous job was being done. Leakage from a detachable plate in the second compartment had to be stopped. Planesmen A.N. Kopylov and P.A. Karpov crawled inside the superstructure, in order to tighten the nuts more securely. They were working in icy water and total darkness, knowing that, should the enemy appear, the boat would dive, not waiting for them to scramble out of the superstructure. They toiled away there for a whole two hours, until they had completed the task.

I gave way to our doctor's insistence and allowed the sailors to hang their wet things on the diesel exhaust manifolds. Soon the diesel compartment was filled with clouds of steam. 'Keep an eye on it; turn it over!' Leading Seaman 1st Class Dogonov urged. But, just the same, something managed to get a bit burnt. While the clothes were drying, our sailors looked like Iroquois, about to begin a ritual dance. Their bodies were painted with brown, yellow and green splotches. This was the handiwork of the medic Kuznetsov and his sickbay attendants. They didn't spare the iodine or the green ointment when treating cuts and scratches, which each one of us now had in abundance.

At 06.00 hours the signal for emergency diving sounded: the signalmen had made out the silhouette of an enemy ship in the pre-dawn haze. We opened the outboard valves. Everything went normally but, again, one of the valves failed to open. The bow of the boat was submerged, while the stern was sticking up on the surface. Now our ship looked like an inflated frog: its head underwater and its rear end quivering outside. It was not until the bow trim had increased to six degrees that the boat went deep.

During the daytime on 14 November we finally made it to the rendezvous point. A fresh disappointment awaited us there: there was no reply to our signals. There was no one to meet us.

'The Last of The Mohicans'

The sea was silent. We were waiting in vain for a signal from the ships meeting us. I heard the Captain ask the Commissar: 'What do you think we should do, Fyodor Alexeievich?'

'Let's surface, Captain. We'll have a look.'

'Stand by to surface!'

It was obvious from the erratic fluctuation of the depth-gauge needle that the sea was choppy on the surface. I put a request to the Captain: 'Vasili Andrianovich, let's surface to periscope depth first, find out the direction the sea is running. Otherwise we might lay the ship on her beam-ends. Added to which, you might get washed overboard.'

We rose. No matter how hard the Bosun tried to hold the boat at periscope depth, he was unable to. We were thrown up to the surface and lay with a list of some forty degrees to port. Without unsealing the upper conning-tower hatch, we turned into the wind. The listing ceased. We blew the central tank completely. Following the well-worn routine, I immediately began to fill the rapid-diving tank. Given the force of the thudding against the hull, you could tell that there was a heavy sea running.

The Captain opened the upper conning-tower hatch and

quickly went out onto the bridge. A torrent of spray flew into the control room. The sky was leaden-grey, with a fearfully low cloud base. Having tied the laces of my ear-flap hat under my chin, I clambered up the ladder. Lavansaari was really close at hand – about five miles away. But right up to the island there was no sea to be seen, just unending foam. I had never seen anything like it in the Baltic before. The wind was tearing off the crests of the waves, reducing them to powder and whirling them away over the boiling sea. The handrails of the conning-tower shield were howling with the strain. Suddenly a huge trough formed beneath the boat's stem, we scudded into this abyss, burying ourselves up to the conning tower in foam. No, this entertainment was not to my liking. Almost on my hands and knees, I made it to the hatchway and down into the control room. Hardly had I left the well of the conning-tower hatch when a waterfall surged into it. In a matter of seconds we had taken on board two or three tons of water. This flood almost knocked Loshkariov off his feet, while Petty Officer Kazakov hastily grabbed at the tap controlling the pneumatic drive of the upper conning-tower hatch's emergency sealing system, and the hatch very nearly shut itself.

The Captain came down from the bridge, wet through. He was gasping, shaking his head. Having barely got his breath back, he said: 'Take her down. We will lie on the bottom where we are. Well, it really is pandemonium up there! There's no way light surface ships could make it out of the harbour! They would sink in two shakes!'

We took on ballast. Six tons of negative buoyancy from the filling of the rapid-diving tank plus the three tons of water in the control-room bilges got us nowhere. The waves were holding the boat on the surface, preventing her from going deep. It was only after giving a boost with both electric motors that we were able to drive the bow beneath the water. Well, from then on it was the same old story: we couldn't hold her back. Before I could turn around, the depth was already eight metres. While we were blowing the rapid-diving tank and starting up the pump to drain the bilges, the boat settled smoothly on the bottom. It began to rain in the control room and in the first compartment: water was leaking through the loosened rivets.

Needless to say, there hadn't been time to ventilate the compartments. We switched on the air-regeneration system. I summoned Petty Officer Lavrikov and said to him: 'We won't manage to charge the battery today, so we will have to economize on the use of electricity. We will have to switch off all the heaters.'

It grew even colder. But the ratings were so exhausted that they would probably have fallen asleep even if they had been up to their necks in water. The ship was plunged into sleep; only those on watch wandered about, trying to warm themselves up, if only a little, by movement.

The following day we leapt out of our bunks at 11.55 hours, woken by Leading Seaman Metreveli's excited exclamation: 'Propeller noise, bearing two-four-zero!'

'Stand by to surface!' – the long-awaited signal reached us from the control room.

'Dit, dit, dit . . .' the Morse code cheeped from outboard. We surfaced. In the opening made by the folded-back upper conning-tower hatch, the autumnal Baltic sky loomed grey. Two submarine chasers had come to meet us. Under their escort we headed for the island harbour.

We moored at the pier. Already waiting for us, huddled up against the piercing wind, were the base commander, Captain Second Rank S.D. Soloukhin, Commissar S.S. Zhamkochian (who later became the head of the submarine brigade's political department) and various other officers.

After the greetings and congratulations, they told us that we would not be going to Kronstadt that day. We were to await the return of 'the last of the Mohicans', the minelaying submarine L-3, under the command of Pyotr Denisovich Grishenko. We would be allowed to lie at the pier at night, while during the day we would lie on the bottom. The enemy air force was not giving the island any peace.

The ratings had climbed all over the superstructure. They had carted to the pier a flattened lead lid, half of a mine's studded upper orifice, and two bucketsful of mine fragments as well. The officers were examining these material proofs of our ordeals with curiosity.

Our thoughtful island hosts provided us with newspapers and magazines. We fell on them avidly: we hadn't had them in our hands for two months, you see. Used to staying awake at night, we sat up reading the newspapers and magazines until six in the morning.

At dawn we went out beyond the harbour entry buoys and settled on the bottom at a depth of thirty-five metres. After having a meal, we composed ourselves for rest.

Sorokin woke me up at 14.00 hours. He announced that the fourth compartment was full of chlorine. I ran there, having snatched up a gas-mask. Only Leading Seaman 2nd Class I.N. Vasiliev, the electrician's section leader, was in the compartment. He was sitting there with his gas-mask on, casting uneasy glances into the hatchway. The batteries were flooded. Sea-water mingling with acid – electrolyte – gives off chlorine.

Sorokin gave me an account of how it had happened. The engine room mechanics had failed to notice that some rusty wire had got under the replacement valve in the fuel tank. While we were on the surface, the water was leaking inconspicuously, but when we dived the outboard pressure increased, and a fountain shot into the gap. They switched on the pump: it got blocked up. While they were removing the cotton waste that had got sucked into the pipe, while they were reassembling the mains, water had flooded the batteries. They had now stopped the leak, but there was no possibility of pumping the water away, since that would increase the production of chlorine. We decided to leave everything as it was until we surfaced, but to relieve the man on watch in the compartment every hour.

At 17.00 hours we surfaced, having previously pumped about three tons of outboard water from the battery pit. We tinkered with the battery until about two in the morning. It was all right, we managed to restore it to order. The charging went off normally. But in spite of the stepped-up ventilation, it still smelled of chlorine in the compartment for a long time afterwards.

During the afternoon of 18 November, while we were still lying on the bottom, some signalling could be heard. I thought that this was a call for us, and hurried to the control room. The Captain stopped me: 'Don't be in a hurry, Viktor Yemelianovich. That signal does not concern us. It is a call to *L-3*. It means that she has reached her destination safely.'

About three hours later we were called too. When we moored

at the pier, *L-3* was lying not far from the mooring wall. Having given orders for the battery to be charged, I went off to call on my friends. Near the moorings I met *L-3*'s first lieutenant, Lieutenant Captain Vladimir Konstantinovich Konovalov, and Lieutenant Captain Mikhail Andronikovich Krasteliov. We congratulated one another on our safe return. 'You can see what kind of a safe return we had,' Mikhail Andronikovich said to me, pointing to the periscope, which was bent and hanging with its full length over the deck.

My friends told me that they had been rammed by an enemy ship. The periscope standard had been turned through forty-five degrees. The captain's periscope had been bent and hung down perpendicular to the ship's side. It would have been impossible to sail amongst the minefields trailing such a 'sweep': all the mines would have got caught up in it. They had surfaced at night and with enormous difficulty, using block and tackle, they had twisted it round towards the stern. And thus they had sailed without periscopes.

I cast an eye over the boat. *L-3* was a minelaying submarine; a superb, mighty and beautiful ship. Before the war I sailed in one of the same type. Now she was unrecognizable. Her rusty side was entirely covered with dents and lacerations. I knew that inside the ship as well there would be few mechanisms that had not suffered the effects of bombardment. But her people had gone on fighting just the same. Two freighters were exploded and sunk by mines laid down by *L-3*.

We left Lavansaari at night with an escort of several ships. It was ten degrees below zero. Beyond Shepelevsky Lighthouse we began to encounter sludge ice and broken pack ice and, once past Tolbukhin Lighthouse, we found ourselves in ice five centimetres thick. The submarine chasers would not have been able to cope with it. *L-3* went first. She broke open a pathway with her mighty hull. The ice rang and grated beneath her stem. The remaining ships moved forward in *L-3*'s wake, stretched out in a long line.

The pier was full of people. It seemed as though all Kronstadt had turned out at this late hour to greet her returning submarines. The first into whose robust embrace I fell was Boris Dmitrievich

Andryuk. We were shaken by the hand, hugged tight, kissed clumsily, the way men do. I saw my friends' faces only dimly: it was dark and, on top of that, my eyes were filled with tears. I couldn't help it: it was freezing, after all!

Our boat was put in dry dock. It was only now, when she was completely out of the water, that we were able to see how badly she had been mauled. One and a half metres of her stem had been torn away, 'lock, stock and barrel'. Along the starboard side of her outer hull gaped a hole over three metres long and nearly two metres wide. It was clear now why the boat had been so liable to unexpected lists in recent times. We looked and we marvelled: how on earth had we managed to sail a ship in such a state?

The ship was in need of extensive repair. Work on her was already in full swing. Used to coping with anything, the dock-workers, assisted by the ratings, were replacing the plating, overhauling the machinery.

And people were in need of 'repair' too. I, for instance, weighed not more than fifty kilos after the patrol. We were all profoundly exhausted. And soon each of us in turn began to be sent to the Hospital for Convalescent Commanding Officers. It was housed in the State Optical Institute building on Vasilievsky Island, along-side the University. Winter was already established in the courtyard, but inside we found ourselves in a sort of tropical oasis. The corridors and wards were green with whole thickets of exotic plants. Bright flowers perfumed the air. There were rhododen-drons, philodendrons, agave, orchids and cacti. Shapely palm trees towered up. Where did they come from and how had they survived in besieged Leningrad?

It turned out that they had been brought there by research assis-tants from the Botanical Gardens. Half-dead from hunger and cold, these enthusiasts had personally brought these rare examples of tropical flora from the hothouses destroyed by bombs and shells, and they cosseted them as though they were pampered children.

A team of hospital doctors, under the direction of Medical Officer Second Rank Verigina, lavished attention and care on the submariners. They fed us with total generosity, to the extent that this was possible in the beleaguered city. I stayed in bed for two weeks, after which they allowed me to undertake modest strolls through the city.

In Leningrad the living was still hard. But the food situation had got a bit better. Enemy aircraft were visiting the city more rarely. Lenin's heroic city was gathering strength, to break the strangle-hold of the siege.

Chapter Four

DESPITE EVERYTHING,
WE WILL BREAK OUR WAY OUT!

A Spot of Leave

I was given permission to visit my family. On the morning of 27 December, a haulage truck took us, thirty submariners, to the aerodrome. A heavy bomber, a TB-3, was already waiting for us. We found places inside the roomy fuselage, where there were some three dozen crates, packed with 'ironmongery' of some kind: besieged Leningrad was producing more arms all the time and shared them generously with the other fighting fronts.

The aircraft was an old one, looking battle-worn. There was no glass in the windows. It was brutally cold inside the cabin. We settled ourselves somehow, wherever we could. I squeezed myself in between two packing-cases, close to a rectangular window. You could see everything from there, but such a ferociously icy blast was blowing that it made my eyes water.

The engines were started up, and we taxied to the runway. Flying low above us, almost hedge-hopping, fighter planes sped purposefully by, having taken off from an adjacent airfield. With the engines setting up a ponderous howl, we rose into the air and, without gaining further altitude, flew towards the north-east. Keeping us company, the 'little hawks' – I-16s – flew past in the opposite direction at an altitude of 500 metres and, executing a jaunty turn, overtook us once more.

Someone tugged at my leg. I saw Captain Third Rank A.I. Marinesko. He was saying something to me, but I couldn't hear him above the whine of the engines. Marinesko pointed to the window. I looked out. The fighter planes had increased in number;

by now there were a dozen and a half of them. They were whirling around like a carousel. I saw flashes. They were firing. There was a real dogfight going on! Our aircraft, having let off two long bursts of tracer fire, turned back in the opposite direction, hugging the ground even closer. We landed safely at the selfsame aerodrome. The flight had lasted about twenty minutes. We went off to make arrangements to stay overnight.

The next day everything repeated itself all over again. After this second attempt, a third of the passengers changed their minds about flying. After a third unsuccessful attempt, there remained fewer than half of us. When we took off for the fourth time, the only ones of us remaining were Roman Vladimirovich Lindenberg, Alexander Ivanovich Marinesko and Pavel Ivanovich Zamotin. After a successful touchdown at Novaya Ladoga, and following that an overnight stay at an aerodrome not far from Moscow, where the majority of the crates were unloaded, everything went well, if you discount the fact that Gorki wouldn't accept us and we were obliged to turn around and land at Ivanovo. Bad weather kept us there for several days.

Having satisfied ourselves that there was not so much as a sniff of flying weather, Lindenberg and I decided to get to Moscow by train. We saw in New Year 1943 lying in the upper berths of an overcrowded railway carriage. We said our goodbyes in Moscow. I got as far as Abdulino station, not far from Ufa, and went further on by cart. There was a real Siberian frost – fifty degrees below zero.

I spent four days in all with my family. The return journey was even more arduous, the temperature fell to fifty-six degrees below zero. It took me more than a week to reach Ladoga. The commandant found me a seat in the cab of a truck loaded with sacks of flour or grain. And we set out across the dazzlingly glittering snow. So this was it, the famous 'Road of Life'! On both sides of the track could be seen the wreckage of half-burnt vehicles; there were gaping holes in the ice and signs of aerial bombardment, carefully signposted. We drove past partly-submerged trucks. They were unloading them directly onto the snow. Special squads of soldiers were swarming around the trucks, trying to drag them onto the firm ice. Women traffic controllers in sheepskin coats and warm felt boots were silently displaying placards with figures and letters on them to the drivers. The drivers would nod their heads grate-fully and wave their hands affably. The sun was shining with all its might. At high altitude a German reconnaissance plane was suspended like a dot. And the endless stream of vehicles rumbled on and on along the ice road.

At Lake Ladoga station five heated goods vans were standing, hooked up to a tiny shunting engine. When the vans were full to overflowing, the train slowly got under way. We were taken as far as Piskaryovka, then had to continue the journey on foot. Deep in the night, having been stopped a countless number of times by vigilant patrols, I reached the floating base *Smolny*. When I at last found myself in my own cabin, I actually pinched myself to see if I was awake: the whole leave seemed like an agonizing and joyful dream. Only my legs aching with fatigue and the pain in my back from the injection – in Kabona everyone travelling to Leningrad was treated to some kind of serum – served as reminders that I had, after all, been away on leave.

We Are Blocked Up In the Gulf

I was appointed Engineer Officer to the 1st Division. A very mixed bag of ships was gathered there: *L-3* and *S-4*, in need of major repair; the minelaying submarine *Lembit*; *S-9*, *S-12*, *S-13* and *D-2*. Ratings were repairing the ships. There was a lot to do.

The floating base *Smolny*'s Engineer Officer, Georgi Petrovich Kulchitsky, complained to me: 'It's tough, Viktor Yemelianovich, there's no light at the end of the tunnel. Everything is a rush job, everything is urgent, it's all go-go-go, and we don't have the materials. We run around like lunatics from Russian Diesel to Electropower, to Northcable. We are not managing to cope with one thing; meanwhile something new is piling up. We have already mastered the vulcanization of electric cable, the welding of aluminium alloy castings, joinery work: things, in short, that our workshops have never had to deal with.'

The headquarters of the submarine brigade was relocated to Kronstadt. Under the cover of bad weather, we safely transferred *Smolny* there too.

My responsibilities were complicated by the fact that part of the division's boats lay at Kronstadt; the rest at Leningrad. And it was essential for me to visit both the one and the other. And the journey to Leningrad and back was not of the pleasantest. The enemy had the Sea Channel under bombardment the whole time.

Throughout the winter the ratings were making ready to put to sea. Meanwhile intelligence reports were bringing ever more disturbing news. Aerial photography, undertaken by reconnaissance planes, provided evidence that the enemy had closed off the whole of the Gulf of Finland with two or three rows of anti-submarine nets. We were constantly seeking ways to overcome them. But, as events proved, all our efforts were in vain. In 1943 we were never able to get out to the sea.

Fruitless attempts to do so cost us dear: we lost several submarines, amongst them *S-12*, in which I had sailed in the autumn of 1942. On that last patrol, the boat went out with a new commanding officer, Captain Third Rank A.A. Bashenko (V.A. Turayev had, at that time, been transferred to a different fleet). The entire crew perished. It took me a long time to get over it. I had become such good friends with those people, each of them had become like family to me. And now they were gone.

Submarines failing to return from patrol in 1943 were *P-408*, *P-406* and *S-9*. Only *P-303*, under the command of I.V. Travkin, managed to break out of the trap, after frightful ordeals.

To avoid further losses, General Headquarters issued an order that, until further notice, no submarines were to be sent into the Baltic. This was the beginning of an agonizing time for us. The whole country was at war. The siege of Leningrad had been broken, a great victory had been won at the Kursk Bulge, our troops had forced a crossing of the Dnieper and, with increasing success, were driving the enemy westwards, while we were 'sitting by the sea and waiting on the weather'.

Naturally, we were not sitting idle. With the help of the plant workers, the submariners were completing the construction of new boats. This was how the minelaying submarine *L-21* and the powerful underwater giants *K-51*, *K-52*, *K-53*, *K-54*, *K-55* and *K-56* had been completed.

The submarine *K-52* was put into commission as early as the summer of 1942, and in that same sailing season she successfully operated at sea. In this connection the fleet's political authorities issued a bulletin. It went as follows:

A splendid submarine has been constructed for the Baltic Red Banner Fleet by the workers. The ship was almost ready, but then war broke out. The submarine remained unfinished.

The submarine remained unfinished, but she had a crew on board, appointed, as is customary, while still in the construction stage. And this crew decided to finish the ship.

When the engineer officer, Captain Third Rank Alexander Petrovich Barsukov, spoke of this to the specialists at the plant, they shook their heads dubiously:

'It's an extremely complicated business.'

'So what? Let's give it a try!' Barsukov replied.

It was indeed a complicated business. But the acrid gunpowder smoke, drifting across the river, was a sufficient reminder of the nearness of the enemy. Not to mention the fact that Admiral S.O. Makarov had once said: 'the Russian sailor is at his most successful when tackling the unworkable.'

The enterprise required a great deal of electric welding work, but the necessary apparatus and instruments were lacking. The submariners managed to find these at the other end of the city. There was no means of transport to convey this equipment to the ship. The submariners divided it up, took it over to the tramway and moved it by hand. There were many turning jobs that had to be done. One of the plants put its disused turning shop at the submariners' disposition. But the workshop had been out of use for a long time, and both neglect and chill held sway there. The ratings had to restore the machine tools to working order. Captain Third Rank Barsukov did not leave the workshop for days on end. Under his direction the Baltic Fleet sailors got the neglected workshop up and running and overhauled the machine tools. Likewise under his direction, the submariners accomplished what was literally a jeweller's work, turning the most delicate of components.

What a wonderful pace this close-knit submarine crew kept up! Twelve months – that was the period projected for such a volume of work, according to the plant's normal pre-war work plan, assuming properly-equipped workshops and an abundance of materials. The splendid submariners brought their ship into commission four times quicker than normal – and they brought her into commission in the most difficult and complex conditions of a Leningrad besieged by the Nazis.

The submarine passed all prescribed trials. Passed them with flying colours! The Bolshevik doggedness of her glorious crew is a guarantee that the coming trials of war patrols too, in deadly

143

skirmishes with the enemy, will be passed outstandingly by the steadfast submariners.

The Military Council of the Baltic Red Banner Fleet awarded Captain Third Rank Alexander Petrovich Barsukov the Order of the Red Star. His most immediate assistants – Senior Lieutenant Yevgeni Ivanovich Semyonov and Chief Leading Seaman Pavel Petrovich Perevozchikov – were presented with medals for 'Military Merit'.

Submariners of the Baltic Fleet!

Your comrades-in-arms – Alexander Petrovich Barsukov, Yevgeni Ivanovich Semyonov, Pavel Petrovich Perevozchikov, and the other ratings, leading seamen and officers of the close-knit crew – have demonstrated that even the hardships of the siege are not obstacles for the leading lights of labour and military enterprise.

Match up to them, comrade submariners!

Prepare your ships for victorious battles!

After the lifting of the siege of Leningrad, we all breathed more freely. Now there was no longer hanging over us like the Sword of Damocles the threat of having ships sunk in the navigational channels between Leningrad and Kronstadt.

The clearance of the navigational channels began from the very first days of spring 1944. Our steam-tugs *Burbel* and *Figaro* began to make regular trips to Leningrad.

It was high time to think about a new training area for the ships. The K-class submarines were coming into operation. It was really difficult for them to sail in the 'Okhtenskoye Sea', as became obvious when one of these ships was pinned against a pier of the main span of the Liteiny Bridge by the current of the Neva.

We had just reached a decision to use the mouth of the Luga River as a training area. Then one evening, while the submarine *K-51* was undergoing speed trials there, a German submarine sneaked in. Fortunately, the enemy missed: the torpedoes passed by. But, after that incident, we put in no further appearances at the mouth of the Luga.

We began to sail in the Krasnaya Gorka Roads. Once I went out there on the minelaying submarine *L-21* with the new Divisional Commander, A.Y. Oryol. Night had fallen. With a long time to go until dawn, we submerged and lay on the bottom. In the morning the training began.

I went from compartment to compartment and I announced:

'First compartment holed on the starboard side! Second compartment deckhead holed! Third compartment battery on fire!' Wherever I passed, there 'fires' sprang up instantly or the pressure hull was 'penetrated by shell fragments'. The imitation smoke stung the eyes in no imaginary way, and water actually shot out from the improvised holes at a pressure of five atmospheres. It was no joke when the fire scorched people's arms, while the water struck them painfully in the face, making the sailors forget that these were merely holes rigged up for training purposes. It was hard going, but essential.

The ship's commanding officer, Captain Second Rank Sergei Sergeievich Mogilievsky, who had been in command of boats of a similar type back when I was sitting at a desk in college, needless to say had no need to be put to the test but, as Captain, he was delighted both with the complexity of the emergency exercises set and with the stringent requirements of divisional headquarters. With considerable satisfaction I noted that, although the boat's crew had been engaged in repair work for a long time, the sailors' high standard of training had been maintained. This showed the worth of an experienced commanding officer. Naturally, it didn't go off without some isolated rough patches, but there really isn't any large-scale activity that takes place without these.

Having spent the entire day submerged and having worked through all the set tasks, towards evening we surfaced. We cruised around in the Roads for a while longer, more than once checking the time it took to blow the main ballast. It is crucial to know this time, especially during the hours of darkness, when the boat surfaces blindly, in pitch-black conditions.

The signalmen reported the approach of a minesweeper. They sent a message from her by semaphore: sailing was forbidden in this sector. Apparently, the duty officer for the Kronstadt sea-defence area had mistakenly given our submarine the go-ahead, without first checking the situation as he should have. In the area where we had been lying on the bottom, a magnetic mine had been detected, whose pulse-count, according to the minesweeper captain's data, was reaching its limit. 'How many runs do you have left to do before it explodes?' the Divisional Commander enquired.

'Three or four. We can't tell exactly.'

The minesweeper, having lowered her magnetic sweep, got under way. We hastened to withdraw from that area. The following day, the divisional minelayer, Lieutenant Captain D.D. Vinnik, told me that on the very first run the day before, the minesweeper had activated a seabed mine in the very spot where we had been proceeding before that.

The Finnish Skerries

In September 1944 Finland withdrew from the war. We were all delighted to hear this. Our submarines got ready to head westwards.

After dinner on 28 September 1944 the Great Kronstadt Roads were humming with activity. Five minesweepers, equally as many patrol boats and three submarines from the 3rd Division – *P-310*, *P-318* and *P-407* – were forming up in escort. Shortly afterwards this first convoy left for distant waters.

On 1 October 1944 we saw the submarines of our division – *L-3*, *D-2*, *S-13* and *Lembit* – off on their journey. Before that, we had spent a sleepless night. During a meeting of the ships' heads of department, Yakov Spiridonovich Kovalenko had announced out of the blue: 'On my *S-13* a crack has been discovered in the portside internal fuel tank. I wanted to ask your advice about it.'

After the meeting I had gone to the boat with him. The outcome of my inspection disturbed me considerably. It was obvious that the submarine could not put to sea with a crack like that. We decided – for the first time in our working practice – to apply electric welding without first pumping the fuel from the tank. I cannot recommend this method, but at the time this turned out to be the right decision. We did the welding using special electrodes, taking every precaution, so as to avoid a build-up of fumes from the fuel which, in combination with air, could explode from the slightest spark. Kulchitsky, *Smolny*'s Engineer Officer, detailed his best electric welder to do this job. Almost the whole night long we laboured over the half-metre crack. But there you are, the job got done, hydraulic tests confirmed the solidity of the join. We breathed a sigh of relief. Now everything was fully restored to order, apart from the total shambles in the compartment. It fell to the sailors on watch that night to do a fair amount of work

146

under the direction of Leading Seaman 1st Class Prudnikov.

A few days later, as part of another division's escorted group, our S-4 left. My burdens grew less. Jokingly, I complained about this to Alexander Kuzmich Vasiliev. His response to that was to say to me: 'Take a day off. After that, concern yourself with the remaining three submarines and the floating base. They need to be in a proper state of readiness for the voyage too, you know.'

'Hang on, Alexander Kuzmich, I have only two submarines left here. How do you make it three?'

'And what about L-55, don't you count her as a fighting unit?'

'Of course I don't count her as a fighting unit but, for the record, she undoubtedly counts as a ship, and is very precious to us.'

'She will make it under her own steam. Keep an eye on her, otherwise the ratings will crank something up again and lose it.'

Alexander Kuzmich was referring to an incident that had occurred on L-55 a few months earlier. During the routine jacking-over of the machinery, a young sailor had overdone it, had set in motion the keel release mechanism. Weighing several tons, the lead keel-piece had come away from the underside of the boat and had fallen to the bottom. Divers I.A. Boichenko and A.A. Raisky had reached the keel, but it was impossible to put it back in place without dock facilities. We came to the conclusion that the old lady would manage, even without a keel, and the lead was given to the shore-base.

We were making preparations for our passage with increasing intensity. The matter was complicated by the fact that the ships which were going to undertake the journey had not sailed for a long time now. And it is well known that machinery deteriorates more from prolonged disuse than it does from use.

We tested Smolny under way. We found no serious short-comings. As for minor ones, however, there were masses. Something let off steam there, something was hissing here, was giving way there, wouldn't shut there . . . Kulchitsky and his men had their work cut out.

On 16 October the tanker Nikolai Ostrovsky came alongside the floating base Smolny for the last time and replenished her supply of mazout.

At 17.30 hours the escort got under way. Four minesweepers

and two submarine chasers were accompanying us. Leading our armada was that indefatigable toiler of the sea, Captain Third Rank Mikhail Oparin, in command of a division of base minesweepers. We set a course for Lavansaari Island. The floating base *Smolny* was following along immediately behind the last pair of minesweepers, which were under way with their sweeps deployed. The weather was amazingly good. The setting sun coloured the waters of the Gulf crimson. But the stillness and peacefulness were deceptive. 'Mine!' yelled a signalman. A dirty-green sphere floated by, a few dozen metres to port of *Smolny*.

Before Peninsaari Island we met with a second floating mine. Shortly afterwards we had to turn out of the navigational channel: we had run into an area ringed in by buoys; four magnetic seabed mines had been found there. As twilight deepened, stern lights were lit on all the ships. We reduced speed.

For more than twenty-four hours we lay at anchor between the islands of Peninsaari and Lavansaari: the minesweepers were clearing the navigational channel. It was a shame about the fuel, but we kept steam up in the boiler: an order could have come from one minute to the next.

The sea began to roughen. Towards midday on 18 October the wind increased to gale force. *Smolny* began to be tossed to such an extent that her anchor chains almost tore loose. We weighed anchor. The minesweepers were thrown about wildly. They abandoned us near Ulko-Tammio Island. A launch with a Finnish pilot approached us.

We were passing through the skerries. All around were islands upon islands, in their tens and hundreds. The wind swooped past in powerful squalls, howling dreadfully in the rigging and antennae. We maintained full speed the whole time, so as not to drift onto the rocks emerging ominously from the water to both starboard and port. The pilot had a confident bearing. The Divisional Commander was tranquil too. Kulchitsky was the one who was the most agitated. Time and again he informed me: 'Viktor Yemelianovich, we're cutting it fine. The mazout is running out. What shall we do?'

'Hold her steady! When the mazout is all gone – report to me. We will take a decision: lie at anchor or burn diesel fuel instead of mazout.'

Gradually Kulchitsky's agitation began to get a grip on me as well. Forcing the pace as we were, our mazout wouldn't last out until Turku. And the wind, as if out of spite, was strengthening all the time. When the sea was revealed between the craggy islands, you could see unbroken foam. But here, in amongst the islands, the water was calm; it was only in the rigging that the heart-rending moaning never died down.

We learned en route that the submarines *P-310* and *Lembit* had already returned to Helsinki from their first war patrols, and that the return of *P-407* was expected. The boats had all scored success in combat. *P-310* had sunk four freighters! *Lembit* had sunk a freighter and a patrol boat. Things had gone wonderfully well!

We reached Helsinki during the evening of 19 October. I was keen to get to know the Finnish capital, but every day we spent there was filled to capacity. We examined the boats as they returned from patrol and compiled repair sheets. Ships in need of serious repair were sent to Kronstadt. Some of it was carried out on the spot. We were grateful to our comrades of the State Control Commission; they helped negotiate business matters with the Finnish bureaucracy. The Finns are a work-loving people. They carried out our orders willingly and conscientiously.

In November the floating base *Smolny* transferred to Turku. Our division would now be based there. It was a convenient place; a well-equipped port with fairly powerful ship-repair plants. The pace of the work quickened. We swiftly established a good working relationship with the plant directors. The repair work began to achieve a steady flow; the ships put to sea on time.
Winter set in. The boats went on sailing and each of them returned with a victory.

In January I had a memorable conversation with the Divisional Commander. Alexander Yevstafievich Oryol gave me a searching look: 'Sit down, Chief, let's have a chat. It is imperative that we dispatch the next submarine in line to the southern Baltic as a matter of urgency.'

'You have *L-21* in mind, I take it?'

'Precisely so.'

'Comrade Captain First Rank,' I said, 'remember that, as far back as a year ago, you promised to send me to sea? This was when the news had reached me that the Nazis had shot my father in Kiev. You said that you would provide me with an opportunity to avenge his death. This didn't happen at the time. Let me go to sea now. I assure you that I will do everything in my power to handle the mission with distinction.'

Alexander Yevstafievich smiled: 'I would willingly meet your request. All the more so since I, myself, have received the go-ahead from the Brigade Commander to put to sea with Mogilievsky. The surface speed of *L-21* is not brilliant. Her best speed is sixteen knots, whereas a convoy moves at a speed of twelve knots. It will be difficult to catch up with them and intercept them. The diesels will be overloaded the whole time by going flat out. And the officer in charge of the propulsion group on the boat is a really young man. Dolgopolov will not have an easy time with him, which is why I intend to request the higher command to allow me to take you on a war patrol.'

'Permit me to put the request to the Brigade Commander. I will explain to him that during my absence the Brigade Engineer's assistant, Alexander Kuzmich Vasiliev, will be here.'

'Wait a little. Don't interfere, otherwise you might spoil everything. You just get yourself ready for the patrol in the most thorough way so that there won't be anything untoward on the technical side.'

The warning was justified. Our submarines were keeping up a strenuous sailing schedule. We were trying to spend as little time as possible on repair work. The machinery had, to a substantial degree, already reached its limit. We were fully aware of this, but we were obliged not to take it into account. By now we were showing the old ships no mercy; we were repairing their machinery just enough for them to stagger on to the end of the war, creaking and groaning. It was therefore essential to keep them under close scrutiny.

The minelaying submarine *L-21* was laid up in dry dock. Her Engineer Officer, Nikolai Sergeievich Dolgopolov, had only just taken over from N.N. Petrov, who had obtained an appointment to *K-54*, currently under construction. Active and energetic, Dolgopolov had rapidly familiarized himself with the ship and was leading the repair work very ably.

The boat came out of dock in the second half of February. The painstaking work of adjusting the pneumatics of the main ballast tank's outboard valves was dragging on. I kept wanting to intervene, but each time I managed to restrain myself. Let the young engineer sort it all out for himself. Dolgopolov knew that I would be going to sea with him, and had candidly asked me not to hover over him too much. He realized that this war patrol would be a kind of examination for him, and he wanted to pass it without prompting.

We loaded mines and torpedoes, took on artillery ammunition, fuel and provisions. In the meantime I was handing over my responsibilities to Alexander Kuzmich Vasiliev. I said to him: 'Get yourself out of your own scrapes, Sasha, you're on your own for a month. Still, the Finns know you very well by now. Remember how you rubbed their noses in it on Christmas Eve?'

At that time, *P-307* had returned from patrol with a smashed propeller and a bent propeller shaft. The plant engineers declared that nothing could be done about the shaft, and called for the manufacture of a new one. Vasiliev, a former lathe-operator at the Izhorsky plant, was outraged. 'Come on, put the shaft on the lathe!'

The Finns did as he asked. It was Christmas Eve. The plant emptied out. Vasiliev and I remained in the workshop. He stood at the huge lathe. We worked the whole night through. The next morning the Finns were amazed: the shaft was as good as new. *P-307* left on her war patrol precisely on time.

'They will carry out your orders,' I said. 'They are a very sensible and businesslike people. It is easy to reach an understanding with them.'

Captain First Rank L.A. Kurnikov arrived from Helsinki on 5 March 1945, to see us off on our war patrol. He asked Oryol: 'Could you perhaps go without Korzh, Alexander Yevstafievich? There is a huge pile of work here, on top of which I need Vasiliev in Helsinki.'

'No, no, Lev Andreievich. Korzh will come on the patrol, as we agreed earlier.'

'Very well then, off you go. The very best of luck!'

Chapter Five

OUR PEOPLE WILL OVERCOME EVERYTHING

The Sea Is Near At Hand

Day had dawned, and the Finnish ice-breaker *Gutsy* had diligently broken up the thick ice in the harbour and provided us with a towing-rope. There was still not even a hint of spring. The temperature was fifteen degrees below zero.

Jerked by the taut rope, our boat pulled away from the pier. Snow covered islands glided by. Blocks of ice collided and somersaulted in the churning wake of the ice-breaker. They thudded and rubbed against the sides of the boat. The noise was so great that it was impossible to talk to one another.

We encountered some Finnish fishermen. They were riding in sledges. Their stocky little horses ran merrily over the hard crust of ice. It was somewhat strange to see such a conveyance out at sea. We asked the ice-breaker to stop. The fishermen drove up to the very edge of the ice. We struck up a conversation. It turned out that they were getting sprats to be smoked. They generously shared their catch with us. The sprats were not sturgeon, of course, and neither were they sterlet, but the ratings nevertheless feasted pleasurably for two days on fish soup and fried fish.

They had put me up in a head of department's cabin. There were two bunks in it. Dolgopolov had obligingly allowed me, as senior man, to take the lower one. The bunks were attached to the ship's side. Although the ship's hull was lined with compressed cork, a frosty vapour blew from it and coated everything with a thick layer of rime. There was a portable electric heater in our cabin. It gave out such a heat that your jacket would start to steam and you would turn over onto your other side. The warmed-up jacket would melt the frost on the inside of the hull, and then freeze to it, and the cold penetrated even through fur. You could stand it for not more than ten minutes without changing position. With the door closed, the temperature in the cabin rapidly rose to over forty degrees (we had a thermometer hanging above the table). When you switched off the electric heater, twenty minutes later your teeth were chattering. So you would sleep like a clockwork toy – in perpetual motion, constantly turning over, switching the heater on, then switching it off, opening or closing the cabin door. Nikolai Sergeievich called this 'automatic temperature control'.

In its turn the second watch began its shift: the officer of the watch was Lieutenant Captain Yuri Sergeievich Rusin, who had been appointed first lieutenant to this boat only a few days before the patrol. In the control room was Senior Lieutenant Nikolai Sergeievich Dolgopolov; with him was the head of the planesmen's section, Leading Seaman 1st Class Leonid Iosifovich Zaborovsky. I was keeping a close eye on my new comrades. The only one of the senior seamen well known to me was Petty Officer Sergei Nikolaievich Ogurtsov, in charge of the planesmen's group. I knew him from a long way back. He was an outstanding expert in his line of work, thoughtful and energetic and he was a Party member; active in public welfare. Everyone respected him.

So far everything was quiet and calm. Dolgopolov, in an undertone, was filling me in on the other people in his department. I was glad to see that the young engineer had such a sound knowledge of his subordinates, their training and their characteristics.

He spoke of Zaborovsky with enthusiasm. Leonid was Polish by nationality, but had lived in Leningrad for a long time. He was working-class and had entered the Navy from the reserve. He came to the minelaying submarine from the front line after having been wounded.

'As you can see it was a complicated route. I actually went through all that too,' said Dolgopolov.

'I already know all there is to know about you, Nikolai Sergeievich.'

'Zaborovsky settled into the ship extremely quickly. His comrades in the planesmen's group respect him and are a bit afraid of him: he is an outstanding specialist, you can't hide anything from him. With his subordinates he is strict and demanding, but within reasonable limits. The ratings behave towards him as they would to a father. Added to which, he is older than all of them – born in 1910, so two years older than you. Not a Party member, but a very upright comrade.'

I asked Nikolai Sergeievich to give me a thumbnail sketch of everyone currently present in the control room. He willingly did so. He described the navigational electrician, Leading Seaman 1st Class M.M. Dubov, the head of the hydrophone unit, Leading Seaman 2nd Class A.N. Buzulukov, a Komsomol member, a lanky fellow with intelligent, deep-set eyes, more like a lab assistant than a seaman.

The head of the propulsion group, Lieutenant Teodor Petrovich Yefimov, stopped by for a minute. He seemed unusually shy and quiet to me. The head of the helmsmen's group, Lieutenant N.I. Redko, ran noisily down from the bridge into the control room, throwing out as he went: 'Comrades, Nyhamn is close by. Diving and trimming any minute now.'

I watched Zaborovsky. Without waiting to be told, he got the water control panel and the trimming pump ready for trimming. He worked calmly and confidently.

I went up onto the bridge. It had got warmer in the open air, already it smelled of the sea rather than of snow. But everyone's feet were frozen from standing on the iron deck for a long time, and they were all dancing about a bit. First Lieutenant Y.S. Rusin was chuckling, because he was properly dressed for the weather. It was immediately obvious: he was an old hand. A broad black band had appeared on the horizon beyond the ice field. From these latitudes on, the Baltic Sea does not freeze over.

The pilot went on foot over the ice to the ice-breaker. The towing-rope was let go. The ice-breaker went ahead, crushing the ice up to the end of the ice field. The Bosun, Petty Officer Georgi Demidovich Ashomok, did a tour around the deck from the bow to the stern for the last time, checking the integrity of the seals on all covers, hatches and removable plates.

Having gone beyond the edge of the ice, we immediately submerged. We got under way using the electric motors. The ship's commanding officer, Captain Second Rank S.S.

154

Mogilievsky, ordered Leading Seaman Gavrilov to write down in the log: 'The passage from Nyhamn Lighthouse to the South Baltic has begun.'

How easy getting out into the open sea had now become! It was not 1942 or 1943, when there were continuous minefields and nets in our path. The moment you emerged from the skerries, there you were – in the open expanse of the Baltic!

Lieutenant Captain Rusin ordered the word to be passed to the compartments: 'First combat shift to report for watch!'

Normal patrol life began. Everybody dispersed to their stations. Senior Lieutenant Alexei Vasilievich Pribavin, the senior navigator, began his shift as officer of the watch and Yefimov his shift as duty engineer.

The off-duty officers gathered in the mess. There was animated conversation at the dinner table. Senior Lieutenant Mikhail Afanasievich Vorobiov of the medical service asked each of us if we were enjoying the meal. He was a thoughtful and anxious person. Vorobiov was the medic on *D-2*. He had been 'borrowed' by *L-21* for one war patrol, to replace the doctor who had been taken ill.

Seizing a convenient moment, Vorobiov said to Captain First Rank Oryol: 'On the *Decembrist*, when there were no people sick, Captain Second Rank Lindenberg always allowed me to stand a signalman's watch. I have wonderful eyesight. I have even developed my own technique for improving signalmen's night vision. I am asking you to let me stand watch with the First Lieutenant on this war patrol too.'

'Well, I don't think that Sergei Sergeievich would have any objection,' said Oryol, casting an enquiring glance at the Captain. 'Of course I wouldn't,' answered Mogilievsky readily and added: 'It is extremely praiseworthy. I like it, when there is no one on the ship afflicted with idleness. But I ask only, Mikhail Afanasievich, that your basic responsibilities won't suffer on account of this doubling-up of duties.'

'You need be in no doubt on that score, Comrade Captain.'

So on the lists of signalmen, in amongst gunners and torpedo-men, appeared the surname of the medic Vorobiov.

Twenty-four hours passed calmly. During the evening of 7 March, when darkness had deepened over the sea to such an extent that you couldn't even see the waves through the periscope, the order was given to the hydrophone operator: 'Listen right round the horizon!'

'Horizon clear!' reported Able Seaman Kovaliov, on listening watch.

We surfaced to the cruising position. There was a moderate swell. A head wind was 'bashing you in the mug', as the sailors jokingly put it. An hour later the wind had become squally, with a heavy swell. Its direction had veered sharply. Rolling had been added to the ship's pitching.

Medic Vorobiov, beginning his watch as a lookout, noticed my white face. 'Viktor Yemelianovich, what's up? Are you unwell?'

'I'm always unwell, Doctor, once the sea gets up.'

'You know, some people are helped wonderfully when it's rolling by eating dried black bread.'

This was a new one on me. I had never yet tried to cure seasickness with dried black bread. Salted cucumbers, herring, sauerkraut, cranberry syrup, dried salt fish, lemon, Vitamin C lozenges – I had tried them all. They helped, but not much. As a rule I gave up smoking as well, from the very outset of war patrols, so that I always had a clear head.

On my order, the cook, Able Seaman F.A. Dmitriev, brought me a handful of pieces of dried black bread from a newly-opened tin. I chewed them with such a loud crunching noise that it seemed as though even my brains were being shaken up. It worked. The queasiness died away.

The wind and the steep swell reached their climax in the middle of the night. The list to port had reached forty to forty-seven degrees. Waves quite often swamped the bridge, howling wildly, pouring water by the ton into the control room each time. On two occasions the Captain had to stop the engines, because the ship, plunging into the waves while under way, had begun to go into a dive. The trim reached five degrees on the bow, and the flat surface of the upper deck was thereby transformed into a huge hydroplane. At such moments, on the Captain's order, people dived down into the control room.

Sailors have two adversaries: the enemy and the raging elements. And it tends to be difficult to judge which of them is the more dangerous.

Because of the heavy list, electrolyte spilled out of the batteries. 'Stop charging,' I advised Dolgopolov.

The Captain decided to submerge and wait out the storm underwater. We hurriedly restored order to the batteries. The squad working in the first battery pit was led by the head of the electrician's group, Leading Seaman 1st Class V.P. Panov, with the electrician P.V. Isakov leading the other squad. Appreciating the importance of this work, I sent Yefimov, the head of the propulsion group, into one of the battery pits, while Dolgopolov took the second under his personal charge. It is good that on a minelaying submarine the batteries are positioned so roomily that you can even stroll about between the rows of tanks. Not stinting on the fresh water, we washed out the battery pits directly with the hosepipe, then we wiped each tank dry. Four hours later, the battery insulation had risen to a normal level.

The electricians, satisfied with the results of their labours, dispersed into the compartments, and out of habit I glanced into the Navigator's cabin to bring myself up to date on the current situation. Senior Lieutenant Pribavin was working on a chart.

'Alexei Vasilievich, what have you plotted here?' I asked, catching sight of the figure 'eight', enclosed in a neat little circle.

'According to the reconnaissance data, there are eight enemy submarines in this area of the sea.'

'Yes. Charming neighbourhood. And what are the depths like here?'

'The depths here are good, of the order of eighty metres.'

We went to the control room together. The ship was travelling at a depth of twenty-eight metres. The clocks were showing 08.25. Five minutes later we were due to rise to periscope depth to scan the horizon. To be on the safe side, I decided to remain in the control room: my help might suddenly be needed.

'Take her up to periscope depth!' Pribavin, as officer of the watch, gave the order, going up into the conning tower. Bosun Ashomok shifted the stern hydroplanes to surfacing. With a stern trim the boat started to come up smoothly. But what was this? The trim didn't fall away, in spite of the fact that the stern hydroplanes had long ago been deflected for diving by the Petty Officer. 'Ease off the stern rudders! Put the bow rudders to full helm for diving!'

157

I all but yelled, seeing with horror how the stern trim was continuing to increase at a catastrophic rate.

Enemy Number Two

Petty Officer Ashomok exerted every effort to hold back the ship's headlong ascent. 'Stop engines! Switch the stern hydroplanes to manual control! Leaping up from his chair, the Petty Officer began to turn the fly-wheel with all his might. But it was entirely in vain. As before, the ship's bow reared skywards.

'The submarine is not responding to the hydroplanes!' yelled the Bosun. Mogilievsky, Oryol and Dolgopolov, one after the other, came running out of the third compartment, down along the sloping deck into the control room. What had happened, we didn't yet know. We only knew that the ship was not under the control of the hydroplanes. The Captain decided to surface. At the same time he ordered the Navigator to set a course for the nearest sandbank, where it might be possible to lie on the bottom undisturbed. We hastily got both diesels ready. We surfaced and immediately got under way.

The Divisional Commander said to me: 'Chief, remain in the control room at all times. Expect the signal for an emergency dive at any moment.'

Petty Officer Ogurtsov was already in position. Even in a moment like that, I could not fail to admire this tireless leading seaman; at any time of the day or night he would be at hand and ready for action.

We headed for the Shtolpe sandbank. We were going along in the surfaced position, at every moment running the risk of coming under attack from an enemy submarine roving around.

Dolgopolov and the Bosun ran to the eighth compartment to examine the drive of the stern hydroplanes. Shortly afterwards this entry appeared in the ship's log: 'The stern hydroplane drive is out of action. The spindle nut-liner thread has been torn off.' Enemy number two – the storm-tossed sea – had done its dirty work.

I went up onto the bridge to report the accident. Having heard me out, Oryol and Mogilievsky were plunged into gloom.

'What are we going to do?' asked the Divisional Commander.

'For the time being there is nothing I can say. I have ordered the drive to be dismantled. Dolgopolov has already put the people in place.'

The sea had calmed down somewhat. But it was still ruffled with white horses. Everywhere I seemed to see periscope bow-waves and the foaming tracks of torpedoes. This, obviously, was because of the figure 'eight', enclosed within the neat little circle on the Navigator's chart. I went down into the control room, expecting every second to hear the order: 'Emergency dive!'

We went on for one hour, then two. It seemed an eternity! I felt like a cat on hot bricks. And time and again I asked them to check the depth with the echo-sounder. Wherever was that Shtolpe sand-bank?

The hydrophone operator announced that, apart from the noise of our own propellers, he could hear nothing. I had also known earlier on that, if your speed exceeded twelve knots, the direction-finder would pick up only the noise of your own propellers, but somehow I had attached no importance to it. Now, however, the very awareness that we could not even hear the approach of an enemy boat reduced me to a tremble. Dolgopolov came running up: 'Here, take a look at what's left of the nut-liner!'

The whole of the thread had torn off. The liner would have to be replaced, but we had no spare. I ordered them to check whether it might be possible to find some suitable component in some other piece of machinery. We would remove it from there and adjust it. I felt partly to blame myself as well, which is probably why I was too ashamed to look Dolgopolov in the eye. 'Which of the sailors have been working on it?' I enquired, not finding any other question to ask.

'Leading Seaman 2nd Class Pyatovsky, Seaman Linnikov and Able Seaman Terentiev. Isn't it worth contacting the bridge?' asked Dolgopolov.

'It's not worth distracting the Captain's attention. I was there. Frankly speaking, it's a bit terrifying going along amongst enemy submarines by day.'

The depths were very slowly diminishing. Pribavin reported to the bridge that there remained ten minutes to the diving-point. For me, those ten minutes were exceedingly long ones.

Having taken an additional half ton of water into the bow tank, we got ready to settle on the bottom with a bow-down trim, so as not to damage the propellers.

Oryol had come down into the control room, then the signalmen and Lieutenant Captain Rusin. Finally the conning-tower hatch clanged loudly behind the ship's commanding officer. 'Emergency dive!' Using inertial thrust, we slipped smoothly beneath the water and settled on the seabed at a depth of thirty-seven metres. Everyone gathered in the cramped stern compartment where the ill-fated drive was. No suitable nut what-soever had been found. What was to be done?

The Divisional Commander took me to his cabin. In a low voice he said to me: 'The combat order for the patrol presents us with two tasks. The first is to lay mines in the Gulf of Danzig and the second – our activities in the enemy's shipping lanes. In our situ-ation it would be enough for us to accomplish just the first task. But for that we need the stern hydroplanes.'

'How much time could you give us for the repair work?'

'I'll give you however much you need.'

'We need two days and nights of undisturbed work, to make sure that no one is harassed or put under pressure.'

'I understand. Work calmly; the Captain and I will wait. Report at regular intervals.'

'That goes without saying. You will be kept informed about the work the whole time.'

So, I had managed to extract two days and nights. But in the meantime I didn't know myself what to do or how to do it. Even in the bow hydroplanes' drive, the nut-liner was of a different form. Dolgopolov and I sat over the drawings, thinking fever-ishly. We were prepared to sacrifice the bow hydroplanes in order to restore the stern ones. 'And what if we were to transfer the whole drive in one piece?' I suggested. Nikolai Sergeievich imme-diately set about taking measurements with a ruler. It turned out that the housing of the drives was different. 'We will remake the housing.'

I was aware myself that this was only said lightly. The stern housing would have to be shortened and reduced in height. And all we had were chisels! Just try hacking at steel with those! And there would have to be a great deal of hacking done. Moreover, there was not much space under the mine tubes and the

160

stern bilge pump wouldn't allow you to swing your arms the way you needed to. But there was no other way out.

We went to report to the powers-that-be. Dolgopolov spread the drawings out on the table in the officers' mess. Oryol and Mogilievsky bent over them. Dolgopolov explained our idea. We would transfer the bow drive to the stern, and secure the bow hydroplanes in the neutral position. There was a great deal of work to do. We would have to shorten the housing by sixty millimetres and reduce its height by twenty millimetres, otherwise the axles would not be centred.

Mogilievsky whistled quietly. And Oryol said thoughtfully: 'This will create a real din over the whole of the Baltic . . .'

'After the very first blows of the sledgehammer, the enemy will have our bearings,' confirmed Mogilievsky.

'That is undoubtedly so,' agreed the Divisional Commander, tensely drumming his fingers on the table. 'But it's a long way to the nearest base. Only submarines would be able to hear us, which do not have depth charges. They are hardly likely to succeed in working out what it's all about. They will not start to torpedo us, because they will think that a foreign submarine would not be hammering away so boldly. We will keep an active listening watch the whole time. If anything crops up, we will take steps immediately.'

'There's just one thing;' the Captain remarked, 'we must select and position people in such a way that they don't just kick up a racket, but hack away in the proper manner, with all their might.'

'Comrade Captain, we will choose strong, skilful chaps. And we will have another shift ready to replace them,' said Dolgopolov, brightening up.

'Well, let's give it a try,' agreed the Divisional Commander and shook his head dubiously. 'In a naval plant it takes a team of metal-workers two weeks to mount, fit and sign off on the stern hydroplanes, while you want to do the lot in two days and nights. Utopians!' But approval had been obtained, and we got down to business.

A team of engine-room mechanics, headed by Leading Seaman 2nd Class P.I. Grigoriev, proceeded to the first compartment to dismantle the bow hydroplane drive. Another team stripped out the stern hydroplanes' ruined mechanism. Dolgopolov marked out the housing with a marking pin. Shortly afterwards the ratings dragged the bow hydroplane drive through the whole length of the ship; an unwieldy, cumbersome object weighing several hundred kilos. They squeezed it underneath the mine tubes to the freed-up housing and tried out the marking. Sledgehammers and chisels were brought. The men were positioned carefully. Once they were fitted in, I gave the order: 'Hack away!'

With rollicking heave-hos, four sledgehammers set to work. The din was unimaginable. The ship's hull hummed and vibrated. After ten minutes the sweat-soaked sailors handed the sledge-hammers over to the new shift. The second shift hacked away, having already discarded their quilted jackets. The third shift removed their canvas smocks, leaving only their striped under-shirts on. Then they removed their undershirts as well. The sailors' backs were gleaming with sweat. The steel of the housing yielded reluctantly. Its coil slowly, very slowly, twisted off in curls and fell into the bilges. I was afraid that the lads would injure one another with the enormous shavings. But there was no stopping them. The struggle with the steel went on. The men got the better of the steel inch by inch, drenching it copiously with their own sweat.

For six hours almost non-stop the surrounding sea was in an uproar. Engine-room mechanics, torpedomen, gunners, planesmen, helmsmen, electricians, the cook and the orderly all took turns working with the sledgehammers. We did not allow the radio operators to take part in this work, so as not to impair their sensitivity of touch. It passes understanding how it could have come about that not one man received so much as a scratch. In vain did the doc set out his bag with its bandages, cotton wool and iodine.

Several times Oryol and Mogilievsky elbowed their way amid the crush of half-naked, sweaty sailors to check how the work was advancing; to encourage the sailors.

Like runners in a marathon, the hammerers used their final efforts to overcome the last dozen millimetres up to the longed-for finishing line – the marked-out edge. Bathed in their own sweat, breathing hard and hoarsely grunting out heave-hos, they would raise the 6-kilo sledgehammers. A few more blows and the hammers were flung down onto the deck plating with a clatter. The faces looked drawn, but the eyes were shining with delight. The housing had been hacked off!

While this frantic work had been going on, the hydrophone

operators had repeatedly reported the approach of enemy submarines, which, like sharks, were circling around, amazed at the monstrous din in the sea but, being unable to solve the riddle, had shied away to the side and hastily taken themselves off as far away as possible.

After the rough hacking-off, the metal-workers – the Grigoriev twins, Zaborovsky, Ponomarenko, Linnikov, Terentiev and Pyatovsky – carried out the clean-up chiselling with hand chisels and filed the housing down with hand files.

We tried it out. Everything was fine. We began to drill the holes. While we in the eighth compartment were preparing for the installation of the drive, in the first they were securing the bow hydroplanes in the neutral position. For added security, they propped up the spindle with the emergency jack.

By 23.30 the work was done. Nikolai Sergeievich and I, filthy with axle grease, checked the assembly painstakingly. We came to the unanimous opinion that everything that had been done could be given the 'thumbs up'.

We ordered the Bosun to run the stern hydroplanes manually through the full range of angles. The drive moved smoothly. The spindle went back and forth without any hindrance.

'Once more!'

When we had satisfied ourselves that there was no jamming anywhere, Dolgopolov ordered the spindle to be lubricated thoroughly with fresh axle grease. After that, we tried out the hydroplanes electrically. Once, twice, three times . . .

'Take a message to the Navigators in the control room: let them come and give their approval,' ordered Dolgopolov, wearily straightening his back.

Senior Lieutenant Pribavin and Lieutenant Redko did not keep us waiting for long; hard on their heels came First Lieutenant Rusin as well. They manipulated the hydroplanes, rejoiced and marvelled.

'We will take it that the hydroplanes have passed the tests when moored. Let us see how they behave themselves when tested under way,' cautiously remarked the First Lieutenant, voicing what we were all thinking.

Dolgopolov and I went to see the Divisional Commander. Oryol, having heard us out, consulted his watch. 'Only thirteen hours in all spent on the repair work. This should be appreciated

163

on its just merits, Captain,' he said to Mogilievsky. 'What splendid fellows! Comrade Dolgopolov, make a note of all who were involved in the work and single out individually the most selfless. Keep this list safe until the end of the patrol. It will stand us in good stead.'

The Captain delightedly shook us by the hand and, by then formally addressing himself to the Divisional Commander, asked: 'May I have your permission to lift off from the bottom?'

'Take her up, Sergei Sergeievich. Let's not waste time. We need to do some proper training, so that the planesmen get used to the new conditions of controlling the ship.'

At 23.50 hours the minelaying submarine abandoned the cosy sandbank and, smoothly gathering speed, set a course for the Shtolpemunde Lighthouse, to pinpoint our position, as it was extremely difficult to keep a plot during anti-torpedo zigzagging, and the Navigator could only guarantee its accuracy to within plus or minus three miles. Such a low level of accuracy did not sit well with us.

Before we surfaced, Lieutenant Redko sat each of the planesmen at the handwheel in turn, so that all of them could get at least a little feel for the way the ship behaved when controlled by the stern hydroplanes alone.

Almost every fifteen minutes Dolgopolov and I ran to the eighth compartment, to under the mine tubes. The bow hydroplanes, the spindle of whose drive was propped up securely on the emergency jack, gave us no cause for concern. But it was wrong of us to put such blind faith in the jack!

We surfaced at 00.45 hours on 9 March, after testing the stern hydroplanes at submerged speeds ranging right up to actual full speed. The roomy bridge was crowded. The Divisional Commander, the Captain, the officer of the watch and four lookouts were there almost constantly.

We reached our position. At this time of year the sea is restless. Visibility is poor. Rain is frequently persistent. Our most pressing task was to locate the Shtolpemunde Lighthouse. It was only towards morning, when there remained not more than an hour and a half until sunrise, that Able Seaman M.V. Yudenkov glimpsed the flashing light of the lighthouse through a foggy haze.

He managed to do this, because he had climbed up onto the upper platform by the periscope standard. Immediately both the Navigators – Pribavin and Redko – climbed up to join him. Having unsealed the upper bowl of the repeater, they took bearings on various courses, until they had obtained a reliable fix. Satisfied, both of them vanished down the conning-tower hatch. I went down into the control room too. The dive passed off serenely. The helmsmen had gradually got used to managing with just the stern hydroplanes.

After dinner the officers' mess emptied out. Only the Divisional Commander, the Captain and I remained at the table. 'Before we set about fulfilling task number one,' said Oryol, 'we must reconnoitre the situation in the Gulf of Danzig thoroughly, especially with regard to the defensive anti-submarine patrols. We will manoeuvre cautiously in the Gulf, so that the coastal observation posts don't detect us. This is particularly important when you take into account the fact that the ship is damaged and unable to manoeuvre normally.'

'Incidentally,' I remarked, 'the planesmen are already handling the ship fairly confidently without the bow hydroplanes.

'That's good. But we must nevertheless observe particular caution.'

On 9 March we went up and down the enemy coasts all day, studying the lie of the land. The results and observations were analysed assiduously. This was used as the basis for planning the minelaying procedure. On a large-scale chart of the Gulf of Danzig we plotted the courses, marked the turning-points and the timing of each run. Our initial point of reference was the Hel Lighthouse.

Unfortunately, the state of the sea did not allow us to set about the accomplishment of our task immediately. It was all the more irritating because, as soon as the wind began to get up, the enemy ships started to make for cover. First the little ones went and, later on, the more substantial ships too. But we were unable to lay mines because, for one thing, the boat might be thrown up onto the surface and, for another, there was no guarantee that the mines would end up at the required depth. So as not to lose time fruitlessly, the Divisional Commander ordered minelaying to be set aside for the time being and the passage to the enemy shipping lanes to be put in hand.

165

At night, in pitch-black darkness, when we were on course for Pillau, Leading Seaman 1st Class T.S. Venderets shouted out: 'I see a light!'

'Helm to port!' Mogilievsky ordered Able Seaman Rubin, on duty at the vertical rudder. Incidentally, that order was interpreted by all non-essential personnel on the bridge as the order: 'All hands below!' Diving down the hatch, the sailors had scattered to their action stations.

Ten minutes later I too could distinguish a solitary little light on the horizon. Oryol and Mogilievsky were peering into the darkness with the aid of night-vision binoculars, exchanging brief comments: 'Long hull, but low-sided.'

'Superstructure entirely displaced towards the stern. See, there's another one. Look more to port.'

'Something more like tankers,' I was thinking. But the Divisional Commander and the Captain had had their doubts aroused by the fact that these vessels were pitching really violently.

'Armed too. See, Captain, they have two guns each.'

'And there couldn't possibly be guns in those positions on tankers . . .'

'Hey! They must be high-speed landing craft!' exclaimed Oryol. 'They have a draught of only one metre. Turn aside, Captain, you won't touch them with a torpedo, and we don't have the muscle to engage them in an artillery battle.' Yes, indeed, they were high-speed landing craft. There was no point in tangling with them. They were not much of a prize, but a big risk. We turned away.

Towards midnight the wind seemed to be beginning to calm down. The moon suddenly emerged from amongst the storm clouds. At that precise moment, Leading Seaman 2nd Class A.F. Ovchinnikov, on lookout duty in the starboard aft sector, shouted: 'Starboard bearing one-three-zero – three submarines!'

We stared in that direction. Along the moonlit pathway in single-file formation, three clear-cut silhouettes with their wake lights burning were moving away about half a mile from us. If our speed had been just slightly greater, we would inevitably have run into the rearmost submarine. The signalmen were rebuked by the Captain for spotting the enemy too late. It was lucky for us that the signalmen on the enemy boats were apparently even more slipshod. Ours might have been late, but they did see something, whereas the Germans had completely failed to spot us; they continued on their way as though on parade.

We received a radio message. Nowadays we frequently received them. They kept us informed about the situation and passed on intelligence about the movement of enemy shipping. The intelligence service functioned flawlessly. This was how we learned straight away that a mixed bag of more than 150 enemy ships were marooned without fuel in the ports of Königsberg and Danzig. We were instructed that our first priority was to destroy tankers attempting to force their way into those bases.

A storm got up during the day on 10 March. Twice we tried to come up, to raise the telescopic aerial mounted on the anti-aircraft periscope. The outcome of these attempts was that electrolyte was again spilt by the ship's rolling and the electricians had to spend several hours taking care of the batteries.

The Captain took the decision to wait out the storm. We would surface when the swell had abated to at least a moderate level. And in the meantime we were cruising at an economical speed at a depth of around seventy metres.

But patience soon ran out. During the night of 11 March we surfaced with the sea running high. We had just blown the ballast when an alarm signal sounded from the first compartment. Leaving Petty Officer Ogurtsov behind in the control room, Dolgopolov and I ran to the torpedomen. During this time the boat had reared up on a huge sloping wave. The bow hydroplanes had been exposed. Then the ship had plunged towards the deep and smacked the rudders against the water with such force that our jack, which was propping up the spindle, had curled up in an instant like a coiled spring, then struck the deckhead like a cannonball and, miraculously hitting no one, had fallen with a clatter into the bilges. With each fresh assault of the waves, the stirrups grew ever slacker, and the swing of the spindle became ever more alarming.

Dolgopolov, having just rushed in with the emergency crew to secure the stirrups, was obliged to give the order not to approach them, and he attempted to prop up the spindle with emergency timbers. But the beams shattered instantly into matchwood.

The Divisional Commander ordered me to move to the control room. Huge waves, swamping the bridge, poured down into the control room in a torrent, sweeping people to the bulkheads and the sides of the ship. Washed out from behind the mains, the emergency wedges and bungs rushed along the deck, striking people painfully on the legs. The waves smashed the glass on the bridge, and it flew towards us with a clinking noise, shattering into tiny fragments on the iron rungs of the ladders.

Twisting clumsily, as though along a gigantic thread, the boat corkscrewed into the waves and, with the diesels running, started to go into a dive.

'All hands below! Stop diesels!' ordered Mogilievsky.

Striving to overcome the tumult of the waves, I shouted through the opening of the lower conning-tower hatch: 'We must get underwater, or else the bow hydroplanes will jam!'

But no one could hear me on the bridge. The diesels were restarted.

Drenched from head to toe, Captain First Rank Oryol came down into the control room. He poured the water out of his leather gauntlets. Dolgopolov came running in from the first compartment. He reported that there was no possibility of the spindle holding. At that moment the submarine corkscrewed into the waves once more. Once more the lookouts came tumbling down from the bridge, and once more the diesels were stopped. 'Dive, Captain,' yelled Oryol, 'before the ship breaks up!' The upper conning-tower hatch was slammed shut and the Captain came down into the control room. 'Emergency dive! Bosun, take her down to sixty metres!'

As soon as the waves had closed over the conning tower, silence immediately reigned, and only the jittery oscillation of the depth-gauge needle for a long time still bore witness to the fact that on the surface the elements were raging.

'What shall we do, Comrade Commander?' asked Mogilievsky. 'I suggest lying on the bottom.' Pointing to the emergency jack, which the ratings had brought from the first compartment, Dolgopolov said: 'The bow hydroplane lashing broke away. The jack didn't hold up. So much wood got reduced to splinters in the first compartment – you could keep a stove running. The bow hydroplane spindle must be made secure again, before they get completely jammed. As matters stand, they are stuck in a position of twenty-eight degrees of dive.'

The Navigator once more looked for a suitable spot. Three hours later the submarine was noiselessly lying on the sandy bottom on an even keel, and we had begun to secure the spindle once more. But how could we get it into the neutral position? We didn't really know how the hydroplanes stood at present. The only way to establish this was by external examination. It's a pity that bright ideas sometimes arrive a bit late: nothing could really have been simpler than to measure and carefully mark the position of the spindle before dismantling the drive. But in the rush we overlooked this, and now it was a matter of guesswork.

'What a disaster,' sighed Dolgopolov, 'we'll have to send down a diver, to examine the hydroplanes from the outside.'

'Who should we send?'

'I'll have to think about it and have a word with Petty Officer Ogurtsov. We'll need a volunteer for this.'

'Apart from that, we'll need the sea to let us. There shouldn't be more than a moderate swell. You go after a volunteer, and I'll speak to the Captain. We'll take a decision later on. But now for some sleep. Everyone should get some sleep. There'll be a lot of work to do tomorrow.'

In the control room the electricians were busy with the electric motors of the auxiliary machinery that had been drenched with water. Chief Leading Seaman Chuikov, Lieutenant Yefimov and Able Seamen Belavkin and Nesterov were hard at it there until the very break of day.

Many volunteers for the inspection of the hydroplanes came forward, but Petty Officer Ogurtsov was insistent in his recommendation of a Komsomol member, Seaman N.M. Gradsky, a planesman. 'I can vouch for him – he's more resourceful than anyone!' That settled it.

When we surfaced with the onset of darkness, Dolgopolov, Ogurtsov, equipped with a portable lamp specially adapted for underwater work, and Seamen Rastorguiev and Gradsky wearing full light-diving outfits, emerged on the upper deck. There was a moderate swell. The water was between cold and extremely cold.

Gradsky entered the water when the boat had completely lost all way and momentum. Rastorguiev was watching out for him, keeping a firm grip on the hemp rope. Gradsky gave a signal to indicate that he was safely in position on the hydroplane. Then the lamp was switched on. A bright patch of light began to glimmer in the greenish water. Gradsky came to the surface, said something to Dolgopolov and once more vanished into the waves. This was repeated several times.

Acting on what Gradsky reported, the sailors in the compartment hoisted the spindle with block and tackle until it was standing upright on the spot, then gripped it in that position with the aid of a complicated construction.

'Well, how is it? Is it secure?' asked Mogilievsky, inspecting the fruits of our two hours of toil.

'Until the next storm,' I replied evasively, remembering how the jack had curled itself into a coiled spring.

Laying Mines

On 12 March we spent the whole day in transit to the mouth of the Gulf of Danzig, on reconnaissance, and on training exercises. The band of stormy weather had passed over, and the enemy's anti-submarine forces had resumed their activity once more, crawling out from their hiding-places.

The space in the control room was crammed with people. The Divisional Commander was there, the Captain, the officer of the watch, the senior engineer, the Bosun, the navigational electricians, the planesmen, and the hydrophone operators (there were two of them on duty at the moment: one on the direct-listening system, the other on the echo-sounding system).

More from habit than out of necessity, I took up my place in my favourite spot, by the ladder beneath the lower conning-tower hatch. Dolgopolov himself was standing at the main water-control panel, ready at any second to use the trimming pump in place of the bow hydroplanes.

Captain First Rank Oryol was sitting on the swivel-stool right by the entrance to the hydrophone operators' cubicle. He moved there as soon as the hydrophone operators reported enemy shipping appearing directly on our course. Captain Second Rank Mogilievsky was standing beside the Divisional Commander. They consulted one another constantly, and the Captain abruptly gave orders to the Bosun at the vertical rudder. There was a tense silence in the compartment, which was why the rudder indicators

170

seemed to tick too loudly whenever there was a change of position.

The clocks were showing 04.00. It was 13 March – a lucky number. That meant we should be successful. 'Hold her steady at sixty metres!' ordered the Captain. Petty Officer Ashomok smoothly shifted the rudders. The bubble in the trim indicator settled on half a degree of bow trim. The depth-gauge needle obediently crept over the dial. 'Starboard four-zero – anti-submarine defence vessel. Bearing steady,' reported Leading Seaman 2nd Class Buzulukov, not removing his headset. We turned aside slightly. The enemy remained astern. But there was another launch approaching to port. Another order to the vertical rudder. Simultaneously we went even deeper. Now the Captain gave another order: 'Bosun, take her down to ninety!'

'Gently does it, Captain,' advised Oryol, getting off the stool, 'otherwise we will bury her nose in the silt.' Now both ships were falling behind us.

It was already nearly six when the Divisional Commander hurriedly returned from the navigational cubicle and said to Mogilievsky: 'Take her up to periscope depth, Captain. It is fifty minutes till sunrise. If there is good visibility, we should be able to see the lighthouse. But go carefully: we are a mile off the coast.'

'Do it, Bosun!' Mogilievsky turned towards Ashomok. 'Only watch out: if you break out onto the surface I'll have your guts for garters!' He was joking; happy that for the time being everything was going really well.

While waiting for the boat to come up to periscope depth, Oryol, Mogilievsky and Pribavin verified once more on the chart the distance from the minefields laid down by our predecessors – *Lembit*, under the command of Captain Third Rank A.M. Matiyasevich, and *L-3*, under the command of Captain Third Rank V.K. Konovalov, – both minelayers from our own division.

Eventually we came up to periscope depth. Judging from the comments coming from the conning tower, we had chosen a very fortunate moment. The visibility was such that it was still not possible for the periscope to be detected from the shore observation posts and, as well as that, the gentle sea swell was in our favour. Once the Divisional Commander and the Captain had scanned the horizon, Senior Lieutenant Pribavin took bearings on the Hel Lighthouse.

171

'Stand by to lay mines!' the order sounded throughout the compartments. Lieutenant B.A. Ordynets, in charge of the minelaying group, prompt, nimble and never downhearted, ran through the control room. Even now, at this tense moment, he smilingly said to the planesmen: 'Lads, don't mess things up! And the minelayers won't let you down!' and he swiftly disappeared beyond the aft bulkhead. We were on the combat course at a depth of twenty metres.

'First mine away!'

The minelayers and the planesmen were working in strict co-ordination with one another. Once each mine had been launched, it was necessary to take a specific quantity of water into the ballast tanks immediately, to replace the weight of the mine.

'Twentieth away!'

'Close the mine tubes!'

'Take her down to eighty metres! Helm to port!'

The mines were laid exactly in the shipping lane. Naturally, we could not foretell at that moment what was to occur in two days' time; how the German submarine *U-367* was to perish on the mines laid by our ship.

The Divisional Commander praised the crew for their outstanding performance of the task. Afterwards he said to Mogilievsky: 'Stay out to sea now, Captain. We must get out of the Gulf of Danzig just as stealthily as we entered it. We will surface in an hour's time.'

Low insulation was unexpectedly discovered in the stern hydroplane motor. We had to take urgent steps. As a general rule, something started to go downhill every single day. Hardly had we dealt with the hydroplane motor when the temperature rose in the forward bearing of the main port electric propulsion motor. And so it went on endlessly . . .

No Luck

The centre from which our submarines were directed at enemy convoys was situated nearby. It was headed by Captain Second Rank P.A. Sidorenko, with whom we were all well acquainted. The direction centre functioned well. We were sure of that by now.

On 16 March Palanga reported that the Nazis were escorting

some vessels under heavy protection through our sector from Pillau. And, indeed, at three o'clock in the morning we spotted the convoy. No attack could be mounted: a destroyer and a motor launch made for us; we barely got away from them.

We went out on the attack again on 17 March. When we got closer, we saw that it was a high-speed landing craft. We turned aside.

At 10.00 hours on 18 March the radio operators received a message about the enemy. There was some delay in our receiving it: the convoy had passed by us three hours earlier. We would not have been able to catch up with it. Besides which, we heard some explosions in the direction in which the convoy had gone. Evidently, someone from amongst our neighbours had put a hefty dose of salt on the enemy's tail, and now the latter was not being stingy with the depth charges. In just half an hour we counted 216 explosions.

In the evening, when we were in the surfaced position, we received another message. On this occasion there was sufficient time for us not to have to hurry to get ready for the encounter. Senior Lieutenant Pribavin was running up to the bridge with ever-increasing frequency. I went up there too. Our doctor, Vorobiov, was acting as a lookout in the port bow sector. The sky had cleared, but there was a haze on the horizon. The moon had gone into hiding about fifteen minutes earlier, so it had become dark at once. We were making wide sweeps, in order not to miss the enemy, intersecting the presumed course of the convoy. 'Eighty degrees to port – a light!' reported Vorobiov. Instantly all binoculars swung in that direction. 'Helm to port! Full speed ahead!' the Captain sprang to life.

Removing his gauntlets and stuffing them under his arm, the Divisional Commander rubbed his hands. Senior Lieutenant Pribavin, cursing beneath his breath, vanished in a flash down the hatchway. Two minutes later he reappeared on the bridge and reported something to the Captain in a low voice.

Holding the binoculars to their eyes, Oryol and Mogilievsky stared for a long time. The light was plainly visible on the horizon. If it could hardly be distinguished through the haze earlier, even I could see it distinctly with the naked eye now.

'It can't be . . .' the Captain uttered out loud.

'Word of honour!' Pribavin affirmed.

'Well, then, check it out on the globe,' ordered Mogilievsky. Pribavin dived down the hatchway once more.

'What's this about, Captain?' enquired the Divisional Commander.

'The thing is, the Navigator is finding out what light we have discovered. It opened up on the wrong bearing.'

'So what on earth is it?'

'Apparently, it's a star.'

'A star?'

'It's Venus,' Pribavin cheerfully announced, barely sticking his head out of the hatchway.

'Doctor, what do you mean by setting up this "venereal attack" for us?' There was both mirth and irritation in the Captain's voice. We resumed our previous course.

'Never mind, Mikhail Afanasievich,' I consoled the shattered medic. 'Worse things happen at sea!'

'Well, a light, that's exactly what it was,' Vorobiov attempted to justify himself.

Ten minutes later it was again he who discovered the silhouettes of five ships on the horizon. 'Oh, that's them!' the Captain exclaimed. 'Fill the main ballast, except for the central group. Helm to port! Stop diesels!'

I dived down the hatchway, to help Dolgopolov below. An attack at night is a tricky business. It is hard to judge distance at sea in the night, when instead of a freighter you see some kind of blurred apparition. Somehow it always seems to me that this vague silhouette fluctuates, quivers, and sometimes rears up queerly, and I can see it more clearly when I don't look at it directly, but some-what to the side.

We launched two torpedoes and dived deep. No explosions. We missed . . .

A destroyer's propellers roared past to one side. Were they going to depth charge us or not? The noise of the destroyer's propellers could be heard again, but by then on the other side. 'They are searching,' Rusin suggested. 'Let them search,' said Oryol. 'We can dodge a destroyer. Far worse to be winkled out by a motor launch: they're more manoeuvrable.'

The destroyer went off to catch up with the convoy and half an hour later we surfaced once more. But by daybreak we had encountered no one else. Having finished charging the batteries, we continued on in the surfaced position for another half hour, ventilating the battery and the compartments. Then the emergency diving signal sounded.

From my favourite spot I had an excellent view of how the lamps indicating the opening of the Kingston valves would light up in unison. But for some reason the signalling system for the opening of the ventilation valves was operating at a delayed tempo. The little lamps for the stern group had completely failed to light up. 'Pass it on to the seventh compartment: open the valves manually!' I shouted, seeing how a bow-down trim was developing.

Seconds went by, while the signalling system failed to work properly. Dolgopolov and Ogurtsov rushed to the valves of the air-control panel, to let air into the mains using the manual reduction valve. We had by now developed a thirty-degree trim, and the ventilation of the stern tanks was still out of action. 'Stop engines! Half astern both!' the Captain gave the order.

The trim indicator was by now showing forty-six degrees. The little lamp indicating the ventilation of the stern group lit up at last. The boat began to level off. 'Ask the seventh compartment why they took so long to open the ventilation manually,' I ordered.

It turned out that it was not all that simple for the sailors to reach the pneumatic operating gear, positioned high up under the deckhead, during the trimming process, switch the valves over, then, operating with a detachable lever, open them up.

'Who is to blame for such a big trim? What happened?' the Captain enquired sternly.

'The automatic reduction gear froze and failed to operate because of the drop in pressure,' Nikolai Sergeievich reported.

'What good is that? You must keep the system in good working order!' The Captain showed his anger.

'Inspection of the compartments!' ordered Dolgopolov.

It was the usual outcome. I could say in advance what and where there would be need to repair and check. Electrolyte had seeped out, torpedoes had shifted and oil had leaked out of the bearings of the main electric motors. This had collapsed, that had been spilt . . .

The freezing-up of the reduction gear is a common phenomenon, especially in cold weather, but we were dealing with the after-effects of the incident the whole day long.

Then we surfaced in the evening into a stormy sea. While turning, the ship suddenly plunged by the stern between a couple of huge waves. The bow of the ship rose, and then crashed down with all its might. Through the voice-pipe the sound of Seaman I.A. Medinsky's voice reached us from the first compartment: 'The bow hydroplane fastening is coming apart! The spindle has pulled out!'

Precisely what I had most feared had happened. When I ran into the first compartment, I saw a dreadful scene of havoc. All our labours lay in ruins: on the deck a heap of twisted steel. The spindle, freed from the strong bonds of the stirrups and the massive supports, had destroyed all our elaborate structure. Then, plunging deep into the conductor pipe, it had jammed in the extreme position. 'Nikolai, what a total disaster!' I said to Dolgopolov. 'The hydroplanes are jammed in the extreme position for diving . . .'

'Yes, now it probably can't be repaired . . .'

Once the boat was lying on the bottom, almost all the officers gathered in the first compartment. Having inspected the chaotic scene, the Divisional Commander asked me: 'Can anything be done here?'

'We will try, but I don't think so.'

'Now we have to give up the whole idea of an attack using the periscope,' announced the Captain.

'Better not even try; she would burst up onto the surface in no time.'

When the ratings had cleared away the twisted metal, the wreckage became less obtrusive. But all our efforts to shift the hydroplanes from their place came to nothing. 'It would really have been better if they had been completely broken off!' uttered Dolgopolov with feeling.

During the night of 22 March the 'diving team', composed of the same crewmen as before, went out onto the upper deck. A moderate swell was hitting the boat abeam. Gradsky went down into the inky water twice and, when Dolgopolov had turned on the portable light for him, the sea was lit up with a weird greenish glow. But we had no time to admire the wonderful lighting display. To lie hove-to at sea, even with the added refinement of lighting effects, is not particularly agreeable. Therefore, as soon as Gradsky had climbed back on board, Sergei Sergeievich without further ado ordered the ship to be got under way using both diesels. The 'diving team' went down into the control room.

Suddenly, dead ahead about fifteen to twenty-five metres away, two of the most powerful explosions boomed out, one after the other. Here and there in the compartments, ceiling lights and lampshades began to rain down with pealing sounds.

'Emergency dive!' Everyone was swept off the bridge, as though by an explosive blast. The lid of the upper conning-tower hatch slammed shut loudly. When everything had calmed down a bit, I asked Mogilievsky: 'What happened out there?'

'Nothing special: just some swine or other dropping a couple of bombs on us. Evidently, the Nazi pilots noticed the light.' Half an hour later we surfaced and continued searching until daybreak, but without success.

During the daytime we trained the planesmen. It was difficult to sail with just the stern hydroplanes, but even more difficult to steer the submarine when, into the bargain, her bow hydroplanes had jammed in the diving position at the most extreme angle possible.

The calculations that we did showed that, at an underwater speed of three knots, the hydroplanes exerted a drag equivalent to 0.81 of a ton, at a speed of four knots – 1.3 tons, at six knots – 3.2 tons, and at full speed using the diesels – 23 tons.

We've Got One!

That evening we surfaced early since, during the training of the planesmen, we had periodically increased the rate of our submerged speed and the density of the electrolyte in the batteries had fallen significantly more than usual.

Once we were on the surface, we carried out another series of trials, studying the behaviour of the boat at various speeds, both in the cruising and the awash positions. We didn't begin charging until 21.30, and twenty minutes later our direction centre informed us of a large enemy convoy putting to sea.

Pribavin promptly plotted the enemy's course on the chart and calculated the time needed for it to intersect with the western border of our quadrant. The Divisional Commander cautioned the Captain that it would not do to attack at the very edge, since we might hinder our neighbours.

Dolgopolov and I were also preparing for the attack. Over and over again we estimated how much water it would be necessary to pump across, in order to compensate for the drag exerted by the jammed bow hydroplanes.

Time moved slowly. The charging was already almost completed. The very darkest hours of the night had set in. In order not to miss the convoy, we were carrying out not only a visual scan, but also one using the echo-sounder. In the cruising position we made one pass after another, almost along the centre line of our quadrant. At last Leading Seaman 2nd Class A.N. Buzulukov, combing the horizon with the echo-sounder, reported: 'Ships on a course eighty degrees to starboard. Plenty of them.'

Leaving Dolgopolov in the control room, I climbed up onto the bridge. All binoculars were trained in the direction indicated by Buzulukov. But in vain: the distance was still too great. Able Seaman Yudenkov was the first to spot the enemy ships. 'Fill main ballast, except for the central group!' ordered the Captain in the control room. The submarine concealed her pressure hull beneath the cover of the waves.

'A destroyer is in the lead,' judged Oryol. 'Captain, hold your course steady on her now, then our conning tower will be at its least conspicuous. Let the destroyer go past, and then lie on the opposite course in her wake.'

'Precisely how I intended to proceed myself, Comrade Commander. Lookouts, maintain a sharper watch out to sea!'

Mogilievsky bent over the hatchway and gave an order below: 'Torpedo attack! Slow ahead both!'

'Starboard seventy – silhouette of a freighter!' reported Leading Seamen 2nd Class Karpenko, a lookout.

Would they spot our conning-tower shield or not? In principle, they could take it for a motor launch of their own. Then they wouldn't raise the alarm. But if the alarm were given, we would have to take to our heels with the utmost speed.

Clutching the handrail, I peered into the darkness as hard as I could, but I was unable to make out anything as yet. Then I suddenly saw a ghostly silhouette to starboard. No more than five cables away. Less than a kilometre from us. 'Silhouette of a freighter dead ahead,' reported Lieutenant Redko, the officer of the watch.

'It's time, Captain!' – Oryol spoke quietly.

Only then did I grasp the plan of attack. The convoy was proceeding in two columns line astern. We were in between them. This was where they would least expect us, and we could select any target. 'Keep your eyes peeled! Don't miss a tanker!' the Captain told the lookouts.

'Port forty – tanker!' Yudenkov reported almost immediately.

'Helm to port! All hands below! Tubes . . . fire!'

The ship's hull shuddered from the triple-torpedo salvo. I had only just jumped down into the control room when through the open conning-tower hatch I saw scarlet lightning, slashing the sky. Then the explosions thundered out. Mogilievsky, slamming the conning-tower hatch behind him, yelled joyfully: 'We've sunk a tanker with two torpedoes!'

To port and starboard, from ahead and astern, depth charge explosions began to crash down. Having reached a standstill, we quietly settled on the seabed. 'It's the freighters, hurling them directly overboard,' Oryol judged, looking at the time. 'The motor launches couldn't have got here so quickly.'

There was no subsequent pursuit, which meant that the depth charges were intended merely for their effect on our morale. This suited us down to the ground.

All anxieties and fears were set aside, a long, long way away. We immediately forgot that the ship was damaged, that the bow hydroplanes were jammed. It didn't matter, we could still fight!

We reloaded the torpedo tubes. The one most delighted of all about this was Leading Seaman Karpenko, in charge of the second compartment. His compartment was now free of the reserve torpedoes, which had been a considerable nuisance to him. The cumbersome steel cigars had obstructed what was already a narrow passageway. The sailors, passing by them, invariably brushed against their rounded sides, wiping off the thick grease. And the exposed metal immediately began to rust, due to the constant humidity. Karpenko had got into trouble with the First Lieutenant on account of this on many occasions. And in the ship's bulletin a cartoon had appeared with the cheeky caption: 'The second compartment, off to the fight, leave the torpedoes covered in blight.'

Now a contented Karpenko would go through the roomy compartment and would receive the torpedomen with the cordiality of a genial host, forgiving the cartoon which, of course, had not appeared in the bulletin without their knowledge and consent.

Appetite comes with eating. The victory achieved during the night of 23 March had enthused the seamen. Everyone became confident that we would chalk up new successes, but for that to happen the requisite hard work had to be done. The senior men were constantly coming to Dolgopolov: 'Allow us to test . . .'

'I ask permission to clean out . . .'

In the compartments everything was being made spick and span. It was a truly excellent affair, but I tried to restrain the most excessive zeal, when it affected people's normal relaxation time. 'We will take a rest, Comrade Chief Engineer. Word of honour, we will take a rest!' the sailors assured me. 'It's not hard work, and already a lot more dirt and rust has appeared. Let them swab it down a bit,' the senior men calmed me down.

'An epidemic of cleanliness!' was how Dolgopolov diagnosed the crew's condition. He walked like a birthday boy amongst the gleaming machinery.

Another One!

Late one evening the radio operators received the information that two hours earlier a convoy, going at a speed of twelve knots, had crossed the western perimeter of our grid position. 'Helm to port! Full speed ahead!' were the first orders to burst from Mogilievsky.

I hurried to the control room. Today our department would have some hard work to do. Dolgopolov and I bearded the Navigator: 'What's the situation? Tell us in detail.'

Pribavin, even though he was in a hurry to get to the bridge, explained: 'We evidently missed a previous radio message. In two hours the convoy could have travelled twenty-four miles, but the total difference between our speeds is only four knots. According to basic mathematics, it works out that we need nearly six hours to catch up with them.'

Yes, our diesels would be hard-pressed. We summoned to the control room Yefimov, the head of the propulsion group, and A.I. Grigoriev, the senior engine-room mechanic (we have three Grigorievs on board, moreover two of them are twins; we find it hard to tell one from the other). We gave them instructions as to how they might organize their work better. We made them check everything, from the stern tube glands to the circulation pumps. Having satisfied myself that everything was in good order, I went up onto the bridge. The Divisional Commander was restlessly pacing up and down. 'Well, how's the machinery?' he asked.

'We've taken all possible steps to safeguard our speed. We've even suspended the charging.'

'Everything is to go to the propellers! Speed, and nothing but speed!'

The diesels were working on full power, yet it seemed as though the boat was barely crawling along. The movement of air was imperceptible, because we were sailing with a following wind. Hour by hour the darkness deepened.

'Is it possible that the convoy might not maintain a speed of twelve knots?' I was voicing a hope.

'We shouldn't count on it,' the Divisional Commander replied. 'The enemy will try to tear through this area under the cover of night. They were not born yesterday either; they've certainly calculated everything and weighed it all up.'

Five hours into the chase, Lieutenant Redko appeared on the bridge. He reported that the echo-sounder had located the enemy: he was ahead of us a bit farther south.

The echo-sounder gave the direction with increasing precision and accuracy, whereas at a speed such as this, the direct-listening system could pick up nothing except the noise of our own propellers. 'Lookouts, be particularly on the alert for anti-submarine motor launches,' Mogilievsky reminded them. But for the time being the sea seemed deserted. No silhouettes anywhere and no lights.

The wind got up, and the exhaust fumes from the diesels which had, by now, been overloaded for many hours on end, began to float over the bridge.

Occasionally glancing down the upper conning-tower hatch into the control room, I could see how first Yefimov, then Grigoriev, ran up to Dolgopolov, both splashed with black engine oil; they wiped their filthy hands on a rag and gesticulated animatedly. 'Port ten – a light!' reported Senior Lieutenant Vorobiov. 'A light, where?' Mogilievsky had rushed over to him. 'It's gone out. Someone must have opened a door. The light lasted half a second, Comrade Captain.'

'Port ten by the compass!' Mogilievsky corrected the course. Lieutenant Redko ran out onto the bridge again. He reported that the echo-sounder had detected a freighter dead ahead, and a second one more to starboard. The convoy was evidently moving in two columns line astern, exactly as they had done the day before. Distance: twenty cables. But the lookouts strained their eyesight in vain. Even using the night-vision binoculars with eight-fold magnification, neither the Captain nor the Divisional Commander could make out a thing. Time dragged heavily.

At 03.40 hours, when the sky and all around had begun to pale into grey, almost everyone was simultaneously able to make out some barely perceptible irregular, formless outlines. With each passing minute, the distance slowly but surely decreased. We switched from the cruising to the awash position. This increased the water resistance, and our running speed was now not more than fifteen knots. 'Torpedo attack!' the order followed from the Captain in the control room. 'Port eight-zero – out to sea – anti-submarine motor launch,' reported Vorobiov, acting as lookout. Able Seaman Rubin added: 'Starboard one-twenty between the freighters – a motor launch, and out to sea – a destroyer or a patrol boat.'

I peered at the silhouettes, creeping along to port and starboard of us. Soon we would have passed through the whole line-astern column . . .

We had to locate a tanker without fail. Four silhouettes had already sailed past to port, three to starboard, but no tankers. 'Starboard five-zero – tanker!' About time too! 'All hands below!' ordered the Captain.

Three remained on the bridge – the Divisional Commander, the Captain and the officer of the watch, Lieutenant B.A. Ordynets. 'Helm to starboard! Stop diesels! Tubes . . . fire!'

The hull's three convulsive shudders testified to the fact that the torpedoes had ejected at five-second intervals. From below we could see how a vivid glow had flared up above the conning-tower hatch. A powerful hydraulic shock rumbled along the hull, followed by a second one. 'Emergency dive!'

A minute later, the waves closed over the boat. Oryol and Mogilievsky came down into the control room in a state of high excitement.

'For some reason they detected us this time even before the sinking of the tanker,' said Mogilievsky. 'We saw rockets.'

'It was a sea of fire! The tanker lit us up.'

The cracking of the bulkheads being crushed in the sinking vessel could be heard distinctly over to starboard. 'Motor launch to port!' reported Buzulukov, poking his head out of the hydrophone operators' cubicle.

Powerful depth charge detonations along the port side threw the ship about roughly. 'Bosun, dive to seventy metres!'

A new pattern of depth charges thrust the boat up almost onto the surface. Some of the lighting in the control room went out. 'Half ahead both!' Ragged explosions thundered around us. We went directly beneath the sinking tanker where, up on the surface, an inferno was raging. We were already at a depth of sixty-five metres when by our side the remains of the tanker began to crash down onto the stony seabed, very nearly crushing us. We manoeuvred constantly.

Fresh explosions struck the hull, like blows from a sledge-hammer. There were many explosions a long way off. These were the depth charges being launched from all the freighters.

Abruptly silence fell. But five minutes later it all began again. It was not until half an hour later that we managed to break away from the motor launches.

A journey that has ended never seems as arduous as all that. So it seemed to us now that the depth charge attack was not so very severe, given that we were intact and nobody had even been hurt. That's very much the fate of submariners; either everyone comes through alive, or fifty souls share a common grave.

Shortly afterwards we surfaced. We had to charge the batteries. We went out onto the bridge and had a look around. There was no one to be seen anywhere. The Divisional Commander drew the

183

Captain's attention to some object that was showing up white on the stern, beneath an antenna stay. A minute later Bosun Ashomok brought over a canvas smock with laces and a naval identification number on the pocket. 'Oho! The tanker has even left us her calling card,' Mogilievsky uttered in surprise, and ordered the Bosun to wipe and dry the trophy.

We set off on the opposite course. At that moment to our starboard two huge fountains erupted and explosions thundered out. 'Emergency dive!'

Head over heels I hurtled into the conning tower, flat on someone's back. Someone's boot was grazing my ear, and I flew towards the anti-aircraft periscope stanchion, pressing my hand to the bruise. 'Depth twenty,' Dolgopolov's voice reached me from below. Mogilievsky was standing beside me, rubbing his elbow. It seemed that he had been hurt as well.

We went down into the control room. The tumult of the emergency dive had already subsided. 'Why did we dive?' Dolgopolov wondered. 'The aircraft had already dropped its bombs . . .'

Mogilievsky laughed: 'I would like to see how you would have felt if, on a second pass, the aircraft had stuck a load of bullets and shells in us, and possibly a couple more bombs.'

We didn't surface again. Up on the surface day was dawning and we, worn out by events, went to lie down for a sleep. For us, night was falling.

Do We Risk It?

There was little opportunity for sleep. At 10.00 hours the hydrophone operator reported that 'the sea is noisy all around': there were freighters on the move. A lot of them. Apparently, the Germans had rushed in a mass exodus out of the ports towards which our troops were advancing. We rose to periscope depth. The sea was calm. The boat was holding up well. And it was hard to believe that the bow hydroplanes were out of action.

'Chief Engineer to the conning tower!' I heard. I went up. Oryol beckoned me to the periscope and let me look through the eyepiece. I took a look and actually recoiled. Brought close by the optics, a huge ship seemed to be absolutely on top of us. Yes, a steamer with a displacement of 5,000 tons was going along right in the periscope-sight, so that it was not even necessary to manoeuvre. 'Should we risk it?' asked the Divisional Commander.

I realized what he was talking about. We had carried out all earlier attacks from a surfaced position. We had not risked firing from periscope depth: we were afraid that, without the bow hydroplanes, the loss of weight from the torpedoes would thrust the boat's bow out onto the surface.

'Let's risk it!' I gave my assent, although I knew that after even a two-torpedo salvo, the turbo pump would not be able to suppress the positive buoyancy. I shared my misgivings with the Divisional Commander and the Captain. Mogilievsky found a way out: 'Put the men in the control room. All the off-watch men in there! We'll do it the way they did on *Snow Leopard* in the First World War.'

A sizeable group assembled, some fifteen men. Hurriedly I gave the sailors their instructions. 'Torpedo attack!' the signal clanged. Events unfolded swiftly, like in a film. Here was the Captain already giving a long drawn-out word of command: 'Fire!'

'At the double!' I urged the sailors on. They ran on winged feet to the bulkhead door. 'Start the pump! Fill the rapid-diving tank!' ordered Dolgopolov. 'Torpedoes away,' Petty Officer Shevchenko reported in a sing-song voice.

It was the third day that his torpedomen were in action, and each time they had coped successfully with the task.

The Bosun was struggling with all his might to hold the lighter boat steady with the stern hydroplanes. But her bow was beginning to ride up. And confusion was affecting our runners. There were many people, and the hatchways are narrow, and they were all trying to elbow their way through them. It took them too long to reach the torpedo tubes. And all that time the depth-gauge needle was creeping inexorably to the left.

I worked it out mentally: at a depth of eight metres – the periscope standard appears on the surface; at five metres – the peak of the bridge shield becomes exposed; at three metres – the anti-aircraft semi-automatic is completely on the surface. Fortunately, by that time, all fifteen runners had turned up in the bow, at the very torpedo tubes. That meant a ton of additional ballast. The ship's bow froze in position, and then began to go downwards.

The Divisional Commander and Mogilievsky were following the run of the torpedoes through the periscopes. There was the crash of an explosion.

'They're hit in the mainmast area!' shouted Mogilievsky. The boat, gathering speed and trim, went below the water. Not a single depth charge. Even the propeller noise ceased.

'The direct-listening system is not working,' Buzulukov reported to the First Lieutenant. 'Can Kovaliov, the senior radio operator, be called here? He will quickly get it sorted out.'

Five minutes passed by: silence.

Eight minutes passed by: silence.

Oryol was getting fretful and pressed the Captain to go up to periscope depth.

Ten minutes passed by: silence.

'Captain, surface. We need to know the outcome of the attack,' said the Divisional Commander, going up into the conning tower. We rose to the surface. We raised the periscopes. From the remarks that Oryol and Mogilievsky were exchanging, we could clearly picture for ourselves what was happening on the surface. The torpedoed freighter was sinking by the stern. Her stern flag was, by then, sticking up out of the water. Right up close to the sinking ship, a second one was standing by. People were climbing over from the stricken steamer; they were throwing some kind of crates over from one ship to the other. 'If only we could slam a torpedo into the second freighter, too,' said the Divisional Commander. But Mogilievsky was not about to attack. He shouted below: 'Emergency dive! Dive!'

The 'Envelope'

The ships of the anti-submarine defence force were attacking us. We could already hear the growing noise of their propellers. We were following a curving course, in order to complicate their search. But the enemy ships were equipped with *Nibelung* echo-sounders. When the pulses they emitted struck the boat's hull, we could hear the high-pitched intermittent *ping*. This indicated that the echo-sounder had come into contact with a target; that we had been detected! There was a howl of propellers, one of the ships was rushing ahead; she was dashing by above us. Terrifyingly

186

powerful blows knocked the deck from under my feet; I fled somewhere else. Broken glass tinkled, shattering wood cracked. Everything that you clutched at was torn from your hand. And the explosions got ever closer and closer. From one minute to the next, the pressure hull might not hold. We manoeuvred this way and that, but we were unable to break loose from the enemy.

The next contact *pinged* in its turn. It was urgently necessary to change our depth. An order to the Bosun: 'Dive to eighty-two metres!'

A pattern of depth charges exploded nearby. But no direct hit; then another contact. 'Take her up to thirty-seven metres!'

The depth charges began to rain down less frequently. The enemy was spending a great deal of time on the search. Since there was no kind of regularity in our manoeuvring through the depths, the enemy was finding it hard to determine where to search for us.

While we were leading the enemy by the nose, constantly changing depth, the Divisional Commander and the Captain never strayed from the hydrophone operators' cubicle. Oryol himself combed the horizon and drew something on paper. Mogilievsky attentively followed the point of his pencil and nodded his head in agreement, then took the headset, listened carefully to the outboard noises and drew on the paper too. I could hear their conversation:

'An envelope!'

'Yes, a genuine envelope – with ships at each corner of the quadrant.'

'And the fifth goes inside . . .'

We were in the centre of a quadrant. As soon as one of the motor launches located us, she rushed in to attack. The fifth launch immediately occupied her place in a corner of the 'envelope'. We found ourselves boxed in at all times from four directions. 'Cunning tactic,' said Oryol. 'However are we going to break out of this trap?'

We continued to manoeuvre; we changed course and the depth of the dive. But the enemy had got a firm grip on us. Wherever we might move, the 'envelope' moved with us. The enemy was calculating that, if he didn't exterminate us with depth charges, he would get us by wearing us down. He was waiting until the batteries ran down and people began to suffocate from lack of oxygen.

I ordered the sparing use of electricity, with immediate effect, as soon as it had become clear that we would not break loose from the enemy pack with the usual manoeuvring, armed as they were with the *Nibelung* system. We were running on one electric motor, operating on minimum revolutions.

The morning of 26 March arrived. The question arose: whether to prepare a meal or to subsist on dry rations? The Captain said that a meal must be prepared, in spite of the need to save electricity. They were not letting us sleep, so we should at least eat normally. The sailors were being worn down. Some of them, in the intervals between explosions, managed to doze sitting up, or even standing. But you don't get any real rest from sleep like that; you just get even more tired.

During the second half of the day, the Divisional Commander convened a 'council of war'. Oryol, Mogilievsky and I were securely battened down in the conning tower. We switched on the apparatus for burning hydrogen and lit a cigarette. Sergei Sergeievich Mogilievsky was a non-smoker but, nevertheless, even he lit up. On the agenda – breaching the 'envelope' and breaking out of the encirclement. In order to resolve this issue, you had to know with which kind of ships you were dealing.

'What sort of ships did you see through the periscope?' the Divisional Commander asked Mogilievsky.

'I couldn't see the ships by then, only their stemposts. I got the impression that I could see even the rivets.'

'Bad business.' Oryol took up the German naval handbook, turned the pages.

What concerned me first and foremost were the ships' propulsion systems. Judging by the propeller noise, these were not launches with high-powered engines. We decided to listen in to the enemy once more. We went to the hydrophone cubicle and took up the headset in turn. I timed one of the ship's propeller revolutions with a stopwatch. And I suddenly heard a distinctive sound: the furnace of a steam-boiler being opened. All was clear: they were *M-40*s, steam-driven minesweepers. We looked in the handbook. The speed of these minesweepers was exactly the same as our surfaced speed. In the most favourable circumstances we might even add half a knot, jamming the diesels' safety-valves with chisels.

We sat. We pondered. Mogilievsky tapped the handbook with his pencil; on his brow, a stubborn frown. 'Listen,' he said, 'what if we play mind games with the German captains? Suppose you were both in command of one of those minesweepers and had already been hanging over a submarine for two days. Suppose the submarine leapt up out of the water all of a sudden, like a shot from a gun. What would you do?'

'Full speed ahead. And – ram her!' answered the Divisional Commander without having to think.

'And what would you do?' Mogilievsky asked me.

'The very same thing.'

'Well then, everything should work out wonderfully,' smiled Sergei Sergeievich. 'Let us think it all through properly. By now we have been plodding along at a speed of one and a half knots for two days and nights. The minesweepers too have been obliged to plod along at a snail's pace, the stokers barely shovelling coal, just enough to keep the steam steady on the mark. Then suddenly the captain sees us and, naturally, immediately gives the order: 'Full speed ahead!' The engineer will unquestioningly carry out the order; he will open the manoeuvring valve to its full extent. What will happen, Comrade Korzh? This is right up your street.'

'The boiler will immediately shut down.'

'Precisely. And the stokers will need at least thirty minutes to raise steam. During which time we will have run nearly eight miles away. How about it?'

'Splendid!' I agreed. 'But they have guns . . .'

'Let us weigh everything up once more,' the Divisional Commander entered the conversation.

Truth develops through a conflict of opinions. In our case it developed over a long time and excruciatingly slowly. There were many contradictory proposals. The help of First Lieutenant Rusin, Navigator Pribavin, Minelayer Ososkov, and of Dolgopolov, the head of *D-5*, was found necessary. When the final version had been accepted and approved, two hours were allocated to complete the preparations. During this time we lay on the bottom.

At midnight I went into the stern compartments. Engine room mechanics A.Y. Vus and B.V. Sabo, both Komsomol members, were labouring over the shaft line and the thrust bearings. They were readying their area of responsibility in such a way as they had probably never prepared it before, virtually checking with pins each opening that might become obstructed at a critical moment. Senior engine-room mechanic Leading Seaman V.A. Golubev and Seaman M.I. Naryshkin were priming the diesels with fresh oil. Senior engine-room mechanics A.I. Sidorov and A.F. Vorobiov were checking the fuelling system, cleaning out the knife-edge filters, so that not so much as a single fuel injector would fail. Over and over again, Pavel Ivanovich Grigoriev, the businesslike and efficient head of the engine-room mechanics' group and a good Party member, examined the blocks.

Dolgopolov and his assistant Yefimov were exercising general supervision.

For the final time I gave the engine-room mechanics, the electricians and the planesmen their instructions as to what they were to do and how they were to do it.

I returned to the control room. It was more crowded there than ever before. As well as those who had their assigned action stations there, twelve ratings were crowded in the passageway. They were holding sub-machine guns and hand grenades were hanging from their belts. Medic Vorobiov was giving two lumps of sugar each, to improve their visual acuity, to everyone who had to go out onto the bridge at the decisive moment. This was a method he had tested on himself and he believed in it, the way a fanatic believes in God.

Mogilievsky was briefing the armed sailors and allocating responsibilities. The whole gunnery crew had gathered here, together with those controlling the firing. Senior Lieutenant A.I. Ososkov had been appointed to control the firing of the 100-millimetre gun, Lieutenant B.A. Ordynets the firing of the 45-millimetre semi-automatic. Everyone's mood was anxious but elevated, militant.

At 01.30 hours the Captain, with a gesture, ordered all the 'troops' to go up into the conning tower. The Divisional Commander, lingering for a few seconds, said to me: 'Well, Viktor Yemelianovich, everything strictly according to plan!'

'The best of luck, Alexander Yevstafievich!'

'Go to hell!' As is customary, according to tradition amongst hunters, the Divisional Commander cursed me affectionately and vanished through the conning-tower hatch.

We waited another half an hour, so that the people in the conning tower, where at present the lights had been switched off, could become acclimatized to the darkness.

Two o'clock in the morning. 'Kolya, now!' I said into the voice-pipe, barely audibly. I watched the tachometer needle. Slowly but surely it crept to the right. It was time! I indicated to the Bosun with gestures that he was to create a stern-down trim. Petty Officer Ogurtsov was already gripping the valve handwheels.

'Blow main ballast!'

'Full speed ahead!'

The depth-gauge needle started with a jerk, jauntily picked up speed. With a lead sledgehammer I struck three times on the battened-down cover of the conning-tower hatch. This meant that the depth-gauge was indicating a depth of three metres. Both diesels had started to operate in the propelling mode. Air was being sucked through the open bulkheads with a whistling sound, while the shaft supplying air to the diesels was being unsealed.

Now both the upper and the lower conning-tower hatches were open. Together with the flood of air into the control room flew splashes of water. Sensing the drops of fresh water on my lips, I rejoiced. Rain! That meant poor visibility.

From the sixth compartment came a deafening cracking noise, like machine-gun fire. It was the diesel safety-valves 'firing', almost 2,000 shots a minute! We were pressing down with a heavy foot. Leaving Yefimov in the diesel compartment, Dolgopolov ran through into the control room, deafened by the firing.

'Well, how's it going?' he asked.

'Like clockwork. You stay here for a bit, while I go up onto the bridge.'

'What? I can't hear!'

'Stay here, in the control room!' I yelled in his ear.

On the bridge the 'troops', armed to the teeth, were patiently getting soaked by the rain, waiting for the enemy pursuit. But there was none. Evidently, the darkest hour of the twenty-four was having its effect, that plus the low cloud cover, plus the rain. The echo-sounder showed that the enemy ships were all still in place.

Ten minutes had passed. The situation remained unchanged. As before, we forced our speed. We didn't even turn on the main electric power; the light bulbs in the control room were burning dimly.

An hour later, with the Captain's permission, we were already carrying out battery charging. The 'boarding party' departed to dry off.

Two hours later the Divisional Commander and the Captain came down into the control room and, convinced by the echo-sounder that the chase was not materializing, decided to settle on the bottom, to allow the exhausted crew to rest. The Captain ordered the watch to be changed hourly.

With the compartments well ventilated, we lay on the bottom, having come nearly thirty-five miles from the spot where we had surfaced. I, too, went to lie down.

We were all woken up by the sound of a disturbance in the control room. It turned out to be a mistake on our part to have settled down so early. It had not even occurred to the enemy to relinquish the chase. He had been tracking us, hot on our heels the whole time, following us with the aid of his radar. Now the Germans were once more seeking us out with echo-sounders. While they still had not found us, the Divisional Commander had taken the decision to surface and to continue onwards in the surfaced position. To find ourselves once more under siege was undesirable for us in the extreme: we had not managed to charge the batteries, and our supply of compressed air was low as well. On top of that, the thread of the nut-liner of our last remaining hydroplanes had become so worn from overloading that it was now no more than two millimetres thick. During the underwater manoeuvres we could have been left completely without hydroplanes. We surfaced and again ran the diesels at full speed.

We reckoned up how many depth charges the Germans had used up on us. It turned out that just the close explosions alone had numbered 178. And, in all, more than 250 depth charges had been dropped on us.

Throughout the day of 28 March, taking advantage of the rainy weather, we went at full surfaced speed, employing an anti-torpedo zigzag. And there were the Finnish skerries themselves. We were home!

On 29 March our minelaying submarine moored alongside the floating base *Smolny*. The first person into whose strong embraces I fell was Captain Second Rank Boris Dmitrievich Andryuk. 'How did it go?' he asked.

'I avenged my father's death!'

The Greatest Joy of All

And once more there was no time to rest. We were keeping eighty per cent of the boats at sea. The moment a ship returned, we tried to get her ready as swiftly as possible for a new patrol.

The submariners were all adding to their battle successes. But our joy was mingled with grief. *S-4* never returned. How and where she perished, no one knows.

I paid a visit to the slipway, where *P-318* was under repair. My friend Captain Third Rank Lev Alexandrovich Loshkariov was in command of her and the head of *D-5* was Lieutenant Captain Nikolai Mikhailovich Gorbunov. The boat had returned severely damaged from her last patrol; the stern smashed and the bow crumpled.

'You see, already the tail with all its entrails has been put back,' Lev Alexandrovich said to me jokingly. 'We shall soon go off to fight again.'

'There was no end of trouble,' said Gorbunov, 'but now it's all over. Any day now we will get off the slipway. All that remains is to complete the watertight trials, touch up the paintwork – and into the water.'

The Director of the plant, Mr Blomqvist, caught sight of me. He spoke Russian poorly; in difficult circumstances we resorted to German, which neither of us knew particularly well. But conversation was achieved. Engineer Blomqvist cordially congratulated me on my return and first of all was concerned to find out whether the repairs that they had done had broken down or not during the patrol.

'Thank you, you did a good job. Please pass this on to your workmen as well.'

'So were there no breakdowns at all?'

'There were. We came under heavy bombardment. From the very outset of the patrol we were left without bow hydroplanes.'

'Oh,' Blomqvist was upset, 'that means you fought un-successfully . . .'

'No, not really. We sank two tankers and a freighter.'

'So many? However did you manage?'

'We repaired everything at sea . . .'

'Splendid! I can only marvel. Your submarines, even falling to bits, fight on just the same and return home safely. It beggars belief!'

'And what else was there to do, in your opinion?'

'What else? Signal *SOS* – and save yourselves . . .'

We burst out laughing: 'No, Mr Blomqvist, our people wouldn't go for that. There's nothing like that in their nature.'

Reports from the Soviet Information Bureau were revealing how catastrophically quickly the territory of Nazi Germany was melting away. And yet for us the news of the enemy's capitulation came as a surprise. The first to burst noisily into my cabin was Georgi Petrovich Kulchitsky: 'Viktor Yemelianovich, victory! It's all over! Rejoice!'

I flung open the cabin window. From the deck a din burst in. Ratings, leading seamen and officers were hugging one another, talking loudly and joyfully.

One after another the submarines began to return to base. The officers of the 1st Division assembled in the base officers' mess. Captain First Rank A.Y. Oryol congratulated everyone on the victory and thanked them for their selflessness and their devotion to duty. We stood silent and uplifted. I looked closely into the faces of my friends. Few remained of those with whom I had begun the war. Many comrades, many ships had been lost in the Baltic submariners' battles. And those who had survived had suffered so much that they would remember it to the end of their days. Yes, it was hard for us. But we held out. Our people have a huge reserve of strength.

Yet to look at, they were totally ordinary lads. Thinner and weary after the patrols, but this was only their outward look. In fact, these were men of steel, not knowing fear, doubt or fatigue.

Amazing people!